With

Hope

D.B. Shubert, Jr.

Hope

What is it? Where is it found?

D. B. (DEE) SHELNUTT, JR.

XULON PRESS ELITE

Xulon Press Elite
2301 Lucien Way #415
Maitland, FL 32751
407.339.4217
www.xulonpress.com

Unless otherwise indicated, Scripture quotations taken from the New Revised Standard Version (NRSV). Copyright © 1989 the Division of Christian Education of the National Council of the Churches of Christ in the United States of America.

Unless noted all hymn references are the The United Methodist Hymnal Copyright 199 by the United Methodist Publishing House.

Illustration: Chapter 19
"Hope" by George Frederic Watts - *public domain.*

Paperback ISBN-13: 978-1-6628-3425-7
Ebook ISBN-13: 978-1-6628-3426-4

In the midst of our political and pandemic darkness, *Hope: What is it? Where is it found?* provides an uplifting alternative. I commend it heartily for its information and inspiration. Dee has done a monumental work in collecting definitions, examples, poetry, songs, images, quotations and real-life stories of hope where there should be none.

To possess this collection equals having a small library for personal and corporate use. The book was driven by the comment of a relative, "You have never given me hope." That haunts me as well; Do I have hope? Do I give hope? Or am I a part of the negative tone that pervades our world? Through the eyes and heart of a caring pastor and human being we are pointed to a brighter future.

Richard Looney –
Bishop, The United Methodist Church, retired

I learned about Dee's book on hope the week that included January 6th, 2021, and the insurrection at our Nation's Capital. Like the COVID Vaccine, hope was something that seemed to be in short supply and needed just as much or more. From a practical perspective, I first wondered how Dee could fill an entire book talking about hope. I should have never underestimated Dee's pastoral skills. As he opened my mind to hope revealed to each of our senses, I knew he would change the way I thought about it forever. After reading his book, I felt I was living with hope, and most importantly I had an understanding of its depth, possibilities and wonders. Dee's book on hope offers sustenance no matter where you are in your life.

Michael Young –
American actor and Emmy Winning Television Host

"In *Hope: What is it? Where is it found?* Dr. D.B. (Dee) Shelnutt, Jr, takes us on a journey searching for a meaning of hope. Challenged by a family conversation, these six words: "You have never given me hope" launch the author on an inquisitive and thoughtful search of discernment. Like a modern-day griot, he shares stories and anecdotes that engage our hearts, minds, and souls with insight, as well as helping us ask the questions of clarity rather than seeking the answers of certainty. Regardless of how you experience hope, this book allows you to launch your own self-discovery in the midst of reading the author's quest for understanding. In many ways, we are led to another six-word affirmation of Christian hope- "Jesus is risen from the dead." A hope without which nothing else makes sense."

L. Jonathan Holston –
Resident Bishop, South Carolina Conference
of The United Methodist Church

Other books by D. B. (Dee) Shelnutt, Jr.

Songs in the Night: Holding on in the Darkness of Life

At the Welcome Tree

Dedication

———⋈———

To all who have offered me hope whether I knew it or not.

&

In memory of:

Virginia Harlow

Teacher, mentor, friend, inspiration

&

Arnold E. Gardner

And the king said to his servants, "Do you not know that a
prince and a great man has fallen this day in Israel?
2 Samuel 3:38

&

Joy Estelle Dyson Privett

Her ways were ways of pleasantness and
All her paths were peace.
Proverbs 3:17

Acknowledgements

My family:

My wife: Kandy – "the wind beneath my wings"

My Daughter: Meredith, husband Jordan Thrasher, their daughters: Georgia, Elizabeth, Anna

My son: Emory, wife Amanda, their sons: Parker and Max

My son: Wesley, wife Melissa

Relatives:

The families of: Lib Harris, Hamilton and Nona Sapp, Herman and Etta Richardson, Eddie and Hazel Jackson, Bill and Willene Savage; Carleen Jackson, Clyde and Pat Underwood, Margarite and Lewis Faw, Florrie Jackson, C. S. and Bessie Jackson; Wilburn and Opal Shelnutt, Gay and Myrtis Shelnutt, Dumas and Tex Shelnutt, George and Jewell Dyson, and Fred and Meriam Shelnutt.; Gladys and Pete Tilley, Elgie and Louise Ruff, Bill and Grace Ruff, Ralph and Charlotte Ruff, Rogers and Mary Austin, Paul and Lennis Matthews.

Friends:

Dave and Marie Allen, Sammy and Judy Andrews, Lowell and Laura Belue, Rusty Bennett, Blanche Beroset, Coby Brooks, Cliff and

Debbie Brown, Dan Brunson, Sandy and Teri Butler, Allen and Cindy Carrington, Alan and Rose Davis, Debbie Foreman, Karl Heinz Gardner, Kevin and Kim Godwin, Mike and Beth (Ware) Harrell, Bucky and Lee Highsmith, Justin and Monique Honnaman, Ron and Lynn Magat, Matt McDade Linda Merrell, Kurt Momand, Brent and Gina Morgan, Dale and Kathleen Morton, Brian and Jacki Munhall, Buck Murphy, Tom and Donna Murray, Stan and Sophia Parrott, Annette and Scott Pendergrass, Betsy Pennington, Jamie Prickett, , Elaine Raulerson, Matt Raulerson, Tony and Karen Rutherford, Jeff and Carrie Safarreyah, Steve Schofield, Todd and Kathryn Shy, Gary and Linda Smith, Kathryn Carper Steiner, Shelby and Jenni Tolliver, Joe and Patti Tuggle, Walter and Lisa Wallace, Prentiss and Elizabeth Wehman, George and Kate Wilson, Dan and Carol Woodley.

The Wise Men:

Don Brewer, Bill Coates, Jack Hodge, Jay Hortenstein, Mark Linkesh, Carol Perry, Tyler Smith, Charlie Strong, and Bill Wittel

My Sunday School Class

The CrossTies Class of Gainesville First United Methodist Church

In Memory:

Charlotte Adams, Liz Adams, Mike Alford, Arlene Bird, Jim and Stella Bowen, Virginia Carlton, Rod Chennault, Jennifer Cody, Rev. Stiles Cobb, Bob and Edwina Cook, Verdery Cunningham, Ruth Dahlberg, Chris Dannelly, Rev. Ervin Dailey, Rev. Mark Earl, Randy Goff, Neill Goff, Phil Gray, Carl Jackson, Bert McDade, B. H. and Talitha Martin, Alberta Merit, Margaret Meyer, Lynn Murphy, Noah Murphy, Kathy Potts, Katie Potts, Hill and Dorothea Redwine, Norma Saunders, Phil Seay, Pat Sloan, Kathy Smith, Maude Snead, Tom and Billie Speed, Donna Stanley, Glenn and Jackie Strother, Boyd and Jewell

Tyson, Liz Watkins, LaUna Williams, Margaret Crist Wood, Cornelia Wohlgemuth.

Special thanks to:

Bishop Jonathan Holston, Bishop Richard Looney, Michael Young

Table of Contents

—————⟨∞⟩—————

"Hope" is the thing with feathers -
That perches in the soul -
And sings the tune without the words -
And never stops - at all -

And sweetest - in the Gale - is heard -
And sore must be the storm -
That could abash the little Bird
That kept so many warm -

I've heard it in the chillest land -
And on the strangest Sea -
Yet - never - in extremity,
It asked a crumb - of me.[1]

Emily Dickinson

———————∝———————

INTRODUCTION

Why a book on hope?

———◇———

After being a pastor for forty years, I retired. I have been enjoying the simpler life of fishing, boating, reading, traveling, being with my wife, children, and grandchildren. One day a close relative of mine called me and during our conversation said to me, "You have never given me hope." I was stunned. Never, has anyone ever said such a thing to me. As the conversation continued, the relative said, "You have given others hope, but not me." That confused me. I thought to myself, "I have not treated any of my relatives differently from this one, in fact, I have spent more time with her than any of the others put together"! Truly, I was at a loss. I have preached sermons on hope, used the word often in visits to hospitals, funeral homes, institutions of chemical dependency, prisons, in letters and in simple conversation. However, I never consciously thought about if I was *giving* someone "hope."

Throughout my life, I have sought understanding to the critical questions of life. Having had many prominent deaths in my childhood and youth, I questioned life's meaning. I spent many years in counseling in order to continually "know myself" and to understand why I do the things I do, and to strive to be psychologically and emotionally healthy during the trials and tragedies that come in ministry. (I recommend all who can afford it to find a counselor and spend time in getting to know one's "self" and especially for all clergy to do the same!)

For many years, I have tried to read a book a day because I want to know everything I can about life: my life, the lives of others, the world and God. The more I read and study the more I realize how little I know! Nevertheless, I have a passion to dive into the depths of as much of life as possible.

I did not enter the ministry to ever hurt a living soul. Because I have had great tragedy in my life, I have wanted to be a "wounded healer" to those who experience the darkness of life. I have always thought ministry was synonymous with hope.

Whenever a person experiences the sudden death of a loved one, or the doctor's report that you or a loved one have inoperable cancer, or your child is chemically dependent or in jail, or your spouse wants a divorce, you have to declare bankruptcy, or other critical situations of life, the questions soon begin:

"Where is God in this?"
"Why did this happen?"
"What did I do to deserve this?"
"Does God really exist?"
"Does prayer really help?"
"What is God's will?"
"Did God make this happen to punish me?"
"How will I get through this?"

It is my strong belief that in times like these, a pastor needs to be the presence and the voice of hope, not one who thinks they have all the answers, because no one does!!! I have tried to point people to the life of Jesus who says that "it is not the will of my heavenly father that any of my children suffer," [2]and "God is like a good parent." [3]Certainly, no good parent will do anything to hurt their children.

And then somewhere in my time together, I make my way to the word "Emmanuel" meaning "God with us." We may not have all the answers, but God is with us, seeking the best for us. Life happens. When it does, we must not offer what I call "cotton candy" theology. Nor should we take the time to preach a sermon in the midst of great crisis (that may come later but not at first). The first, and most important thing a pastor can do in such times, is to be present, to speak calm words of assurance of God's everlasting love and presence with us, and to pray and offer words of healing and *hope*! More than anything, hope is the most important thing that can be offered to those in peril. That is what I have spent my life trying to do. I thought, sincerely thought, that I had offered my relative hope through my presence (my time), calm words of assurance of God's everlasting love for her and her family, and with prayers for healing. Why then, did these things not bring her hope?

While wrestling with this, questions began to flood in my mind and heart:

"What is hope?"
"Where is hope found?"
"Should others expect hope from me?"
"What does hope look like?"
"What is the definition of hope?"
"Who has given me hope?"
"How do we know when we have received it?"
Is there a difference between "hope" and "Christian hope?"
What is "new" hope?
How do we "give" hope?
What does it mean to put our hope in God?

In Paul's first letter to the Corinthian Church, he says (I Corinthians 13:13) "Three things remain forever: faith, *hope* and love, but the greatest of all is love." Isn't it interesting that all three of these everlasting things are invisibly visible! We speak of having faith and hope, but we rarely hear anyone say that they "have" love, rather we hear "we are IN love" or "I love you."

Hope permeates all of Paul's letters, but take note, in his letter to the Galatians, Paul says, "the fruit of the spirit is **love**, joy, peace, patience, kindness, **faith**fulness, gentleness, generosity and self-control." [4]Love is listed as #1, faithfulness is listed as #6 and hope did not make the list!!! Why? This leads me to ask, "Did Paul mean that there are *only* these nine fruits or was this a starting point?" Isn't *hope* a fruit of the Spirit?

Then, Paul says in Romans 5:1-5:

> *"Therefore, since we are justified by faith, we have peace with God through our Lord Jesus Christ, through whom we have obtained access to this grace in which we stand; and we **boast in our <u>hope</u> of sharing the glory of God**. And not only that, but we also boast in our sufferings, knowing that suffering produces endurance, and endurance produces character, and **character produces <u>hope</u>, and <u>hope does not disappoint</u> us,** because God's love has been poured into our hearts through the Holy Spirit that has been given to us."*

How does character produce hope?

Can hope disappoint us?

Like a rock in my shoe, I became irritated and troubled by the words of my relative. So, I came downstairs to my home-office and wrote her a letter. Here is the jest of it:

Dear relative:

- It would be advantageous to me if you would articulate the following:
- What do you mean by "hope"?
- What did you expect from me that I did not give you?
- How did I give other relatives hope but not you?
- How do <u>you</u> give hope to others?
- Who has given you hope in your life? What was it like? Help me know what they said or did. I would love to know how.

- What did you hope to gain by sharing with me that "I never gave you hope?"

Your words have set me on a journey to strive to understand what hope is, how it works, what is the evidence of it, and how to give and receive it. I am eager to hear from you.

Sincerely,
Me

This book is the outcome of my studies and inquiry. I "HOPE UPON HOPE" that it is helpful! It is not written to "put down" my relative nor to justify myself. It is written with an intense search and thirst to understand a word I have used my entire life, yet not really given much thought to what it means in relation to whether or not I have passed it along to another.

I remember in college taking a class in Abnormal Psychology. The professor said to the class, 'We cannot get up every morning without subconsciously thinking that today will be better than yesterday. That is hope."[5]

He also said, "a person might consider suicide when they have no hope." In other words, if anyone loses all hope, life no longer seems to have meaning.

Basically, hope is our driving force to life. We cannot live without it. As Ilia Delio says, *Hope is the main impulse of life.*[6]

I am grateful that someone has given my relative hope, even if I did not. Sadly, she never responded to my questions.

Her words made me wonder if others in my years of ministry felt the same way that she did. I pray not! With all of my heart, I pray not!

Perhaps this book will stir you to take a good look at your own life and ask,

"How do I define hope?"
"Where have I been offered hope?"

"Who has offered me hope?"
"Am I responsible for other's hope?"
"Where does my hope originate?"
"What's the difference between hope and wishing?"

I certainly do not have all the answers but let me point us in a direction that will *hopefully* set us in process to think theologically, psychologically, and sociologically about this powerful little word that is **the** driving force that enables us to live. This book is a combination of autobiography, commentary, life lessons and a resource of numerous ways one might understand hope. At its core, it is written from a pastor's heart for all to know the world is tinged with hope that never, never goes away. It is a pleasure to join you on this journey.

D. B. (Dee) Shelnutt, Jr
Sweet Harbor
Summer, 2021

On you I depend from birth;
From my mother's womb
You are my strength;
Constant has been
my hope in you.

Psalm 71:6

International Symbols of Hope

—∝—

The swallow:

Tradition has it that often sailors would have one swallow tattooed on their body before settng out on a voyage, and the second swallow tattooed upon his return to the home port, once completing his journey. This led many sailors to start embracing the swallow as a symbol of hope and the succesful completion of a long voyage. Since swallows do not travel far out to sea, when sailors saw one, they knew that land was near, thus they carried a message of hope.

The anchor:

The anchor is the oldest symbol of hope! During a storm, sailors clung to the anchor, once the shipwreck was imminent. As such, the anchor was associated with hope. The anchor symbolized the support against the complications that life presented. In Christianity, the anchor became a symbol of hope duirng the Roman persecution.

The Dove:

In Hebrew scripture, a dove was released from Noah's ark and when it returned with an olive branch, it showed that the flood was over. Still today, the dove in Judaism is a symbol of peace and healing. In Buddist tradition, the dove is a symbol of fidelity. Doves are usually white in color which symbolizes purity, love and peace. In the New Testament a dove descended upon Jesus at his baptism as a symbol of the Holy Spirit coming upon him, ushering in a new era, a new covenant with God.

The Butterfly

The Christian religion sees the butterfly as a symbol of resurrection. Around the world, people view the butterfly as representing endurance, change, hope, and life. Butterflies symbolize life struggles that people have endured to emerge as a better person.

Iris

The iris is represented in Greek mythology. Iris was the goddess of the rainbow and a messenger for Zeus and Hera. Many believe that the flower is named after her. She carried messages from heaven to earth on the arc of the rainbow and was a companion to female souls on the way to heaven. To this day, Greeks plant purple irises on women's graves so that Iris will guide them to their resting place in heaven.

Associating irises to the goddess of the rainbow, like the Ancient Greeks did, is fitting because there are over 200 species of irises that come in a wide variety of colors. Specific iris symbolism depends on the flower color:

- Purple irises symbolize royalty and wisdom.
- Yellow irises symbolize passion.
- Blue irises symbolize faith and hope.
- White irises symbolize purity.

Ram

In many ancient societies, the ram has been a long-held symbol of determination, action, initiative, and leadership. The ram is also a symbol of Aries, which is an astral symbol of rulership. It is also associated with power and strength.

Yellow

It is the lightest hue of the spectrum, signifying joy, happiness, betrayal, optimism, caution, idealism, imagination, hope, sunshine, summer, gold, philosophy, dishonesty, cowardice, jealousy, covetousness, deceit, illness, hazard and friendship.... In Japan, yellow represents bravery, wealth, and refinement.

I find these international symbols of hope fascinating. Like me, do you wonder who came up with them? The anchor, dove, and butterfly are ones most people would associate with hope, but why a swallow, a ram, the color yellow and iris?

Chapter 1

Can hope be defined?

————⋈————

The fact that jellyfish have survived
For 650 million years despite not having
brains, gives hope to many people!

Since my relative is the only person in my life to ever suggest I have not given "hope," I have taken this very seriously in order to be more acutely aware of what hope is and how I can do better. Naturally, I went to the dictionary. In The Merriam-Webster Dictionary of the English Language, hope is defined this way: "Hope is a feeling of expectation and desire for a certain thing to happen." [7] Another defined hope this way, "Hope is the emotional state, the opposite of which is despair, which promotes the belief in a positive outcome related to events and happenings in one's life." [8] Yet another, "Hope is looking forward with confidence to a future good."[9]

If that is the case, there are a whole lot of folks who get let down. Think of those who:

* expect/desire a raise at work and do not get it.

* the students who expect/desire an A on a test and do not make it.

* the athlete who has trained diligently and devotedly who expects/ desires to make the team and does not.

1

* the one who expects/desires the doctor to give a great health report and is told there are serious medical problems.

What about:

* the spouse who expects/hopes to be loved and adored by the spouse and instead is often pushed aside for sports or work or other family members?

* the parents who expect/desire their little ones to grow up to be doctors and lawyers who grow up to be chemically addicted and incarcerated?

* those who live in war-torn countries under evil dictatorships?

* those who watch their children die of starvation and thirst?

* those whose children are taken away from them at the border of this country and live in substandard housing?

* the indigent farmer who makes forty cents a day working on farms where the produce they collect will go to corporations where the CEO's make millions of dollars.

Where is hope for those:

  * trapped by diseases who have no medical insurance? (As I write these words, our world is in "shut-down" from the deadly Corona - Covid 19 virus. Millions have been infected and there have been numerous deaths. There is great fear enveloping us, both from contracting the disease and what it may do our health, and how the medical bills will be paid with many businesses having to shut down.)
  * abused by the church, and by people who are supposed to protect and defend all people?
  * the physically, emotionally, and spiritually abused who are underage and must remain silent?

Where is the hope for the people in these and other such situations?

Hope is a simple four-letter word that can mean so much to anyone going through a difficult time. It can certainly make the difference between hanging on and giving up.

As I have reflected on hope, I am not certain it can be defined, but only experienced. In my life I have witnessed the evidence of hope in the lives of some who had no hope for a future in this world.

Judy

She was 37 years of age dying of Hodgkin's disease. She had suffered with it for fifteen years. Her husband and eleven-year-old son were constantly there for her. Her doctors told her if she could live another six to ten months, there would be medical improvements that would basically make the disease non-threatening. The last month of her life, she asked to be at home. I went by one day to visit her and the family. She was wrapped in a quilt with a notebook in her hand. I asked what she was doing, and she said, "We need a new kitchen floor. This one is so outdated. I am ordering a new one today!" And she did! A week later, the new linoleum blue floor was put in her kitchen. Flowers were in a vase on the table and she had a smile on her face and peace about her. She died a few days later. Hope wasn't just a new kitchen floor but doing something better for her loved ones. She received a feeling of satisfaction, joy and feeling normal even as she approached the end of her life.

Jennifer

She had just turned seventeen-years-old and had battled cancer since turning four. No person ever diagnosed with this disease lived to be twenty. The day before her death, she was in her bedroom and in great pain. Her father came in the room and asked, "What can I do for you young lady?" She said, "I want to go to Wal-Mart." Though unable to physically take her there, her parents instead said, why don't you go there in your mind, what would you look for? What would you buy?

3

She began to name the things she would have chosen. She felt normal again and when the invisible shopping spree ended, she slowly slipped into a coma and died.

I have talked with the dying who wanted to know more about a sermon series I was going to preach or bible study that would be offered by the church just days or hours before they died. Talking about "normal" or "routine" things of life, brought them hope that tomorrow would be better than today.

Dan

He was in the hospital at the point of death. When he saw me walk into the room, he took out a cassette tape and said, "I want you to hear me play the piano when I was performing in concerts." Slowly, he fumbled with the tape player, put in the tape and when the music began, he relaxed on his pillow and his fingers moved in the air playing an imaginary piano (I imagine the most beautiful concert grand piano of all). His face was radiant. When the tape was over. He ejected it and put it in my hand. He said to me, "Think of me when you listen to it." He died a few hours later. Music was a great part of his hope as he faced the great unknown. Giving me the tape was in some way of saying "I live on, my life counts for something, my music is immortal."

There is hope that we will be remembered after our deaths. That is one kind of hope, and there is another that Cynthia Bourgeault calls "mystical hope" that exists for us in this life. Richard Rohr says of Bourgeault's thought:

Because we are so quickly led to despair, most of us cannot endure suffering for long without some sliver of hope or meaning. However, it is worth asking ourselves about where our hope lies. Cynthia Bourgeault makes a powerful distinction between what she calls ordinary hope, "tied to outcome.... an optimistic feeling... because we sense that things will get better in the future" and mystical hope "that is a complete reversal of our usual way of looking at things. Beneath the 'upbeat' kind of hope that parts the seas and pulls rabbits out of hats, this other hope weaves its way as a quiet, even ironic counterpoint."[10]

Let me share from Bourgeault's own writings:

We might make the following observations about this other kind of hope, which we will call *mystical hope*. In contrast to our usual notions of hope:

1. Mystical hope *(or what I would simply call "Christian hope")* **is not tied to a good outcome, to the future.** It lives a life of its own, seemingly without reference to external circumstances and conditions.

2. It has something to do with *presence*—not a future good outcome, but the immediate experience of being met, held in communion, by something intimately at hand.

3. It bears fruit within us at the psychological level in the sensations of strength, joy, and satisfaction: an "unbearable lightness of being." But mysteriously, rather than deriving these gifts from outward expectations being met, it seems to produce them from within...

[It] is all too easy to understate and miss that hope is not intended to be an extraordinary infusion, *but an abiding state of being.* We lose sight of the invitation—and in fact, our *responsibility*, as stewards of creation—to develop a conscious and permanent connection to this wellspring. We miss the call to become a vessel, to become a chalice into which this divine energy can pour; a lamp through which it can shine.

We ourselves are not the *source* of that hope; we do not manufacture it. But the source dwells deeply within us and flows to us with an unstinting abundance, so much so that in fact it might be more accurate to say we dwell within it.

The good news is that this deeper current does exist and you actually *can* find it. For me the journey to the source of hope is ultimately a *theological* journey: up and over the mountain to the sources of hope in the headwaters of the Christian Mystery. This journey to the wellsprings of hope is not something that will change your life in the short range, in the externals. Rather, it is something that will change your innermost way of seeing. The journey to the wellsprings of hope is really a journey toward the center, toward the innermost ground of our being where we meet and are met by God.[11]

We do not simply "obtain" hope, it is "an abiding state of being." When we stay connected to the "wellspring" we become an instrument into which "this divine energy can flow." I love her words, "*a lamp through which it can shine.*"

Bourgeault is right when she emphasizes that we must stay close to the "center – the innermost ground of our being where we meet and are met by God" so that hope abides. How this happens is mysterious and "mystical." It is not something we can make happen because it is in the relationship of our openness to meet God, the source of all hope.

It is here that we see the difference between *hope* and *wishing.* Hope is not necessarily futuristic, but something that resides in us (*an abiding state of being*). Wishing is most used in the past:

I wish I had not said that.
I wish I had studied harder for that test.
I wish I had made a better choice.

When "wish" is used futuristically, it almost always deals with the impossible:

I wish I will win the lottery.
I wish I drove a Rolls Royce.
I wish I could be a celebrity.

There is nothing significantly wrong with "wishing," however, it is far from having "hope." We can *have* hope always flowing within us. There does not have to be a specific outcome, rather a gradual reshaping of our lives as flowing streams smooth rocks over time. Just as no two rocks are the same, our relationships with God are all unique and beautifully so. Thus, hope means something different to all people.

I would love to know the images of hope that come to the minds of those who live in the Amazon? the People's Republic of Congo? In Antarctica? The Soviet Union? The UK? South Korea? North Korea? Vietnam? Iraq? North Dakota? Canada? Hawaii? Belize? Or those in jail? Homeless? Starving? Those suffering from disease?

In our home, there is a small table on the glass porch where I sit each morning for my time of devotional reading and prayer. From my chair, I look out over beautiful Lake Lanier. The view never ceases to inspire me of the beauty of creation. Water has a calming effect on me. So, during my time of devotional and study each morning, I have thought about how I have experienced hope and I realize that often I have experienced hope, with and without "a feeling of expectation and desire for a certain thing to happen" as the dictionary suggests, and I have experienced "mystical hope" throughout my life where I am *hope-filled* because of my love for God and others and their love for me.

As I have meditated on hope, I decided to sit down and be intentional about where I have experienced hope by putting pen to paper. Here are some of the ways:

a tiny smile in the face of a devastating diagnosis
a wave from the hand of a child when feeling sad
finding a penny on the ground
a person offering a free piece of chocolate or cologne
when my wife prepares my favorite meals (I clean, I don't cook!)
the face of a grandmother or grandfather
an organ donor has been located

feeling the sun and warmth on my face after a long and bitterly
cold winter
receiving a letter or email from an old friend
a "vacancy" sign on a hotel when it is late, and exhaustion has set in
seeing a rainbow after torrential storms
feeling the tug on a fishing pole after hours without one
turning the calendar to a new year
money back from the IRS
my political party candidate is elected
being selected for the team
the smell of hamburgers and hot dogs cooking on a grill
spying a nest of infant birds
forgiveness from a person I have hurt
the hand of a child in mine
when the prodigal comes home
the letter of acceptance from the college of my choice
knowing I am loved
the steeple on a church
heat on a cold day and cold on a hot day
when she said "I do"
hearing the windchimes make music as the wind tickles them
the soft glow of a candle in darkness
a hand clasped in prayer
the laughter of a baby
the thrill of a touchdown
a new puppy
the music of the Beatles
someone remembering my birthday
the smell of a new vehicle
seeing the ocean
a pair of glasses
a refrigerator full of food
the job I love
when relatives gather for special events
a new song whose tune goes over and over in my mind

medicines for illnesses
the bank telling me I have more money in my checking than I thought
going on vacation
looking at the changing colors of leaves in autumn
an Easter lily, butterfly, and other symbols of Easter
a friend lets you borrow a cup of sugar when our cupboards are bare
watching a movie with my wife
seeing the capitol of my nation or state
the blessing of a meal
when I have enough batteries on Christmas morning
saying "yes"
saying "no"
when my wife makes banana bread with my late mother's recipe
remembering special events in my life
my relationship with God
Christmas morning
the promise of God to be with us always
wedding pictures
seashells
a good novel
watching my grandkids enjoy the lake, the boat, fishing
the sound of my wife's voice
a cathedral
beautiful organ music
dancing at a wedding
the smiling face of the nurse and doctor when I am afraid and sick
having a dependable vehicle to drive
my favorite restaurant
time to reflect
praying for world peace and working toward it
a Moon Pie and an R C cola
hearing "O Holy Night" sung beautifully during the Christmas season
a Christmas cactus blooming right on time!
the smell of a freshly cut lawn
being called D-Dad by my grandchildren

family togetherness
remembering loved ones now departed from this life
bringing joy to a person in need
a just judge
the smell of vanilla flavoring
walking in a sanctuary when the pews are polished and
candles burning
smell of cinnamon rolls and hot Krispy Kreme Donuts
pictures of my grandparent's home
symbols: a dove, the cross, butterfly, anchor, baptismal font,
bread/wine
snuggling up with a child and telling them a bedtime story
the sixty-six-book library called the Bible
the baptism of a child
when the dentist says "no cavities"
when a third grader receives a Bible from the church
a boy scout receiving the eagle scout award
the word "chaplain" on the door in the hospital
being with someone you love
planting a tree
holding a newborn baby
going to the zoo
the Big Chicken in Marietta, Georgia
(I knew I was near grandparent's home!)
front porches
farmland
birthday parties
missionaries
watching deer move across my yard
sunsets on the top of the boathouse with my wife and a glass of wine
a book sale
the library known as the Bible
scales that show I have lost weight
pictures drawn by my grandkids on the refrigerator
smell of homemade bread

photo albums filled with pictures of loved ones
Christmas ornaments – especially the ones made by my children
and grands
the writings of Henri Nouwen, Richard Rohr, Leslie Weatherhead,
and others
seeing a teenager carrying their Bible into worship
the teachings of Scott Peck
a toddler getting his first haircut
beautiful flowers and trees that come alive in springtime
surprise visits to our home from a friend or family
my computer turning on each morning for me to read the paper
praying the daily hours
sharing exciting news to another
the cleaners
opening a letter of affirmation
my cell phone
aunts and uncles and cousins
the statue of liberty
teachers
my closest friends
doctors without borders
mountains
friends
the smell of freshly cleaned church pews
Cedric the entertainer
a hospice worker
To Kill a Mockingbird
a dark sky full of beautiful stars
unexpected visitors
hygienists
hearing someone call my name
works of art
the tenor voice of Alfie Boe
the light on the porch welcoming me home

My list continues as I go about day to day living. I am more alert to hope than ever before in my life.

Recently, I have been going through boxes in the basement that I have not opened in years. In one, I found some of my old yearbooks. The oldest one I have is from my seventh-grade year while a student at Darlington in Rome, Georgia. As I opened the yearbook, I thought of all my old friends, wondered about many of my classmates, and began hoping that I might reconnect with some of them in the future. (I am quite aware that none of us will look the same. I once had black, solid black hair, and lots of it. Today, I have little hair and what is left is white!)

With each page I saw teachers, staff and students that in their own way, were hope to me. One in particular came to mind: the secretary to the headmaster lived in my neighborhood. She called me to her office one day and said, "I have a job opportunity for you if want it." She told me about her next-door-neighbors who were in their eighties who needed someone to bring in firewood and kindling into their home each day during the cold months. It paid $5.00 a week! I took the job and worked for them for three years. They became "second" grandparents to me. I worked there throughout every season. In the summer I painted, or cut grass, or weeded in their garden. In the autumn, I raked leaves and cleaned their gutters. Winter was bringing in firewood, and springtime was spent helping put in new flowers. There was always something to do and I loved it.

Sometimes our best vision of hope is looking backwards! What great hope I was offered to not only make a little money, but the blessings of knowing these wonderful people. I had forgotten, and now the memory fills me with a sense of thanksgiving and joy. Hope leads to gratefulness, joy and peace.

We keep our grand dogs from time-to-time and recently I noticed that while we were eating at the table, our son and his wife's chocolate Labrador sat quietly beside my chair watching every bite I took. As I looked closer, she was salivating and there were drops running off of her mouth onto the floor. She was anticipating, (hope-filled) that some scrap would come her way.

Humans are not much different! We salivate as we watch our meals being assembled. Notice how many times we swallow while waiting on our food to arrive!! We salivate anticipating: a birthday party, a raise at work, waiting for the person we want to date to say "yes," seeing a loved one who has been away for months or years. All of these, and many more, are aspects of hope.

Let me encourage you to make your list of what brings you hope. Compare it to mine. Compare it to those in your family or friends at work. You may discover that what brings you hope may bring the exact opposite to another. What is one person's "heaven" can be another's "hell." Perhaps you offered hope to someone, and they never understood it that way.

I love music of all kinds. Growing up with a preacher-father, I deeply love the great hymns of the church, the old gospel songs, and organ and piano music. When I was in college, while I studied, I loved to listen to soft organ music. One of my roommates did not grow up in the church and he despised it when I had on a record of organ music or church hymns! Usually, I would change to the music of our decade when he was in the room, but at times he would come in while I was studying to classical music and say, "Turn that stuff off! It's horrible."

Basically, hope is one little word with NO true definition!

Though we cannot really define hope, it is like what someone said when asked "What is pornography?" replied, "I cannot define it, but I'll know what it is when I see it."

We cannot define love, but we know "God is love."[12] Paul, in his letter to the Corinthian church writes about the "nature" of love" in what has become known as the "love chapter of the Bible," but he does not and cannot define love.[13]

From cover-to-cover the Bible shares about God's undying faith in humanity, but the Bible never defines "faith" rather, we are given the nature of faith in multitudes of ways.

Similarly, the Bible never defines "hope" rather, points to it as the continuous work of God. In essence, God is faith, hope and love. Further, humanity, made in the *image* of God, share these qualities, these "natures. They are already within us, and we can offer faith, hope and love without consciously being aware of it. However, when we *intentionally* do so, the world becomes a better place, and there is a deeper sense of purpose and meaning as we go about life day-to-day.

Hope is all around us. It is like the air we breathe, ever-present, but hardly noticed until something blocks it from us, and we know we must have it to survive or else we will die.

Perhaps hope is what enables us to have faith and to love. Hope is the undercurrent of all that allows us to "get up in the morning expecting today to be better than yesterday." Soren Kierkegaard once said, "hope is passion for what is possible."[14] Helen Keller said it this way, "optimism is the faith that leads to achievement. Nothing can be done without hope and confidence."[15]

Something as simple as going to the grocery store is an exercise in hope that the place will carry the things we need. The same with going to the doctor, dentist, buying clothes, affording a new vehicle, mailing a letter, trying AA, going to a restaurant, and studying for a test. Practicing day after day on the football field is an exercise in hoping that the player will be able to get in the game and maybe, just maybe, the team will win.

Hope is at work in EVERYTHING we do and will do!

Without hope, we cannot go forward in life. Indeed, hope permeates our lives! Hope is something we choose! Joanna Macy says "active hope is a practice...*it is something we **do** rather than **have**.* Since active hope doesn't require our optimism, we can apply it even in areas where we feel hopeless. The guiding impetus is intention; we choose what we aim to bring about, act for, or express."[16] Vaclav Havel says it this way,

> *"Hope is a state of mind, not of the world. Either we have hope within or we don't; it is a dimension of the soul not essentially dependent on some particular observation of the world or estimate of the situation. It is an orientation of the spirit, an orientation of the heart; it transcends the world that is immediately experienced and is anchored somewhere beyond its horizons."*[17]

When we choose hope, then we can "sit by a window and wait for one more dawn, despite the fact that there is not one ounce of proof in the black, black sky that is can possibly come." [18] Hope is not necessarily based on outcome, but perceived outcome. Hope is trust that the future will exist, and it will be good.

Hope locates itself in the premises that we don't know what will happen and that in the spaciousness of uncertainty is room to act... ***Hope is an embrace of the unknown and the unknowable.***[19]

When parents walk toward the emergency room to see their teenager who they know is in critical condition from an automobile accident where under-age drinking was involved, they embrace an unknown future. They hope, despite the odds, that their child will live and thrive, that they can survive the monetary burden of hospital bills, and that they will not be sued for other damages. In the deep darkness, subconsciously, they have chosen hope; hope for their child, hope for themselves, and hope for a bright future despite the tremendous odds against it.

The Apostle realized this when he wrote:

> "...*that suffering produces endurance, and endurance produces character, and character produces hope*" (Romans 5:3-4)

How does this happen? Take an athlete for example who decides to strive for the Olympics. There can be no "endurance" without pushing the body; not stopping to rest the second the body feels weak. Such "suffering" builds endurance which leads to growth!

Taking this illustration a step further, to be the best athlete means saying "no" to harmful things (such as getting little sleep, eating and drinking harmful things to the body, and being lazy). It means saying "yes" to a lifestyle of focusing on the goal and not allowing anything to prevent it. Thus, endurance produces character.

The athlete with "character" is one who lives on an even plane of being. There is no wavering from the lifestyle no matter the number of wins or losses along the path to the goal. It is this inner character that produces hope; hope that sustains us no matter what happens to us in life.

One of my childhood friends was diagnosed with glioblastoma. The physicians laid out for him and his wife what this disease looked like:

- It was not curable by medical treatment.
- The odds of living beyond eighteen months are minimal.
- What makes it so deadly is it looks like an octopus: the tumor has tentacles that go all over the brain that are inoperable.
- There are several medical centers working diligently on ways to cure.
- The medical team can do what surgery they can and then give chemo/radiation.

We know this disease as the one that took the lives of John McCain and Ted Kennedy. Perhaps you know another who has had or has this horrible disease.

Knowing the future is unknown, knowing there is not "one ounce of proof" for survival, he chose the surgery. He is taking both chemo and radiation. The cancer is spreading. He is embracing the unknown and cherishing time with his family and friends. It is hope that enables him to face each minute as he journeys through this disease. Witnessing his hope gives his wife, children and grandchildren encouragement that translates as hope.

Within the past couple of weeks, he has spiraled downward. He is now in a hospital bed in his living room and given morphine to keep him comfortable. He has a two-year-old granddaughter who adores him. In his immense pain, with eyes closed, he senses her presence. He gently moves his hand from under the sheet and his beloved little cherub reaches out and holds his finger. A smile lights his face. No words between them, but incredible love and hope fill the room.

Hope is what gives us incentive to live against all odds and even to do so with joy and expecting a tomorrow. The Apostle Paul wrote to the church in Corinth, "Love bears all things, believes all things, *HOPES* all things, endures all things."[20] Love hopes! Life hopes! Without it, we cannot live. It is as essential to life as breath itself.

Hope can mean anything you want it to be!

———✝———

Chapter 2

The Opposite of hope

————⋈————

Hope is a song in a weary throat.

Pauli Murray

Besides the Lord's prayer, my mother insisted that I, along with my siblings, memorize the prayer of St. Frances of Assisi. It has taken on several mutations over the years, but the one I memorized is this:

Lord, make me an instrument of your peace
Where there is hatred, let me sow love
Where there is injury, pardon
Where there is doubt, faith
Where there is despair, hope
Where there is darkness, light
And where there is sadness, joy
O Divine Master, grant that I may
Not so much seek to be consoled as to console
To be understood, as to understand
To be loved, as to love
For it is in giving that we receive
And it's in pardoning that we are pardoned
And it's in dying that we are born to Eternal Life
Amen[21]

The way I memorized the first section was to think in terms of opposites:

Opposite of love – hate, (I have learned over time that the opposite of love is apathy) opposite of doubt – faith, opposite of despair – hope, opposite of darkness – light, and the opposite of sadness – joy.

The dictionary says "despair" is "utter loss of hope."[22] Jurgen Moltmann says that "despair, presupposes hope. What we do not long for, can be the object neither of our hope nor of our despair (Augustine) The pain of despair surely lies in the fact that a hope is there, but no way opens up towards its fulfilment."[23]

My heart hurts that my relative was in despair and she felt she did not receive any hope from me. The vision that keeps coming to my mind is seeing her drowning in a lake. I am throwing her a rope that lands right in front of her. All she has to do is grab onto it so she could be pulled to safety, but she doesn't get it. Either she is too scared to reach out and take it or she doesn't see it, or she is looking elsewhere. For whatever reason, the rope of my hope doesn't seem to rescue her.

As a pastor, it has been my life's passion to be a "rope-thrower" to those drowning in despair. I have been there myself drowning in despair, and amazingly, there was always someone to rescue me.

I have seen those who have experienced despair along my life's journey:

- The man who lost his job, then his family, and was homeless for over three years.
- The woman who desperately wanted to give birth and have a household full of children, rushed to the hospital during her first pregnancy, lost the child and had to have an emergency hysterectomy. She would never give birth to her own children.

- The husband, shortly after marrying the woman of his dreams, discovers he has testicular cancer. As he prepares for surgery, the doctors discover the cancer is not only in one, but both testicles. They are removed. He will never father a child. They divorce.

- The woman whose husband died. She was a "kept" woman: large house, swimming pool, expensive cars, jewelry, clothing, and vacations. Suddenly her husband died, and she never knew his investments. Upon his death, he owed millions of dollars. At age 60, she lost everything she had and moved in with her 80-year-old parents. She never recovered from her poverty.

- The mother of three small children who became extremely sick, went to the doctor for help. He ran tests on her and when she came for the results is told that she has AIDS. She had never been promiscuous. She confronts her husband and discovers he had led a secret life. He gave her AIDS. They both died leaving their children to be raised by a relative.

- The couple who raised five children into adulthood. Four of the five held post college degrees and were outstanding citizens. The middle child was homeless and lived on the streets of Atlanta, severely chemically addicted. They tried everything in their power to reach him, but to no avail. He died at age 28 from his addictions.

- The family who had two sons. The oldest son married and had a little girl. When his daughter was two years old, he discovered that his wife and his brother were having an affair! To add insult to injury, she was pregnant by his brother. He and his wife divorced, and his brother married the ex-wife. The family is irreparably shattered. The parents are beyond devastated. The brothers vow never to see one another again.

- The family shattered by a brother who secretly had his father, (in the early stages of dementia) sign a new will leaving everything to him. When the father died and the will was read, the rest of the family discovered what had happened. The brother showed no remorse, received all the money, land, houses, and personal belongings of his parents and the rest of the siblings received nothing.

- The children whose mother died, and the father remarried eight months later taking his new wife on a European honeymoon. While there, he dies, and she has him cremated. When she returns home, the children are informed that everything belongs to her, and they will receive nothing. To this day, twenty years later, they have never been able to have even one thing from their parent's home, personal items that would hold no value to the wife but would mean the world to them. They fear she killed him for his money and possessions but can never prove it.

- The patient who is told that the tests came back positive: stage four cancer that has metastasized to several vital organs and has only weeks to live.

- The worker who has given over twenty-five years to the company and finds a pink-slip in his office. He will not receive all his pensions, health insurance canceled, and no severance. He is over fifty and cannot find any work.

- The man who has lived a troubled life because of "sins" from his youth. He hates himself for having had sexual relations with his sister when they shared a bed in his early teen years. The family lived in poverty. They lived in a small house with three rooms. His parents lived there with their five children. He had to share a mattress with his younger sister.

- The man who went to the doctor early one morning to receive the report of his recent physical. The doctor told him that he had cancer and would need to be hospitalized for further tests and surgery. He leaves the physician's office and heads to work only to receive the news that the company needed to downsize, and he was without a job. In frustration, he heads home to wait for his wife to return from work, decides to water the vegetable garden and when he reaches down to turn on the hose, is bitten by a copperhead. He is rushed to the hospital where he knows he needs immediate help but knows he will not be able to pay the bills.

We have read and studied about the despair caused by:

- the Holocaust,
- child abuse from thousands of Roman Catholic priests and clergy from other denominations.
- the sinking of the Titanic where the poor were locked in the bowels of the ship where they could not get out and all drowned.
- Severe poverty
- Communism
- The great political divide
- recessions

Confronting America's silent disease: Suicide

Suicide is the tenth leading cause of death in America![24] Let that sink in.

Based on the CDC's analysis, the occupational groups with the highest suicide rates are:

1. Farming, fishing and forestry: 84.5 suicides for every 100,000 people in the occupation
2. Construction and extraction: 53.3
3. Installation, maintenance and repair: 47.9
4. Production: 34.5
5. Architecture and engineering: 32.2
6. Protective service: 30.5
7. Arts, design, entertainment, sports and media: 24.3
8. Computer and mathematical: 23.3

9. Transportation and material moving: 22.3
10. Management: 20.3[25]

Medical doctors have the highest suicide rate of any profession. **One doctor commits suicide in the United States every day!** It is higher than among those in the military, which is considered a very stressful occupation.

Contrary to what many believe, the cold winter months are not the months with the most suicides! The highest rates are in the light of spring, not the darkness of winter.[26]

Also, "In April, May and June, the suicide rate goes up and is the highest."[27] These numbers can be two to three times higher than in December, when suicide rates are the lowest.

Suicide statistics:

I.   States with the highest rate of suicide:
  1) Alaska
  2) New Mexico
  3) Wyoming
  4) Nevada
  5) Colorado

II. Men commit suicide at a higher rate than women.

III. The second highest rate of suicide is between the ages of 15-35.

IV. Though dentists are not ranked in the top rankings of professions who take their lives, they are prone to depression because "they are in a profession where nobody wants to see them, and they are the last place people want to come back to."[28]

As I write this chapter, the coronavirus, Covid-19, is plaguing the world. As I have already stated, millions have already died, and many millions are infected. Numerous businesses have had to close their doors, schools have shut down, and the stock market has taken a huge hit. Two dentists in our city have taken their lives.

Religion and suicide:

One of the most important facts about the Bible is it is never afraid to address any subject. Murder, adultery, greed, sexual deviancy, incest, war, and just about every known sin to humankind are found within its pages. And though most who have read the Bible remember two suicides best: King Saul and Judas Iscariot, there are actually seven suicides in the Bible.

1. [Abimelech] called hastily unto the young man his armor-bearer, and said unto him, Draw thy sword, and slay me, that men say not of me, A woman slew him. And his young man thrust him through, and he died (Judges 9:54).

2. And Samson said, "Let me die with the Philistines. And he bowed with all his might; and the house fell...upon all the people that were therein" (Judges 16:30).

3. Saul took a sword and fell on it (1 Sam. 31:4).

4. When [Saul's] armor-bearer saw that Saul was dead, he fell likewise upon his sword, and died (1 Sam 31:5).

5. When Ahithophel saw that his counsel was not followed, he... got him home to his house, to his city, and put his house in order, and hanged himself, and died (2 Sam. 17:23).

6. It came to pass, when Zimri saw that the city was taken, that he went into the palace of the king's house, and burnt the king's house over him with fire, and died (1 Kings 16:18).

7. [Judas] cast down the pieces of silver in the temple, and departed, and went and hanged himself (Matt. 27:5).

I have devoted my whole adult life to the church and the study of Scripture. I strongly believe that the "church is of God and will be preserved until the end of time."[29] The church has done much good over the numerous centuries of its existence. In short, I owe my life to the church!

However, I have witnessed churches who have done much damage.

- The woman who came to the church where I was serving as pastor who was "kicked out" of her church when she was a teen because she was pregnant and unmarried. The elders publicly shamed her in front of the congregation.

- The couple who worked diligently in their church for the prevention of abortion discovers their fourteen-year-old daughter is pregnant. They realize that some social issues look differently when the issue is your daughter, and she is sitting across the kitchen table crying. They know they cannot go back to the church where they attend because now, they are struggling with the issue of abortion.

- The young man who came to my office one day to share that he would never trust a clergy person again. When he was in the sixth grade, his youth leader sexually molested him when driving him home from a youth event.

- The couple who gave their church a quarter of a million dollars only to discover the pastor had stolen it and used it to purchase a large home. They would never give through the church again.

When I was in college, a professor who was dearly loved on campus, took his life. He was an advisor to my fraternity, and we were all stunned and deeply bereaved. On the day of his funeral, many of us went to the funeral home. When I walked in, this professors' aunt came up to my brothers and to me and said, "Thank you for coming here today. You know he is in hell. That's what the Bible says." She had learned in her church that suicide was believed to be a "mortal sin" punishable by eternal hell.

One of the most tragic funerals I ever attended was of a man who took his life. He was married with two children. He and his family were deeply involved in a church of another denomination. One day his wife came home to find a note from her husband. He told her that he had taken all their savings out of the bank and was on his way to Florida where he planned to live it up and engage in homosexual activity. He told her he loved her and the children, but he had lived a lie and wanted to live his life in this new way. One week later, his body was found in a hotel room. He left a note. He shot himself in the head. He was an only child, and his parents were not to be consoled.

At his funeral, the clergy preached on sin and evil. They never mentioned how this man lived nor how he died, only to say that he was in hell where he belonged. His in-laws, dear friends of mine, came to me following the burial and said, "Will you go and minister to our daughter and her children? They need to hear the Good News of Jesus Christ, and to remind them that though their father had issues, he loved them." Then they said to me and with tears running down their faces, "They didn't even say his name."

It is imperative that we know that God loves us: body, mind and soul. Jesus said, "I have not come to those who are well, but to those who are sick."[30] Anyone who takes their lives, has the sickness of hopelessness. It is the greatest despair of all.

Let me first address scriptures that articulate the importance of the body and its care. Also, scriptures that show how God is with us in our worst of times. And lastly, where people get the idea that taking one's life will send you to hell.

Scriptures showing God's value of humanity, the care of the body and God's everlasting presence with us:

Psalm 34:17-20

When the righteous cry for help, the LORD hears and delivers them out of all their troubles. The LORD is near to the brokenhearted and saves the crushed in spirit. Many are the afflictions of the righteous, but the LORD delivers him out of them all. He keeps all his bones; not one of them is broken.

1 Corinthians 6:19-20

Or do you not know that your body is a temple of the Holy Spirit within you, whom you have from God? You are not your own, for you were bought with a price. So, glorify God in your body.

Jeremiah 29:11

For I know the plans I have for you, declares the LORD, plans for welfare and not for evil, to give you a future and a hope.

Proverbs 3:5-6

Trust in the LORD with all your heart, and do not lean on your own understanding. In all your ways acknowledge him, and he will make straight your paths.

Psalm 147:3

He heals the brokenhearted and binds up their wounds.

Romans 10:13

For "everyone who calls on the name of the Lord will be saved."

Romans 8:38-39

For I am sure that neither death nor life, nor angels nor rulers, nor things present nor things to come, nor powers, nor height nor depth, **nor anything else in all creation, will be able to separate us from the love of God in Christ Jesus our Lord.**

Deuteronomy 30:19

I have set before you life and death, blessing and curse. Therefore, choose life, that you and your offspring may live,

John 10:10

The thief comes only to steal and kill and destroy. I came that they may have life and have it abundantly.

John 10:28

I give them eternal life, and they will never perish, and no one will snatch them out of my hand.

2 Corinthians 12:9

But he said to me, "My grace is sufficient for you, for my power is made perfect in weakness." Therefore, I will boast all the more gladly of my weaknesses, so that the power of Christ may rest upon me.

Romans 12:2

Do not be conformed to this world, but be transformed by the renewal of your mind, that by testing you may discern what is the will of God, what is good and acceptable and perfect.

Romans 5:2-8

Through him we have also obtained access by faith into this grace in which we stand, and we rejoice in hope of the glory of God. More than that, we rejoice in our sufferings, knowing that suffering produces endurance, and endurance produces character, and character produces hope, and hope does not put us to shame, because God's love has been poured into our hearts through the Holy Spirit who has been given to us. For while we were still weak, at the right time Christ died for the ungodly....

Matthew 6:34

"Therefore, do not be anxious about tomorrow, for tomorrow will be anxious for itself. Sufficient for the day is its own trouble.

Isaiah 41:10

Fear not, for I am with you; be not dismayed, for I am your God; I will strengthen you, I will help you, I will uphold you with my righteous right hand. *This has always been a favorite of mine. The hymn, "How firm A Foundation" is based on this text.*

2 Corinthians 4:8-9

We are afflicted in every way, but not crushed; perplexed, but not driven to despair; persecuted, but not forsaken; struck down, but not destroyed.

1 Peter 5:7

Casting all your anxieties on him, because he cares for you.

Psalm 55:22

Cast your burden on the LORD, and he will sustain you; he will never permit the righteous to be moved.

John 16:33

I have said these things to you, that in me you may have peace. In the world you will have tribulation. But take heart; I have overcome the world."

Psalm 138:7

Though I walk in the midst of trouble, you preserve my life; you stretch out your hand against the wrath of my enemies, and your right hand delivers me.

Psalm 34:18-19

The LORD is near to the brokenhearted and saves the crushed in spirit. Many are the afflictions of the righteous, but the LORD delivers him out of them all.

Hebrews 13:5-6

Keep your life free from love of money, and be content with what you have, for he has said, "I will never leave you nor forsake you." So, we can confidently say, "The Lord is my helper; I will not fear; what can man do to me?"

1 Peter 5:6-7

Humble yourselves, therefore, under the mighty hand of God so that at the proper time he may exalt you, casting all your anxieties on him, because he cares for you.

John 14:1

"Let not your hearts be troubled. Believe in God; believe also in me.

Matthew 11:28

Come to me, all who labor and are heavy laden, and I will give you rest.

1 John 4:4

Little children, you are from God and have overcome them, for he who is in you is greater than he who is in the world.

Psalm 23

The LORD is my shepherd; I shall not want. He makes me lie down in green pastures. He leads me beside still waters. He restores my soul. He leads me in paths of righteousness for his name's sake. Even though I walk **through** the valley of the shadow of death, I will fear no evil, for you are with me; your rod and your staff, they comfort me. You prepare a table before me in the presence of my enemies; you anoint my head with oil; my cup overflows. Surely goodness and mercy will follow me all the days of my life and I shall live in the house of the Lord forever.

We may never get "over" the death of a loved one, but we can get "through" it.

Joshua 1:9

Have I not commanded you? Be strong and courageous. Do not be frightened, and do not be dismayed, for the LORD your God is with you wherever you go."

Isaiah 40:31

But they who wait for the LORD shall renew their strength; they shall mount up with wings like eagles; they shall run and not be weary; they shall walk and not faint.

Philippians 1:6

And I am sure of this, that he who began a good work in you will bring it to completion at the day of Jesus Christ.

Revelation 21:4

He will wipe away every tear from their eyes, and death shall be no more, neither shall there be mourning, nor crying, nor pain anymore, for the former things have passed away."

Hebrews 11:1-40

Now faith is the assurance of things hoped for, the conviction of things not seen. For by it the people of old received their commendation. By faith we understand that the universe was created by the word of God, so that what is seen was not made out of things that are visible. By faith Abel offered to God a more acceptable sacrifice than Cain, through which he was commended as righteous, God commending him by accepting his gifts. And through his faith, though he died, he still speaks. By faith Enoch was taken up so that he should not see death, and he was not found, because God had taken him. Now before he was taken, he was commended as having pleased God....

2 Corinthians 1:10

He delivered us from such a deadly peril, and he will deliver us. On him we have set our hope that he will deliver us again.

Job 10:12

You have granted me life and steadfast love, and your care has preserved my spirit.

Romans 8:1-2

There is therefore now no condemnation for those who are in Christ Jesus. For the law of the Spirit of life has set you free in Christ Jesus from the law of sin and death.

Luke 18:1

And he told them a parable to the effect that they ought always to pray and not lose heart.

Genesis 2:7

Then the LORD God formed the man of dust from the ground and breathed into his nostrils the breath of life, and the man became a living creature.

Isaiah 55:11

So shall my word be that goes out from my mouth; it shall not return to me empty, but it shall accomplish that which I purpose, and shall succeed in the thing for which I sent it.

Psalm 42:5

Why are you cast down, O my soul, and why are you in turmoil within me? Hope in God; for I shall again praise him, my salvation

Romans 15:13

May the **God of hope** fill you with all joy and peace in believing, so that by the power of the Holy Spirit you may **abound in hope**.

Romans 8:28

And we know that for those who love God all things work together for good, for those who are called according to his purpose.

1 John 1:9

If we confess our sins, he is faithful and just to forgive us our sins and to cleanse us from all unrighteousness.

Philippians 4:13

I can do all things through him who strengthens me.

Psalm 30:8-12

To you, O LORD, I cry, and to the Lord I plead for mercy: "What profit is there in my death, if I go down to the pit? Will the dust praise you? Will it tell of your faithfulness? Hear, O LORD, and be merciful to me! O LORD, be my helper!" You have turned for me my mourning into dancing; you have loosed my sackcloth and clothed me with gladness, that my glory may sing your praise and not be silent. O LORD my God, I will give thanks to you forever!

Genesis 28:15

Behold, I am with you and will keep you wherever you go and will bring you back to this land. For I will not leave you until I have done what I have promised you."

Psalm 34:1-35:28

Of David, when he changed his behavior before Abimelech, so that he drove him out, and he went away. I will bless the LORD at all times; his praise shall continually be in my mouth. My soul makes its boast in the LORD; let the humble hear and be glad. Oh, magnify the LORD with me, and let us exalt his name together! I sought the LORD, and he answered me and delivered me from all my fears. Those who look to him are radiant, and their faces shall never be ashamed....

John 5:24

Truly, truly, I say to you, whoever hears my word and believes him who sent me has eternal life. He does not come into judgment but has passed from death to life.

1 Peter 4:6-5:10

For this is why the gospel was preached even to those who are dead, that though judged in the flesh the way people are, they might live in the spirit the way God does. The end of all things is at hand; therefore, be self-controlled and sober minded for the sake of your prayers. Above all, keep loving one another earnestly, since love covers a multitude of sins. Show hospitality to one another without grumbling. As each has received a gift, use it to serve one another, as good stewards of God's varied grace:...

Psalm 138:7-139:24

Though I walk in the midst of trouble, you preserve my life; you stretch out your hand against the wrath of my enemies, and your right hand delivers me. The LORD will fulfill his purpose for me; your steadfast love, O LORD, endures forever. Do not forsake the work of your hands.

O LORD, you have searched me and known me! You know when I sit down and when I rise up; you discern my thoughts from afar. You search out my path and my lying down and are acquainted with all my ways....

Luke 1:37

For nothing will be impossible with God."

Psalm 51:17

The sacrifices of God are a broken spirit; a broken and contrite heart, O God, you will not despise.

<u>Now for the tough ones:</u>

<u>Ephesians 5:29</u>

For no one ever hated his own flesh, but nourishes and cherishes it, just as Christ does the church.

This is one that gives a lot of trouble, because far too many "hate their own flesh." We live in a culture that idolizes youthfulness. The beauty industry is a multi-billion-dollar industry. I cannot begin to count the number of men and women who have come to my office who shared how much they hated something about their bodies. Indeed, many have "hated their own flesh."

I had a friend growing up who was severely obese, had acute acne all over his face, arms, back and chest, and sores that caused him to have a distinct odor. Often, he would lament to me how much he hated his body. Today, he is still obese, bears the scars of acne all over his body and continues to hate how he looks.

In one of my pastorates, there was a man who was born with Proteus syndrome. This is a bizarre condition that is horribly disfiguring. Usually, the person who has it has growths all over the body resembling boils or giant tumors like Joseph Merrick, the 19th Century Englishman who became known as the Elephant Man. (If you have never seen the movie *Elephant Man,* I highly recommend it.)

He came to see me one day and told me about growing up with this disease and how he was pushed to the margins of society. He was quite lonely and depressed. Interestingly, he married, and he and his wife adopted four children. He refused to have biological children for fear he would pass along this dreaded syndrome. He was a wonderful man but hated to look at himself in the mirror. He told me he had severe growths over one hundred percent of his body!

More than a few women have shared with me how much they hated their bodies, their hair, their noses, or their figure. I have had men say,

"I feel so lucky to have married such a beautiful woman with the way I look." Then there are those who refuse to work out in a gym for fear of showering and others seeing them naked. Their insecurities prohibit their achieving better health.

Truly, there are many who hate their flesh. Today, youthfulness and beauty seem to be at the forefront of what is acceptable appearance. Far too many "bullies" harass those who are skinny, fat, short, tall, non-athletic, non-achievers, who don't drive a "cool" vehicle, who dress differently than the "norm" and who can't afford to participate in all the extra-curricular programs in school and community. In short, we have an epidemic in this nation of those who "hate their flesh."

One of the church's responsibilities is to teach the importance of knowing we are all made in God's image (as presented in Genesis 1) and it is good. There is beauty in every person. We are more than how we look. Perhaps it is time to eliminate beauty pageants, dating shows where all the women and men look like models, and television shows that criticize and condemn others for their appearance. It is time to appreciate every person's individuality no matter what! Red, yellow, black, brown and white we are precious in God's sight. Let me encourage all of us to celebrate not only who we are and how we look but let us celebrate others and affirm them no matter their appearance.

Mark 16:16

Whoever believes and is baptized will be saved, but whoever does not believe will be condemned.

The emphasis seems to be on "belief" and "baptism."

Throughout my life, I have had people use the term "believer" to describe someone who is follower of Jesus. It isn't that this is wrong, but it can sometimes be used to condemn those who do not "believe" as we believe. What does it mean to "believe?"

I have been a pastor to some who are addicted to illegal substances, who have hurt their families by stealing from them to purchase drugs, who have broken the law, and found themselves in prison. And yet, when I visit many of them, they talk of being a "believer." Are they? What is the criteria of being a "believer?" Am I to judge that?

There have been those in churches who sing in the choir, serve on various important committees in the church, teach Sunday school, and are regularly in worship who commit adultery, get arrested for drunk driving, who fudge on their taxes, who tell lies, and love to condemn those who think, act, and look differently from them. Are they really believers? What is the instrument we should use to measure this?

I have also known those who confess Jesus as Lord of their lives who have never been baptized. Some have died without having participated in this ritual. Should they be condemned?

Luke 23:43 tells the story of Jesus on the cross between two thieves. He says to one of them, "*Today you will be with me in paradise.*" We do not know if the thief has been baptized. Jesus did not ask him whether he had or not! In fact, there is no reference to Jesus ever baptizing anyone, nor asking anyone if they had been baptized.

We are certainly not to discount the meaning and importance of baptism, for Jesus himself was baptized. It was a defining moment in his life and changed the meaning of baptism from simply being for the forgiveness of sins to being a sign of God's eternal love. In Christendom, baptism means we are marked for life with God's eternal love, and is the entrance into the church.

Many churches have a baptismal font at the front of the church to help all who enter remember their baptism. It is customary to dip a finger in the bowl of water and put the sign of the cross on the forehead as a reminder.

I cherish my baptism. My parents had me baptized when I was six months old. The picture hangs in my home: My father, mother, my two sisters (who still had the scabs from chicken pox on their legs) and me.

In my office, I have the little white pants I wore that day and the certificate from the church. Often, I remind myself that I am baptized, I am a member of the family of God known as the church, and <u>that there is nothing I can do for God to love me more or less.</u>

The Bible, from cover to cover, shares the greatest story of love ever written. God is hopelessly in love with humanity. Symbols help us remember that love, such as baptism and communion. But God's love is not dependent on whether we eat bread and drink wine in worship, have water put on our heads, or even if we attend church. Those things can be instruments of affirmation, nevertheless, we are of great value to God without them.

If we read more from where this verse comes from, we read that those who believe will have signs that accompany them: *"they will cast out demons, speak in new tongues, pick up snakes in their hands and if they drink any deadly thing it will not hurt them, they will lay hands on the sick, and they will recover."* (Mark 1616-18) Did Jesus mean this literally?

It seems to me Jesus is saying that when we follow him, we are empowered to live differently from the world. We will *"cast out demons"* by standing up against evil and injustice. We will *"speak in new tongues"* by using more healthy language that uplifts others rather than condemns. We will *"pick up snakes and drink poison and it will not hurt us"* which implies we can go to the poisonous of the world, the deadly of the world and live the good news of Jesus before them without fear. That is the purpose of the church! We are to make disciples of Jesus by going INTO the world where there is evil and sickness and strive to make people whole (well). The word "salvation" in Hebrew means to "be made whole." The root word of salvation is "salve" which is a substance to put on a wound to aid in the healing process. We are to go where people are hurt, wounded and *"lay hands on them"* the hands of welcoming, assurance, comfort and care. This is the work of the church.

I have been at the side of parents who lost a child in birth or youth, and even in adulthood, who were never baptized. Are they condemned?

Condemned to what? Basically, the word "condemned" means to disapprove. It does not mean "cast aside or cast out." I disapproved of my children's behavior when they disobeyed. I would never cast them out.

If the church condemned all who are in it because of their sin, no one would be left to attend! The church must, and I mean must, share the good news of God's grace. Why? Because there are too many who sometimes think they are better off dead.

A member of one of my churches was a fine man. He loved his wife and daughters. He loved the church. I do not think he had an enemy. However, he had a deep struggle. He was an alcoholic. He tried several times to quit. He had treatment and went to AA.

One day, I received a call that he had committed suicide. His note simply said, "I cannot overcome this disease of alcoholism. I love you all, but I am better off dead than an albatross to you. Forgive me." I will never forget his brother's prayer when we all gathered at his home. He said, "O God, we know you did not take him, but you have received him." I love that prayer. God received him. God did not condemn him!

I think that is what Jesus did with the thief on the cross. What really mattered in that crucial hour on the cross was not about the man's belief, but God's belief in him. It was not about whether the thief had been baptized, but God's love for him. This is the essence of the meaning of God's grace. God receives even those we think should be condemned.

Proverbs 11:17

*A man who is kind benefits himself, but a **cruel** man hurts himself.*

I was at a home where a woman had taken her life and her forty-eight-year-old son said to me, "This was cruel of mother to do this. She did not leave a note and without any warning shoots herself." I reminded him that when someone is in such pain, the only thing they can think about is relief. I do not think she wanted to die; I think she wanted relief from her despair. It was not a healthy way of dealing with her depression, nevertheless, she did not mean to be "cruel."

In my many years as a pastor, those who have taken their lives have done so usually out of fear such as not being able to overcome addiction, knowing their spouse no longer loves them, financial woes, health issues, or self-hate. None that I am aware of have taken their lives to punish another or to be cruel. I am confident that there are those who have done so, but it is not the norm.

One of the ways some with depression "act out" is by cutting themselves. I have seen the scars of those who have taken razor blades and cut their wrists, their thighs, their feet, and other areas of the body. They are not intentionally being "cruel" to their bodies, they are trying to cope with their emotional issues.

There are those who "unintentionally" hurt themselves by smoking, excessive drinking, taking illegal and harmful drugs, overeating, never exercising, over working with little rest. Often family members see what is happening and even try to address the issues but are unable to get through to them.

In the movie *The Da Vinci Code* one of the members of the group Opus Dei (a clerical group that seeks to achieve perfection) would go in his cell and completely undress, then take a cord of whips and beat himself with it. For him, it was a means of religious dedication to God and a means of punishing himself for his sins. Nowhere in holy scripture can we find any reference to doing such things to ourselves.

Despair often leads to hurting others and ourselves. It is imperative that the church in general and local churches in particular work to ensure all that God does not need "cruelty" to our bodies, and that the body is sacred. When that is permeated into our whole being, we will begin to see a much healthier society.

1 Corinthians 3:17

If anyone destroys God's temple, God will destroy him. For God's temple is holy, and you are that temple.

This is the main scripture that is used by many to suggest that God will eternally destroy a person who takes their life. However, it is not good Biblical scholarship to take one verse of scripture and isolate it from the rest of the Bible. We must learn to study the Bible in its context and the world from which it came. It is but one sentence out of the entire Bible that suggests God's disfavor with those who would destroy God's temple.

However, we must remember that the character of God is full of grace and forgiveness. Once again, let me reiterate the scripture where Jesus says that God is like the good parent. **No good parent would sentence their child to a permanent place of torment.** Indeed, the words *eternal punishment* are inconsistent with the meaning of punishment. When a parent *punishes* a child, it is to help the child understand what was done wrong so that it can be corrected in order to live harmoniously in the family. To punish a child eternally would defeat the very intention.

Since Jesus taught that we are to forgive 70 x 7 times (or unlimited forgiveness),[31] wouldn't it be understood that God forgives us eternally!! God's ability to love and forgive is far greater than our human minds can comprehend.

The word *destroy* in this scripture is an interesting one. It implies that if we hurt God, God will hurt us. That is not the way of God. God is not hostile. There is no place for hostility in any relationship. One of the reasons for America's high divorce rate is hostility. This occurs when a spouse feels hurt by the other spouse. Instead of confronting the spouse with the hurt for healing to take place, what often happens is the injured spouse seeks to hurt the other. That is hostility. You hurt me, I hurt you. This defeats Jesus' own words to love our enemies, to do good to those who hurt us. What good does it do to love only those who love us, even the *mafia* does that! (Luke 6:32ff; italics mine)

Paul never defines the word *destroy* in this passage. I think of the times my folks would say to me "You do not want to know what I have in mind if you continue your behavior." They meant business. They did not take lightly what I was doing. Neither does God take lightly our behavior. This is true individually and for the church. Remember, Paul was writing to the *church* in Corinth. He referred to the church as the *body* of Christ. The church must strive to never get off track. Woe be to those who would destroy the body of Christ. Whether individually or corporately, hurting the *temple* is of ultimate importance to God. However, God will not obliterate anyone! If we are to have unlimited forgiveness shouldn't God? The use of exaggeration (by the word "destroy) is meant for emphasis only.

Paul seems to define *temple* in the sense that God resides within us. Therefore, our bodies are a temple of God, holy and sacred.

We also must be careful not to define suicide as just those who shoot themselves, swallow a bottle of pills, or close the garage door and die from carbon monoxide poisoning. Many take their lives by years of unhealthy living: smoking, alcohol and drug use, over-eating, laziness, and emotionally through bitterness, anger, and hate. Are we to judge these as also "going to hell?"

The church quickly becomes unhealthy when its members live in unhealthy ways through greed, gossip, hate and selfishness. It is essential that in striving to interpret this passage, we broaden our understanding of the words *destroy* and *temple*.

"Sickness unto death"

"Sickness unto death" is what the nineteenth -century Danish theologian Soren Kierkegaard calls **despair.** But it is despair that comes from not being who we are. It is the ever-present knowledge that one day we will die (Could it be today?). Humans, unlike animals, know that death is coming our way. We live knowing our days will one day come to an end. However, we do not "live" in this tension every moment, but it is always with us. We, all humanity, have the sickness of the unknown. Kierkegaard says it this way:

"just as a physician might say that there very likely is not one single living human being who is completely healthy, so anyone who really knows mankind might say that there is not one single living human being who does not despair a little, who does not secretly harbor an unrest, an inner strife, a disharmony, an anxiety about an unknown something or a something he does not even dare to try to know, an anxiety about some possibility in existence or an anxiety about himself, so that, just as the physician speaks of going around with a sickness of the spirit that signals its presence at rare intervals in and through an anxiety he cannot explain. In any case, no human being ever lived and no one lives outside of Christendom who has not despaired, and no one in Christendom if he is not a true Christian, and insofar as he is not wholly that, he still is to some extent in despair."[32]

Serene Jones simplifies Kierkegaard's theology in these words:

"Despair is a fundamental feature of all human life. No one escapes it. But people manage it in dramatically different ways—some destructive, some healthy. Kierkegaard tells us that everyone, by virtue of being alive, has to confront a terrible but inescapable contradiction. On the one hand, we are *finite*; we are born, we die, we have bodies and must grapple with circumstances we don't control. These features of our lives—whatever form they take—are simply givens. They comprise our destiny, those things about us over which we have no control. OF course, the hardest truth for us to accept is the unavoidable fact that we will die. Our lives are finite because they have a definite endpoint. However, death arrives, the day will come for all of us.

On the other hand, we are *infinite,* insofar as we are self-aware and can imagine ourselves living other lives, doing other things, being other people. We can also imagine higher realities like God, truth, and goodness. We can even imagine-- and yearn for-- the possibility of living forever, immortality. We know time keeps going one earth after our death, and we imagine what it might be like to keep living, on and on.

Kierkegaard explains that this tension between our finitude and our capacity for imagining infinity—the tension between our given destine and our imagined freedom—creates enormous anxiety in us. No one escapes it. It is an endemic part of our humanity. We know what we are and imagine always what we might have been or could be. From this unavoidable anxiety is born despair, especially when we face the hard truth of death. We will die, having lived only a fraction of what we imagine was possible."[33]

Kierkegaard then provides four-character sketches of how different people manage this internal struggle with despair and death. Serene Jones puts them into her own thoughts in the following ways:

- **The "flitterers"** – those who refuse to acknowledge it. They flit about, untroubled by it but also not thinking about anything. Although in despair, is so innocent, and can be comic!

- **The "Cravers"** – these recognize despair but tamps it down by attaching themselves to things like jobs, families, art or in far too many cases, alcohol. They "pawn themselves to the world."

- **The "Ragers"** – they recognize the inevitability of despair for what it is –inevitable—but furiously rages against the fact that they do not control their own destiny. Consumed by their anger, they fall into lives of desperate misery. They are constant victims of their own failed desires, they hate themselves or, avoiding that, hate the people around them.

- **The "Bigger"** – those who, when confronted with their despair, are able to see themselves as part of something bigger. They recognize this something "bigger" not by more rigorously asserting themselves but by releasing their rage and losing themselves s as they let themselves become part of that bigger reality. Some call this "bigger" thing God.[34]

I am confident that we know people in each of these "sketches." I have had parishioners who "flitted" around in life. They had no grounding other than to think that life centered around them, and God's attention was almost totally on them. They are the "non-thinkers" which can lead to "non-feeling" of significant depth for others and the world.

There are far too many "Cravers" who consume their time with activities, so they do not have to think of the deeper things of life. They are always looking for the next task, the next party, the next investment, the next sporting event, thereby eliminating any time to contemplate their own mortality. These are the ones who usually do leave their "houses in order" because they are too busy.

The "ragers" are every pastor's nightmare. They are the ones who find easy targets to torment and hate. They hate those of other races, other religions, the poor, the immigrant, the liberals, the conservatives, LGBTQ, and those who have what they do not. Kierkegaard would say their hate is misdirected. Who do they really hate? They hate themselves and their inability to control others.

I had a woman whose son was diagnosed with AIDS in the mid-1980's. I drove her to the hospital to visit him as he was dying. On the way home, she wept. She said to me, "I don't understand why people hate gay people." To my surprise, in her next breath she said, "I just wish he wasn't surrounded by so many Black nurses and doctors." Interestingly, she was a "rager." She could not let go of the need to control, she could not strip away her own hate, and become a person of grace.

I am ever amazed at those who are "bigger" in character. They are willingly first responders. They are the ones who will give their lives to rescue a person in the throes of tragedy and death.

One of the people I will always remember was a man who was virtually unknown. On a cold winter morning, January 13, 1982, the plane he was aboard crashed in the icy waters of the Potomac River in Washington, D.C. Seventy-four people were killed. One of six people to initially survive the crash, Arland Dean Williams, Jr., helped the other five escape the sinking plane before he himself drowned. He had no thought of simply being rescued and leaving others behind. His actions that fateful day were broadcast all over the world. Not long afterward, the 14th Street Bridge over the Potomac River at the site of the crash was renamed in his honor.

Jurgen Moltmann says "hope makes us ready to bear 'the cross of the present. Owning our own despair, taking responsibility for our "sickness" and seeking the power of God's very presence with us lifts us from 'settling for a level of despair that we can tolerate and call it happiness.'"[35]

He continues "We bear the sickness unto death, knowing that one day we shall all die, in the eternal present. Time is ever moving. There is no 'this instance' for this 'moment' is an atom of eternity.[36] It was Goethe who said, "All these passing things we put up with; if only the eternal remains present to us every moment, then we do not suffer from the transience of time."[37]

Truly, the opposite of hope is despair, but the kind of despair that all humans suffer, knowing we will die, but also knowing that God is with us "until the end of the age." The question is how we live with this "despair."

Once again, Kierkegaard says:

This despair can be so hidden where no one can see it and even the person is not aware of it. "and when the hourglass has run out, the hourglass of temporality, when the noise of secular life has grown silent and its restless or ineffectual activism has come to an end, when everything around you is still, as it is in eternity, then...whether you were man or woman, rich or poor, dependent or independent, fortunate or unfortunate, whether you ranked with royalty and wore a glittering crown or in humble obscurity bore the toil and heat of the day, whether your name will be remembered as long as the world stands and consequently as long as it stood or you are nameless a dun nameless in the innumerable multitude, whether the magnificence encompassing you surpassed all human description or the most severe and ignominious human judgment befell you...eternity ask you and every individual in these millions and millions about only one thing; whether you have lived in despair or not, whether you have despaired in such a way that you did not realize that you were in despair, or in such a way that you covertly carried this sickness inside of you as your gnawing secret, as a fruit of sinful love under your heart, or in such a way that you, a terror to others, raged in despair.[38]

There are those in life who constantly live in fear of their deaths. They do not enjoy life because death is always looming over them like a black cloud. They live in despair.

There are those who live life to the fullest with an innate awareness that they are mortal and will one day die, but they see death as a vital part of life. They co-exist with this "despair." It does not rob them of their zest for life.

All of humanity lives with this "sickness unto death" but it does not have to be paralyzing. We do not lose hope, because God is with us. Martin Buber once said that the translation in Exodus where Moses asks God for God's name, has been mistakenly written as "I am." Buber says that the better translation is "I shall be there."[39] I love that! God shall be there in our birth, our lives, in our deaths and in life beyond death.

We can absorb the most intense pain without abandoning our sense of hope because we know with certainty that God shall be there with us, every step of the way! Thanks be to God!

Work Without Hope

All Nature seems at work. Slugs leave their lair—
The bees are stirring—birds are on the wing—
And Winter slumbering in the open air,
Wears on his smiling face a dream of Spring!
And I the while, the sole unbusy thing,
Nor honey make, nor pair, nor build, nor sing.

Yet well I ken the banks where amaranths blow,
Have traced the fount whence streams of nectar flow.
Bloom, O ye amaranths! bloom for whom ye may,
For me ye bloom not! Glide, rich streams, away!
With lips unbrightened, wreathless brow, I stroll:

And would you learn the spells that drowse my soul?
Work without Hope draws nectar in a sieve,
And Hope without an object cannot live.

Samuel Coleridge
Composed February 21, 1825

Chapter 3

How do we "give" hope?

———◇———

Hope is our destination,
Faith is trusting in that destination,
And love is how we get there.

Matt Rawle

Now that we know that hope is, for the most part, unable to be defined, yet basic and vital to life, what does it mean to *give* hope? I was told that I had not "given" my relative hope. What did she expect? If she knew what she needed from me and didn't get it, could she have received it elsewhere?

How do we *give* and receive hope? Can we give hope and not even know it?

I would suggest that:

> **We are powerless to *give* hope to anyone,**
> **rather we can *offer* hope to others**
> **in multitudes of ways,**
> **most of them without our even knowing it.**

Recently, during the Advent season, my home was flooded with requests for money from colleges/universities, churches, and missional organizations. Here are some of their slogans: "Hope Grows Here," "Plant Seeds of Hope," "Wait in Hope," and one that said, "This Christmas, give hope"! What does it mean to "grow hope? What does it mean to "plant seeds of hope?" What does it mean to "wait in hope?" And how do we "give" hope? For these organizations, it meant giving a monetary gift. Such gifts would enable children and youth to receive gifts for Christmas or assist in their educations, thus bringing them *hope* during their lives away from family and friends.

Sending money for the purpose of helping children in need is a wonderful ministry. The children will never know who gave the money for them to receive their gifts. Some children will not equate such a gift with hope, and that is okay. Some will think they are entitled to such gifts. Then there are some who will be deeply grateful, and the gift will become more to them than just a bicycle or a doll, rather symbols of generosity that might influence them in some way when they are older to be able to present such offerings to others.

Interestingly, in the church, the time of collecting money is referred to as *the offering*. The congregation *offers* their money, time, talents, and other gifts to the glory of God and for human need. We offer hope through such acts of giving but are powerless to make hope happen. Only the recipient can determine whether or not such gifting brings hope.

Max Lucado tells the true story of the aftermath of the Armenian earthquake in 1989. Over thirty thousand people were killed. A father raced to the elementary school to save his son and when he arrived, he saw that the school had been leveled. He had made a promise to his child that "he would always be there for him." Though he was told that all of the students were dead, the father began to work removing the stones and debris. He worked some thirty-eight hours. His hands were raw, and his energy gone. But he refused to quit. He called his boy's name, "Arman!" "Arman!" and a voice answered him, "Dad, it's me." Then the boy said these priceless words, "I told the other kids not to worry. I told them if you were alive, you'd save me and when you saved me, they'd be saved too. Because you promised, no matter what, "I'll always be there for you."[40]

This father offered his son "hope" through a promise. That one thing helped to keep his son alive.

I believe, as Joyce Rupp says, "Hope resides at the core of who we are. We are meant to be hope-filled people."[41] Perhaps we are born with an innate ability to be hopeful. A baby's cry is in essence, a cry of hope for someone to feed them, change them, hold them, and care for them. Though not always mentally aware of it, all cries in need are for hope.

Pope Francis said, "If there is no hope, we are not Christian. That is why I like so say: do not allow yourselves to be robbed of hope. Hope-filled people inspire and boost the enthusiasm of others. Jesus was a *carrier of hope*. We are meant to be the same.[42]

We can be "*carriers of hope*" by being who we are! In multitudes of ways, we offer hope to others simply by our presence. A parent seated in the stands watching their child play a sport offers hope to the child, to other parents and coaches.

When a pastor sees parishioners coming in the door of the sanctuary, hope abounds in the possibility of ministry these people might undertake to make the world a better place. There is also the possibility that lives will be changed through some aspect of worship. The people themselves are not conscious of this, but by their very presence, they are offering hope to the pastor and other congregants. Such hope strengthens the church!

I feel conflicted about churches that have a separate place where children worship and another place where youth worship. My reasons:

- The children and youth miss the hope that adults can offer to them.

- They need to see those who are married, single, widowed, elderly.

- They miss the total worship experience of being with people of all ages.

- They miss out on baptisms.

- They miss out on holy communion with the whole church.

- They misunderstand that worship is not about being with folks just like us or all our same age.

- Adults need to be with children and youth in worship so they can glean hope from them.

- We need each other.

I have vivid memories of being in worship when I was a child and seeing the parents of a child who died walk down the aisle and sit in the pew in front of me. I knew their hearts were heavy with grief, but they were in church. They were models for me that I would not have had if I had been in "children's" church or "youth church." Each week, they were there. Over the years, others who had severe losses also were in worship.

In the United Methodist Church, there is an annual conference where each year clergy and laity gather to worship, to ordain new clergy, and to go about the business of the church. The opening worship service always begins with the singing of the hymn "And are We Yet Alive." Notice the words to these particular stanzas:

> And are we yet alive,
> And see each other's face?
> Glory and thanks to Jesus give
> For his almighty grace!
> What troubles have we seen,
> What mighty conflicts past,
> Fightings without, and fears within
> Since we assembled last?
> Yet out of all the Lord
> Hath brought us by His love.

And still, he doth his help afford,
And hides our life above.
Then let us make our boast
Of his redeeming power,
Which saves us to the uttermost
Till we can sin no more.
Let us take up the cross
Till we the crown obtain
And gladly reckon all things loss
So, we may Jesus gain.[43]

As I look around, I see the faces of many clergy who are fervently singing this great hymn of our faith who have lost a spouse, a parent, or a child. There is:

- My friend whose eight-year-old son was killed when the school bus driver thought she had seen him cross the street and pulled out, running over and killing him instantly.

- my uncle who had three of his seven children to die.

- A clergy whose son was killed when a car hit his bicycle

- My seminary friend whose three-year-old son inhaled a balloon and died

- A close friend whose daughter went to catch a frisbee, fell, suffering an aneurysm and dying on the spot.

- Another whose two-year old fell off a balcony and died.

- Our close family friend whose daughter died from a drug overdose in her early twenties.

- The dear friend whose wife left him to raise their three small sons.

- A new friend who has lost four babies shortly before their births

- The life-long friend whose son died at one-year from meningitis.

- The friend whose home burned to the ground, leaving nothing behind
- The clergy couple who has two children in jail
- A number of clergy with various cancers, some who have lost their hair and they appear thin and in pain.

They are all standing and singing together the great hymn of our faith with great conviction of soul, their faces and voices looking upward with the assurance that God is with them.

I can barely sing the words as tears form in my eyes remembering the loved ones I have lost and knowing the pain that many others are feeling remembering their loved ones who are now in the church celestial. Their presence, their faith (even with "fears within") strengthen me. They are "carriers of hope" and they are not even aware of it or as Cynthia Bourgeault says, "they are "lamps" to us."[44]

We can also be "carriers of hope" by what we do. Henri Nouwen tells about Donald Reeves who was pastor of St. James Anglican Church in Piccadilly, who was an activist, a contemplative, a social worker, an artist, a caring pastor, a restless mover, a visionary, and a pragmatist who converted a practically lifeless downtown Anglican parish into a vibrant center of prayer and action. It is a place that welcomes traditional Christians as well as people who feel alienated from the Church. It is also a place for mediation, counseling, art events, concerts, peace-making, book publishing and hospitality. On the cover of Reeve's ten-year plan for the church were these words:

A vision without a task is a dream.
A task without a vision is drudgery.
A vision and a task are the hope of the world.[45]

Let me concentrate on those two words: "vision" and "task" as essential for the offering of hope in the world, especially through the church and in our politics.

To have "vision," we must be willing to take the blinders off of our eyes and to see the brokenhearted and downtrodden of the world. Who are they? Why are they in the positions they are in, and how do we offer hope?

Centuries ago, a man named Moses had his eyes opened (*vision*) to the torturous conditions of slavery. He did not want to become involved because he had a speech problem, he stuttered. How could he be a leader and stutter? A reading of the book of Exodus shares how his brother Aaron helped him to have the courage to approach the evil pharaoh and when nothing could be accomplished, he led a *resistant movement* that took the slaves out of bondage into a forty-year escape route through the "wilderness" to the promised land. Moses' vision (and task) is the central theme of the Old Testament. Moses' liberation of the Israelites, (the exodus) parallels the life of Jesus whose life, death and resurrection liberate humanity into a new life (eternal living) now and always.

Throughout biblical history, there are multitudes of accounts of those who had a vision for justice and mercy, who put their lives in danger to offer hope for the well-being of humanity. A quick synopsis is found in the book of Hebrews chapter 11. (Let me encourage you to stop and read this chapter.)

It was Saint Augustine who first suggested that hope is a woman with two daughters whose names are COURAGE and ANGER.[46] They are born:

> "against all odds, in situations of hopelessness and powerlessness, the offspring not of men but of faith, of fruitful waiting and hoping against hope. They are born through the powerful intervention of Yahweh, who brings life into barrenness, lifelessness, and futureless-ness – when all hope is gone. Yahweh is the 'unmistakable agent... the one who can

turn barrenness into birth, vexation into praise, isolation into worship,' creating 'a new historical possibility where none existed.'"[47]

The image of a "mother" in Augustine's theology is the one who stands up for those who cannot stand up for themselves. She is the advocate for the weak and vulnerable. She is not content to merely speak, but she exposes how the powerful and privileged exploit them.

Indeed, throughout history, it has been the "mother" and her children, Courage and Anger, who have helped to lead movements of radical change. They not only dream of a different world but work to make it happen.

Martin Luther saw (*vision*) corruption in the hierarchy in the Roman Catholic Church. Fueled by his *anger*, he was filled with *courage* to address the issues, so he posted his 95 Thesis to the door of the Wittenberg Church. His life was threatened. The Church leaders became enraged, but Luther was not to be outdone. His *actions* began the Protestant Reformation. The movement saw changes in Catholicism and the formation of many Christian denominations known as protestants.

We see such anger and courage manifesting themselves in the civil rights movement that has continued for decades in America. During my lifetime, I have seen the elimination of separate water fountains, separate public schools, and separate dining places for people who are Black. Yet, there are still major systems of racism in place that continue to discount and undermine their safety and freedom.

Hope dreams of a different world even when those who would seek to rule would desire otherwise. Sometimes it seems overwhelming to dream when the odds are so great.

Jonathan Sacks, in *The Dignity of Difference: How to Avoid the Clash of Civilization,* shows:

"*the average American consumes five time more than does a Mexican.

*The average American consumes ten times more than a Chinese person.

*The average American consumes thirty times more than an Indian.

1.3 billion people (or 22% of the world's population, live below the poverty line.

841 million are malnourished.

880 million are without access to medical care.

1 billion lack adequate shelter.

1.3 billion have no access to safe drinking water.

2.6 billion go without sanitation.

113 million children (2/3 girls) go without schooling.

150 million children are malnourished.

30,000 children die each day from malnutrition.

In 18 countries (all in Africa), life expectancy is underage 50. (In Sierra Leone, it is a mere 37 years)

Infant mortality rates are higher than on in ten in 35 countries.

By the end of the second millennium ce, the top fifth of the world's population had 86% of the world's GDP, while ethe bottom fifth had just 1 percent.

The assets of the world's three richest individual billionaires were more than the combined wealth of the 600 million in habitants of the least—developed countries.

The Walton family, the six heirs to the Walmart empire, 'possess a combined wealth of some $90 billion, which is equivalent to the wealth of the entire bottom 30% of U.S. society.'

One billion people around the world go to bed hungry each night."[48]

Let me encourage you to stop and to go back to the top of this page and reread these statistics. What are you feeling as you read them? What will you do about them? How will you live differently so the world can change for the better?

Though I do not know who said this, I agree with the person's words, "this is an assault on the creation of God, the dignity of God's children and in that assault the assault on the worthiness of God." Indeed, "We cannot read the Bible without immediately learning that God does not stand for injustice!"[49] Indeed, from cover-to-cover, the Bible displays multitudes of stories of the "sisters" Anger and Courage who stand up with action against abuse, injustice, and entitlement of the powerful to oppress.

"Hope makes herself known in encounter with suffering and struggle."[50] That is why it is imperative we have good VISION and rise to the task with COURAGE that leads to ACTION.

In almost every presidential election in my adult life, I have heard some people say, "I will vote for the candidate that will put the most money in my pocket." Each time, I hear this, I cringe. Is that the response Jesus would say? Do we vote from a perspective of what the candidate/government can do for me, or do we vote from a perspective of what the candidate/government can do for the betterment of all? Can we truly follow Christ and not be concerned about the well-being of all?

I have tried to model my years in ministry, as well as my life from Matthew 25:31-46:

> *"When the Son of Man comes in his glory, and all the angels with him, then he will sit on the throne of his glory. ³² All the nations will be gathered before him, and he will separate people one from another as a shepherd separates the sheep from the goats, ³³ and he will put the sheep at his right hand and the goats at the left. ³⁴ Then the king will say to those at his right hand, 'Come, you that are blessed by my Father, inherit the kingdom prepared for*

you from the foundation of the world; [35] *for I was hungry and you gave me food, I was thirsty and you gave me something to drink, I was a stranger and you welcomed me,* [36] *I was naked and you gave me clothing, I was sick and you took care of me, I was in prison and you visited me.'* [37] *Then the righteous will answer him, 'Lord, when was it that we saw you hungry and gave you food, or thirsty and gave you something to drink?* [38] *And when was it that we saw you a stranger and welcomed you, or naked and gave you clothing?* [39] *And when was it that we saw you sick or in prison and visited you?'* [40] *And the king will answer them, 'Truly I tell you, just as you did it to one of the least of these who are members of my family,* [a] *you did it to me.'* [41] *Then he will say to those at his left hand, 'You that are accursed, depart from me into the eternal fire prepared for the devil and his angels;* [42] *for I was hungry and you gave me no food, I was thirsty and you gave me nothing to drink,* [43] *I was a stranger and you did not welcome me, naked and you did not give me clothing, sick and in prison and you did not visit me.'* [44] *Then they also will answer, 'Lord, when was it that we saw you hungry or thirsty or a stranger or naked or sick or in prison, and did not take care of you?'* [45] *Then he will answer them, 'Truly I tell you, just as you did not do it to one of the least of these, you did not do it to me.'* [46] *And these will go away into eternal punishment, but the righteous into eternal life."*

How does our "nation" and all the "nations" of the world:

- Feed the hungry?
- Provide drink to the thirsty?
- Cloth the naked?
- Welcome the stranger?
- Care for the sick?
- Care for those in bondage?

When we take seriously this "task" we will see a world that can thrive. Yet, when we neglect any ONE of these, we see destruction and turmoil. **The *language* of hope, thus, is also the language of resistance:**

- This is the God who said to Pharaoh, "let my people go." (Exodus 9:1)
- This is the God of Hannah; "For not by might does one prevail" (I Samuel 2:9)
- This is the God of Isaiah; "For the tyrant shall be no more!" (Isaiah 29:20)
- This is the God of Amos; "let justice roll down like water and righteousness like a mighty stream." (Amos 5:24)
- This is the God of Jesus; "The spirit of the Lord is upon me, because he has anointed me to bring good news to the poor. He has sent me to proclaim release to the captive and recovery of sight to the blind, to let the oppressed go free, to proclaim the year of the Lord's favor." (Luke 4:18-19)[51]

The language of hope is:

- standing up against communism.
- standing up against Nazism.
- standing up against racism.
- standing up for the rights of the disabled, the oppressed, the diseased, the stranger, the poor, the marginalized, the weak, the preservation of earth and taking seriously the environment.
- Grieving at what grieves the heart of God, participating in the suffering of God.

Let me share more ways we can *offer* hope individually, and then corporately. In doing so, I would like to take Don Follis' work and where it is necessary, I will insert the word "offer" beside his word "give." His insights are significant and vitally important:

Don Follis suggests *10 Great Ways to Give (offer) People Hope*, which are:

Acceptance. The need for acceptance is met when we willingly and unconditionally love someone. Can you look beyond a person's faults and still care for them? There's not a better way to give (*offer*) a person hope than by accepting them for who they are, not for what they do.

Love. The need for love is met by expressing care through physical touch and tender words. Tell people you love them. Tell your spouse, your children and your colleagues. Tell people in the hospital, at weddings, at funerals. Try calling someone today and say, "I wanted to give you a quick call to tell you thank you for being part of our church family and for being a good friend. I love you, and I'm proud to call you friend."

Appreciation. The need for appreciation is met through expressing thanks and praise, especially in recognizing someone's accomplishments.

Approval. The need for approval is met by building up or affirming a person and acknowledging the importance of the relationship.

Connection. The need for connection is met when we enter another person's world. There is no substitute for spending time with someone. And it's not just time—it's time and really listening to people from your heart. If you will truly listen to someone, whether they are happy or sad, they will feel blessed. Pastor David Augsburger says, "Being heard is so close to being loved that for the average person, they are almost indistinguishable."

Comfort. The need for comfort is met by responding to people with appropriate words and physical touch. If a person is grieving, there really are only two things to say: "I'm so sorry," and "I love you." Place your hand on the shoulder of a person in pain and tell that person you're on his side.

Encouragement. The need for encouragement is met by urging people to hang in there, to persist toward the goal they so want to achieve. Send notes, phone someone, pray with someone, take someone to dinner or a movie. People are dying for someone to say, "I'm so proud of what you are doing. You make this world a better place to live in."

Respect. The need for respect is met by honoring and regarding people as important. Do you show deference to your spouse's opinion? Do you listen to your children? Do you respect people's time? Do you respect people from different backgrounds and religions?

Protection. The need for protection is met when we establish harmony in relationships and show people, they are free from fear or threat of harm. Are those for whom you are financially responsible secure in knowing that you will provide for them? Do you relate to people in a consistent way? Do you treat your employees the way you want to be treated? Do people know what to expect from you? Can they read you?

Support. The need for support is met when you come alongside someone and give them your complete attention. Anticipate and notice when someone is experiencing periods of stress.[52]

Arlin Cuncic adds a few more:

Remind people that they deserve happiness

Remind the person in your life that no matter how his life has gone, he deserves happiness. In fact, choosing to be happy is less selfish, because it allows him to be more generous and compassionate with others.

Hope is fueled by optimism and the belief that you have the power to make positive changes in your life, says Shane Lopez, Ph.D., author of "Making Hope Happen." When giving others hope, focus on helping them define realistic goals, offering support and being a hopeful person yourself.

Sharing Successes

Help give a person hope by sharing how you have found success in your own life, writes Paul Huljich, author of the book "Stress Pandemic: The Lifestyle Solution, Natural Steps to Survive, Master Stress and Live Well" in a "Psychology Today" article. Perhaps you have already achieved something that the other person is striving for, such as a happy relationship. Share the secrets of your success.

Admitting Failures

Share failures in your life to show the other person that the path to success is rarely straightforward. Hopefulness requires being adaptable and changing course when faced with obstacles, according to Lopez. Tell your friend about your difficult break-up or your sister about the time your best friend let you down. Others will feel more hopeful knowing that not everything in life comes easy -- and that obstacles can be overcome.

Change Takes Time

Remind others that positive change takes time, suggests Huljich. Let your girlfriend know that although you are having problems right now, a year from now things could be completely different. Show her that the issues don't need to be solved overnight, but rather that the two of you need to be working together in the same direction. Hope requires sustaining optimism over the long term, rather than giving up too quickly.

Change Is Within Reach

If your best friend is struggling to lose weight, let her know that the change she desires is possible, says Huljich. Sometimes people lose hope because they believe that a situation cannot be improved. Be a positive influence and show her how she can reach her goals, and how others in her position have been successful. Knowing that change is within reach can increase hopefulness and reduce feelings that what a person wants is not possible.

Narrow Down Goals

It is easier to be hopeful when you have a narrow set of goals, says Lopez. If you try to achieve too many goals at the same time, or add additional goals to your already busy list, you set yourself up to fail. Help others be more hopeful by working through the process of narrowing down goals with them. For example, help your boyfriend decide whether to apply to college or enter the workforce directly after school.

Find Passions

People who are excited and passionate about something in their lives are more hopeful, says Lopez. Help others to discover their passions, to instill a sense of hope. If a friend doesn't enjoy math class but blossoms when taking out her art supplies, suggest that she might not want to follow the path of becoming an accountant, as her parents have suggested. People are most hopeful when they are driven by passion.

Be Hopeful Yourself

Help others to be hopeful by exuding hope yourself -- your attitude will be contagious and will rub off on others. Talk in hopeful ways, such as saying things like, "I am really excited about our plans for this weekend," or "I can't wait for summer -- we will have so much fun at my cottage." Be specific, be hopeful and talk about what you are looking forward to. Others will often follow suit.

Offer Help

In the case of a friend who is feeling down, offer resources or help. If a friend is sick, offer to bring homemade soup. If your boyfriend is struggling with algebra, help to find him a tutor. Sometimes a lack of hope can be a downward spiral that is hard to escape. Do the legwork to find resources or support that will give someone the boost to be more hopeful.[53]

Offering hope comes in multitudes of ways: consciously through intentional acts that better humanity and acts of kindness and actions that lift another to greater comfort, peace and assurance of their value. We have looked at intentional ways, let's look at some unconscious ways we are offered hope without even thinking about it:

What comes to my mind are cafeteria workers in the lunchrooms where my grandchildren live. Every day they show up to cook and serve healthy meals for hundreds of children. Are the children aware of the hope that goes to provide their lunches each day?

The auto workers who, day after day, stand in an assembly lines putting parts on the automobiles we drive. We take it for granted and think little of it until something goes wrong.

All of those who work in the medical world who spend countless hours giving medicines to the sick.

Scientists working diligently to find cures for diseases.

The postal folks who deliver our mail (through rain, snow, sleet, and heat)

The pharmacists who fill our needed prescriptions.

The mechanic who repairs our vehicles, lawn mowers, and other things.

The ambulance drivers and first responders.

The teachers, administrators, volunteers at schools, colleges, universities.

Those in law enforcement dedicated to the protection of all people.

Clergy who sincerely love people and work diligently on sermons, visit the sick and care for the needy.

Those in the entertainment industry who spend countless hours memorizing lines and filming programs that educate and also amuse us.

Insurance providers.

Politicians who work for all people, especially the least, the last and lost of the world.

Pilots, flight attendants, and those who make it possible for us to travel the friendly skies.

Taxi drivers, Uber drivers, Lyft drivers, parents who drive their kids.

The business world that offers us varieties of things to help us live comfortably.

Philanthropists who give above and beyond their taxes to charities that benefit the mind, the body and the emotions.

Various charities that provide relief to the needy

Churches through worship, education, mission and nurture

Farmers who grow the food that eventually makes it to our tables.

Sanitary workers who collect our garbage.

These are but a few of those who offer hope "round the clock" that we hardly notice, much less consciously note their importance in our world.

We can be instruments of hope by simply walking into a meeting, a charitable event, a school, workplace, religious organization, sporting events, and especially in our homes. Without even saying a word, we can offer hope!

Sometimes, we offer hope the best in non-verbal expressions such as smiles, hugs, handshakes, the nod of the head, a thumbs up, hands folded in prayer, clapping, the writing of a note or email or text, the sharing of a donut, a gift left on a desk, flowers delivered to friend or loved one, the wave from a car, the offering of a seat, holding a door, motioning for someone behind you in line to get ahead of you, through art and music.

I was in the grocery store parking lot recently and witnessed an elderly woman walking toward her car pushing a cart full of groceries. She was having issues with trying to hold her cane, her purse, and her umbrella (sprinkling of rain) while she made her way to her car. A young man came walking toward her. He had tattoos on his neck, arms, and hands. His hair was black and blue. Earrings and a nose ring were very visible. His clothes were dirty and ragged. When he saw the elderly woman, he rushed to her and motioned for her to go on to her car. The elderly woman was skeptical but handed the cart to him. She opened her trunk, and the young man unloaded all the groceries, closed her trunk, and turned the cart around and headed back toward the front of the store.

The woman said, "Let me give you a tip." He smiled and nodded with a "no" and then gave her a thumbs up. When she saw that I had witnessed this, she said to me, "That reaffirms my faith in this old world." My response, "Mine as well!"

He never said a word to her. His <u>actions</u> *offered* her hope.

I have witnessed people seeing a rabbi or a priest and how they ran to them with expectation of what they could mean to them. Their very presence offered hope.

I have witnessed the same with folks who see a nurse, doctor, dentist, veterinarian, teacher, tow-truck worker, garbage collector, plumber, mechanic, or just about anybody who can meet a need in our lives.

Frederick Buchner once said, "The place God calls you to is the place where your deep gladness and the world's deep hunger meet.[54] "When that happens, we are agents offering hope.

In short, we can offer hope in unlimited ways through our "God-calls" meeting the world's needs, but just as importantly, through being ourselves as we go about each day performing random acts of kindness consciously and unconsciously.

What about corporate/institutional hope?

Interestingly, in times of great crisis such as an earthquake, hurricane, tornado, tsunami, or a pandemic "virus", the first sign of hope is usually this one:

AMERICAN RED CROSS

Most likely, they are the first to arrive on the scene offering medical relief, and comfort. The big red cross is known all over the world as an organization that brings quick relief to those in great need.

Another corporate symbol that is meant to bring calm in the storms of life is:

A CROSS ON A CHURCH STEEPLE

For many passing a church on the busy highways of life, the steeple bearing a cross is a "positive" sign that God is at work in the world, seeking the best for humanity. The cross symbolizes that God can bring life out of death, light our darkness, hope from despair, joy from sadness, and pardon from sins.

Numerous folks over the centuries have glanced at a steeple with a cross on the top and stopped their agenda and entered into the church. What they need varies as some stop to pray, to ask for prayer, to light a candle, to seek out a clergyperson or to worship.

On September 11, 2001, the world watched in horror as America was attacked. Thousands lost their lives. Fear engulfed us and terrorism was real and near.

The church where I was pastor quickly gathered the staff and clergy and we put together a worship service that would begin at 7:00 that evening. There was little time to try to "get the word out." At 7:00, the sanctuary was filled, and people were aligning the walls. It was natural for the community to find a communal way of handling this great tragedy.

THE AMERICAN BALD EAGLE

The American bald eagle is a symbol for the United States of America. For many, it signifies all that is good about this nation and at the forefront, freedom. Many who have returned from war, or from traveling to other countries want to "kiss the ground" in gratitude that, though America is not perfect, it offers what most countries do not in the way of being the "land of the free." There is great hope in the very concept of freedom.

THE SALVATION ARMY

The Salvation Army is known for its worldwide care of the homeless, the elderly, the poor, and rehabilitation for alcohol-related addictions. It has a membership of close to two million and is present in 131 countries. Though most do not know this, it is a protestant church that derived from Methodism. Most see it as a sign of hope from their thrift stores and the bellringers at Christmas.

SUSAN G. KOMEN

When Susan Komen died at the age of 33, her sister, Nancy believed that if patients knew more about cancer and its treatment, then less deaths would occur. She has devoted her life to that end, forming the Susan G. Komen Breast Cancer Foundation which is now named the Susan G. Komen for the Cure.[55]

UNITED WAY

United Way Worldwide is a nonprofit organization that works to identify and resolve vital issues confronting communities such as education, income and health. They do this in partnership through schools, government agencies, civic groups, the business community, faith communities and neighborhood associations. Wherever the sign "United Way" appears, it is seen as a symbol of hope for a community.

For many, images of the United States Capitol, Ronald McDonald House, a sunset or sunrise, horses grazing in a pasture, the Bible, a white-framed country church, candle-lighting on Christmas eve, a flower growing in a concrete sidewalk, a couple on their wedding day, the baptism of a child, puppies, students on graduation day with their robes and hats, flowers in bloom, a fisherman pulling in a catch, sailboats on a lake, hot-air balloons in the sky, little league ballgames, a military soldier, the face of a grandmother, the Lincoln Memorial, holy communion, the AIDS quilt, Niagara Falls, seashells, Uncle Remus, the grand canyon, soup kitchens, families sitting down to eat at Thanksgiving, the presence of a physician or nurse, pictures of Mother Teresa and Martin Luther King, Jr, kids trick-or-treating, a new house under construction, people of all nations, races, religions, together in one place with respect and love for one another, a rocket launched into space, pictures of earth from miles away, trees and streams and clouds and rain and snow and changing seasons, and numerous more offer hope.

Other signs also can offer a sense of hope while traveling the highways:

REST AREA AHEAD

FOOD – GAS- LODGING

CITY LIMIT

VACANCY

BEACH

These are just a few of the numerous signs that offer hope to large amounts of people. Let me encourage you to look for more signs along your travels each day. It might surprise you how many there are that give us a sense of peace, confidence, and most of all *offer* us *hope*.

They say a person needs just three
things to be truly happy in this world:
someone to love
something to do
and something to hope for.

copied

Hope is a strange invention

Hope is a strange invention –
A Patent of the Heart –
In unremitting action
Yet never wearing out –

Of this electric Adjunct
Not anything is known
But its unique momentum
Embellish all we own –

Emily Dickinson

———————✕———————

Chapter 4

Hope and the Bible

———◇———

"If you lend to those from whom you hope to receive,
what credit is that to you?"

Luke 6:34

the only place in the gospels Jesus
mentions hope, but his whole life and ministry
were all about it.

The Bible never defines hope yet hope permeates all sixty-six books contained within it! Interestingly, the first time the word "hope" is mentioned in the Bible is in the eighth book called Ruth. It is in the context of Ruth's mother-in-law, Naomi, feeling very depressed after the deaths of her two sons. Naomi knew she must return to her native land where she could find support, as women had few ways of making a living in those days, as well as, being protected. She says to her two daughters-in-law, "*I have no hope.*"[56] She expresses what we all feel sometimes in life.

The story turns out that one of her daughters-in-law, Ruth, accompanied her on the journey home and marries a local man. Naomi is taken into their care, and all is well. Hope was there all the time!

But let us go back to the first book of the Bible, Genesis, which begins with the story of creation and God's delight in making a world;

sun, moon, stars, vegetation, animals, fish and birds, then humanity and finally, a day of rest. For many, Sabbath has become the TGIF of the workforce! We do love our weekends!

Following the creation of male and female, the drama of being human began with betrayal, lies, murder, greed, adultery, idol worship, and multitudes of other sins. There is covenant-making on the part of God and covenant-breaking on the part of humanity. However, God does not leave humanity alone, rather God continually offers grace: forgiveness, redemption, and new life. God is always at work in the world.

Even after Adam and Eve break God's trust by eating of the fruit from the tree of knowledge, God is angry, but merciful. They are extracted from the Garden of Eden and sent out into the world to work by "the sweat of their brow."

Then we meet Abraham and Sara, Jacob, and Esau, and read of Noah and the flood. Throughout these stories, hope is seen in the ways God is present with them and working with them.

Moses comes on the scene in turbulent political times and the Exodus is a long account of the Israelites journeying through the wilderness to the promised land. During their forty-year hike, the people get frustrated, worship an idol, complain, and criticize their leaders. (sound familiar?) Nevertheless, God is with them, bringing them out of the desert into the land "of milk and honey."

After the death of Moses, we read of good and bad judges, the life of King David and Solomon, the Psalms where many are laments with hope in God's abilities to act in overthrowing enemies and disease, the prophets and the multitudes of trials and heartaches that happen when God is not central in life. Vivid is the picture of the valley of dry bones in the book of Ezekiel where the prophet dares to believe that these bones could live again (have new life), Hosea wooing his unfaithful wife back to him (the wife being symbolic of the wayward people of Israel), then Jonah and God's salvation of Nineveh. Isaiah, Jeremiah, Daniel, Amos, all bring a glaring light to the waywardness of God's people but offer hope in God whose love remains steadfast. All these prophets proclaim in their unique ways that God never gives up on humanity. Never! All thirty-nine Old Testament books reflect God's hope in humanity.

In various places of the Old Testament, it is essential for the people of Israel to *remember* the exodus and the covenants of God. This is *the* central point of their faith. God is always faithful. (Remember the rainbow in the story of the great flood, Abraham's descendants, the land, circumcision, and Moses' leading the Israelites through the wilderness to the promised land?) Before they can go forward, they must go back and remember who they are in the sight of God.

**Thus, hope can be found in looking backwards,
remembering what God did for "their people"
to move forward into a future.**

Here are *some* specific places where *hope* is mentioned in the Old Testament:

Lamentations 3:24	"The Lord is my portion," says my soul, "therefore I will hope in Him"
Job 11:18	and you will have confidence, because there is hope
Job 13:15	though he slay me, yet will I hope in Him
Psalm 33:18	hope in steadfast love
Psalm 38:15	in Thee O Lord, do I hope
Psalm 39:7	my hope is in God
Psalm 42:11	Why are you cast down, O my soul and why are you disquieted within me? Hope in God: for I shall again praise him, my help and my God.

Psalm 43:5	hope in God
Psalm 62:5	For God alone my soul waits in silence, for my hope is <u>from</u> Him
Psalms 71:5	you are my hope
Psalm 71:14	I will hope constantly
Psalm 78:7	set your hope in God
Psalm 119:114	I hope in your word
Psalm 130:5	In wait for the Lord, my soul waits, and in His word, I hope.
Psalm 130:7	O Israel! Hope in the Lord!
Psalm 146:5	Happy are those whose help is the God of Jacob, whose hope is in the Lord their God.
Proverbs 10:28	hope of righteousness
Proverbs 23:18	surely there is a future, and your hope will not be cut off
Proverbs 24:14	hope not cut off
Jeremiah 29:11	For I know the plans I have for you...to give you a future with hope
Habakkuk 3:17-18	Though the fig tree does not bud, and there are no grapes on the vines, though the olive crop fails, and the fields produce no food, though there are no sheep in the pen, and no cattle in the stalls, yet I will rejoice in the LORD, I will be joyful in God my Savior.

Probably the most quoted scripture in the whole Old Testament is Psalm 23.

When I was a child in Sunday school, I had to memorize this text. Its words have remained in my heart because they are timeless. As a pastor, I have had numerous requests of people who were dying who asked me to read this Psalm to them and to have it read at their funerals.

The LORD is my shepherd, I shall not want.
He makes me lie down in green pastures.
he leads me beside still waters.
he restores my soul.
He leads me in the paths of righteousness
for his name's sake.
Even though I walk through the valley, of the shadow of death,
I will fear no evil;
for you are with me.
Your rod and your staff—
they comfort me.
You prepare a table before me
in the presence of my enemies.
You anoint my head with oil
my cup overflows.
Surely^{J} goodness and mercy shall follow me
all the days of my life,
and I shall dwell in the house of the LORD
forever.

One of the verses of this great Psalm that has especially meant much to me is *"yea though I walk* **THROUGH** *the valley..."* Having had many tragedies in my life, I have come realize that a person never gets "over" them, but we can get "through" them.

Candy Lightner's thirteen-year-old daughter was killed by a drunk driver several years ago in California. Candy was angry and bitter and said in her house for almost a year plotting various ways to get revenge on the driver who killed her daughter. She realized one day that all her anger and venom were not serving anyone any good. She realized that she would never get over her grief in losing her beloved child, but she could get over it. She chose to do something constructive with her grief and began the organization M.A.D.D. (Mothers Against Drunk Driving). Through her efforts, thousands of people have been brought safely home.

King David, the author of Psalm 23, also wrote another of my favorite Psalms. This one was written after the death of his own son. I love how his words reflect his journey from darkness to light and sadness to joy. Psalm 30 is also one that remains timeless:

> *Sing praises to the LORD, O you his faithful ones,*
> *and give thanks to his holy name.*
> *For his anger is but for a moment;*
> *his favor is for a lifetime.*
> **Weeping may linger for the night,**
> **but joy comes with the morning.**
>
> **You have turned my mourning into dancing;**
> **you have taken off my sackcloth**
> **and clothed me with joy,**
> **so that my soul may praise you and not be silent.**
> **O LORD my God, I will give thanks to you forever.**

Some of the greatest words of hope are contained the books of the prophets. Let me zero-in on Isaiah 40:28-31:

> *Have you not known? Have you not heard?*
> *The LORD is the everlasting God,*
> *the Creator of the ends of the earth.*
> *He does not faint or grow weary;*
> *his understanding is unsearchable.*
> *He gives power to the faint,*
> *and strengthens the powerless.*

Even youths will faint and be weary,
and the young will fall exhausted;
but those who wait for the LORD shall renew their strength,
they shall mount up with wings like eagles,
they shall run and not be weary,
they shall walk and not faint.

Another Psalm I had to memorize was for an elementary school play. I learned it from the King James Version of the Bible and have savored its wisdom throughout the years.

Blessed is the man that walketh not in the counsel of the ungodly, nor standeth in the way of sinners, nor sitteth in the seat of the scornful.

But his delight is in the law of the LORD; and in his law doth he meditate day and night.

And he shall be like a tree planted by the rivers of water, that bringeth forth his fruit in his season; his leaf also shall not wither; and whatsoever he doeth shall prosper.

The ungodly are not so: but are like the chaff which the wind driveth away.

Therefore, the ungodly shall not stand in the judgment, nor sinners in the congregation of the righteous.

For the LORD knoweth the way of the righteous: but the way of the ungodly shall perish.

In times of temptation and discouragement, I have remembered those words loudly and clearly *"Blessed is the man that walketh not in the counsel of the ungodly...and he shall be like a tree planted by rivers of water, that bringeth forth his fruit in his season...whatever he doeth shall prosper..."* Those words have given me hope to stay grounded, to keep the faith, to keep on going.

81

One last one that has proven trustworthy for me comes from the last book of the Old Testament, Malachi.

Will anyone rob God? Yet you are robbing me! But you say,
"How are we robbing you?" In your tithes and offerings!
You are cursed with a curse,
for you are robbing me—the whole nation of you!
Bring the full tithe into the storehouse,
so that there may be food in my house,
and thus, put me to the test, says the LORD of Hosts.
See if I will not open the windows of heaven for you
and pour down for you an overflowing blessing.

The expression *"open the windows of heaven"* is an image that deserves our reflection. When you imagine heaven's windows opening, what do you see? What do you feel when you think on that image?

I think of the windows in my elementary school. They were huge and to open them took a lot of strength. Once opened, it was if the whole side of the building became a part of the outside. Fresh air floated into the room, the sun was brighter, and the smells of nature, flowers, and trees enveloped us. I wanted to get up and rush outside and run around, skip, roll in the grass. I wanted to get out there and play baseball, tether ball, and soccer. I wanted to jump in a swimming pool or swim in a lake. Open windows let me be outside while at the same time being inside.

Opening the windows of heaven, lets us glimpse God in ways never experienced before, that is equally as exciting as a third grader opening a school window and digesting the world outside. Malachi suggests this thrill and special experience comes through giving, cheerfully, generously, and regularly to God.

I had a member of my church one time to say to me, "If I didn't tithe, I'm afraid I would miss something!" ***Givers are happier people***. There is a joy that is unexperienced until the heart is open for God to use what we have. Try it and see for yourselves.

When I put money in the offering plates at worship, I know that for every dollar I give, some of that money goes to operate colleges, universities, children's homes, facilities for the elderly, seminaries, missionaries all over the world, and programs to assist the poor and homeless. When I give, the windows of heaven open and I can catch a glimpse of God at work in the lives of thousands of people. I am a co-worker with God in the field of human need.

The New Testament

All the writings of the New Testament center on the person of Jesus. His radical message of "good news" turned the world upside down in his day and continues to do so in ours. His death and resurrection are hailed as the pivotal point of humanity. Through him, the church is born and has remained strong throughout the world for some two thousand years!

The greatest sermon ever preached is contained in the first book of the New Testament (Matthew 5-7). It is profound. It offers us the best way of living life to the fullest. I will not share it all, but highlight some of its verses:

> "Therefore, I tell you, do not worry about your life, what you will eat or what you will drink, or about your body, what you will wear. Is not life more than food, and the body more than clothing? Look at the birds of the air; they neither sow nor reap nor gather into barns, and yet your heavenly Father feeds them. Are you not of more value than they? And can any of you by worrying add a single hour to your span of life? And why do you worry about clothing? Consider the lilies of the field, how they grow; they neither toil nor spin, yet I tell you, even Solomon in all his glory was not clothed like one of these. But if God so clothes the grass of the field, which is alive today and tomorrow is thrown into the oven, will he not much more clothe you—you of little faith? Therefore, do not worry,

saying, 'What will we eat?' or 'What will we drink?' or 'What will we wear?' Indeed, your heavenly Father knows that you need all these things. But strive first for the kingdom of God and his righteousness, and all these things will be given to you as well.

"Ask, and it will be given you; search, and you will find; knock, and the door will be opened for you. For everyone who asks receives, and everyone who searches finds, and for everyone who knocks, the door will be opened. Is there anyone among you who, if your child asks for bread, will give a stone? Or if the child asks for a fish, will give a snake? If you then, who are evil, know how to give good gifts to your children, how much more will your Father in heaven give good things to those who ask him! "In everything do to others as you would have them do to you; for this is the law and the prophets.

Jesus' law was built upon grace, mercy, forgiveness, new life, redemption, peace, joy, and eternal life. Jesus wanted all people to have the best of life, to experience God's holy kingdom on earth, and to treat others the way we wish to be treated. If those who say they are followers of Jesus even lived this way for a day, the world would see significant change for the good, and there would be more hope for humanity.

Knowing the difficulty of loving our neighbors, much less our enemies, Jesus tells a fascinating story that summarizes how his followers are to live this out. It is found in Luke 10:25-37:

Just then a lawyer stood up to test Jesus. "Teacher," he said, "what must I do to inherit eternal life?" He said to him, "What is written in the law? What do you read there?" He answered, "You shall love the Lord your God with all your heart, and with all your soul, and with all your strength, and with all your mind; and your neighbor as yourself." And he said to him, "You have given the right answer; do this, and you will live."

But wanting to justify himself, he asked Jesus, "And who is my neighbor?" Jesus replied, "A man was going down from Jerusalem to Jericho, and fell into the hands of robbers, who stripped him, beat him, and went away, leaving him half dead. Now by chance a priest was going down that road; and when he saw him, he passed by on the other side. So likewise, a Levite, when he came to the place and saw him, passed by on the other side. But a Samaritan while traveling came near him; and when he saw him, he was moved with pity. He went to him and bandaged his wounds, having poured oil and wine on them. Then he put him on his own animal, brought him to an inn, and took care of him. The next day he took out two denarii, gave them to the innkeeper, and said, 'Take care of him; and when I come back, I will repay you whatever more you spend.' Which of these three, do you think, was a neighbor to the man who fell into the hands of the robbers?" He said, "The one who showed him mercy." Jesus said to him, "Go and do likewise."

Of great note is that the hero of the story is the Samaritan. In that day, Jews and Samaritans did not get along well. Jews thought Samaritans were "less than" and disgusting. In today's world, the hero of the story would be whoever you think is your worst enemy!

Jesus had an uncanny way of illustrating what it is like to live in the realm of God. God's kingdom is the opposite of what we would think it might be. Our enemy is the hero of the story!!!! Preposterous! Unsettling!

Jesus goes a step further with a story of a loving father found in Luke 15:11-32:

Then Jesus said, "There was a man who had two sons. The younger of them said to his father, 'Father, give me the share of the property that will belong to me.' So, he divided his property between them. A few days later the younger son gathered all he had and traveled to a distant country, and there he squandered his property in dissolute living. When he had spent everything, a severe famine took place throughout that country, and he began to be in need. So, he went and hired himself out to one of the citizens of that country, who sent him to his fields to feed the pigs. He would gladly have filled himself with the pods that the pigs were eating; and no one gave him anything. But when he came to himself, he said, 'How many of my father's hired hands have bread enough and to spare, but here I am dying of hunger! I will get up and go to my father, and I will say to him, "Father, I have sinned against heaven and before you; I am no longer worthy to be called your son; treat me like one of your hired hands."' So he set off and went to his father. But while he was still far off, his father saw him and was filled with compassion; he ran and put his arms around him and kissed him. Then the son said to him, 'Father, I have sinned against heaven and before you; I am no longer worthy to be called your son.' But the father said to his slaves, 'Quickly, bring out a robe—the best one—and put it on him; put a ring on his finger and sandals on his feet. And get the fatted calf and kill it and let us eat and celebrate; for this son of mine was dead and is alive again; he was lost and is found!' And they began to celebrate.

In Jesus' day, no good Jewish father would stand for a son, much less a "second" son to get an inheritance before his death. To even ask for it was to suggest that the son wanted his father dead! Shocking as that is, the father gives his second son his share of what he would receive when the father dies.

The son goes into a far country and squanders the money in living life to the hilt. I will leave that to your imagination what that looks like! When he is making a living with pigs (Jews thought pigs were very unclean!) and basically not getting enough to eat, he "comes to himself" and decides to go home.

Those listening to the story think that Jesus will say that when he gets home, the father turns his back on him or the father has him severely punished, or the father makes him a slave. But that is not what happens. The father runs to meet his son (he had been looking out for him every day since he left) and does not even let him apologize. He sends his servants for a robe (symbol of sonship) and ring and kills the fatted calf, so that there could be a party with the best of steak and wine and dancing. After all, his son who was lost is found, was dead and is alive!

It was a wonder that Jesus was not put to death after telling such an outrageous story! God is the father in this story. God's love is filled with faith, hope, and love. What hope there is for all who have gone astray to come home to the ONE who loves us no matter our sins.

The greatest account of hope in the whole Bible is in all four gospels. It is the resurrection of Jesus after his crucifixion. I have selected John 20:1-18:

> *Early on the first day of the week, while it was still dark, Mary Magdalene came to the tomb and saw that the stone had been removed from the tomb. So she ran and went to Simon Peter and the other disciple, the one whom Jesus loved, and said to them, "They have taken the Lord out of the tomb, and we do not know where they have laid him." Then Peter and the other disciple set out and went toward the tomb. The two were running together, but the other disciple outran Peter and reached the tomb first. He bent down to look in and saw the linen wrappings lying there, but he did not go in. Then Simon Peter came, following him, and went into the tomb. He saw the linen wrappings lying there, and the cloth that had been on Jesus' head, not lying with the linen wrappings but rolled up in a place by itself. Then the other disciple, who reached the tomb first, also went in, and he saw and believed; for as yet they did not understand the scripture, that he must rise from the dead. Then the disciples returned to their homes.*

> *But Mary stood weeping outside the tomb. As she wept, she bent over to look into the tomb and she saw two angels in white,*

sitting where the body of Jesus had been lying, one at the head and the other at the feet. They said to her, "Woman, why are you weeping?" She said to them, "They have taken away my Lord, and I do not know where they have laid him." When she had said this, she turned around and saw Jesus standing there, but she did not know that it was Jesus. Jesus said to her, "Woman, why are you weeping? Whom are you looking for?" Supposing him to be the gardener, she said to him, "Sir, if you have carried him away, tell me where you have laid him, and I will take him away." Jesus said to her, "Mary!" She turned and said to him in Hebrew, "Rabbouni!" (which means Teacher). Jesus said to her, "Do not hold on to me, because I have not yet ascended to the Father. But go to my brothers and say to them, 'I am ascending to my Father and your Father, to my God and your God.'" Mary Magdalene went and announced to the disciples, "I have seen the Lord;" and she told them that he had said these things to her.

His disciples left him to die alone. All of them betrayed Jesus, but one more than the rest. Judas accepted payment for telling where Jesus would be so the authorities could arrest him. His friends left him to die alone. Those for whom he had healed, taught, preached, and loved, left him to die alone. His family looked on from a distance. To the world, he seemed a dismal failure. Indeed, a three-year ministry "down the drain"!

As he was dying, he was mocked, spit upon, and his clothes were taken off of him and the soldiers gambled to see who would get them. His words from the cross are recorded:

> *Father forgive them; for they know not what they do.*
> *Today you will be with me in paradise.*
> *Woman, behold, thy son! Behold, thy mother!*
> *My God, my God, why hast thou forsaken me?*
> *I thirst.*
> *It is finished.*
> *Father, into thy hands I commend my spirit.*

Numerous sermons have been preached on these words, there are libraries full of books written about them and they have been the subject of multitudes of scholarly discussion. Together, they offer hope for those in need of forgiveness, eternal life for those who think their lives are worthless, homes for the homeless, trust in the face of suffering and death (the Psalm that Jesus quotes "My God, my God why hast thou forsaken me" ends in praise and trust of God![57] Finally, his words became an acknowledgment that his work had ended, and he entrusted his future, his very being to God's eternal mercy.

And then, while it was still dark, women went to the tomb and discovered that he was not there, for he had risen from the dead. They became the first evangelists of the resurrection as they ran to tell the other disciples. The word was out. The world has never been the same! Some of the greatest words of hope are found when Jesus appeared to the disciples after his resurrection while they were huddled up in great fear of being arrested and put to death by the government because Jesus' body was missing!

He appears in their midst and like the father in the story of the prodigal son, Jesus does not punish nor admonish them for leaving and betraying them. He never mentions these things. Instead, his first words to them are words of peace! They are stunned! We are stunned just thinking about it.

Then he did something even more bizarre. He gave them the power to continue his work of forgiveness. Fifty days later, His Holy Spirit came upon them, and the church began. For almost two thousand years, the church has been an instrument of hope in a world of despair. The cross is the symbol that reminds us that God can turn our suffering into salvation, our negatives into positives, and death into eternal life.

The words of the New Testament are a "testimony" to hope. Later on, a man named Paul would write almost one-half of the New Testament. His words found in these excerpts from Romans 8:31-39 accent the hope found in God through Jesus:

What then are we to say about these things? If God is for us, who is against us? Who will separate us from the love of Christ? Will hardship, or distress, or persecution, or famine, or nakedness, or peril, or sword?

No, in all these things we are more than conquerors through him who loved us. For I am convinced that neither death, nor life, nor angels, nor rulers, nor things present, nor things to come, nor powers, nor height, nor depth, nor anything else in all creation, will be able to separate us from the love of God in Christ Jesus our Lord.

He would also write the most famous verses in the world on the nature of love found in I Corinthians 13:

If I speak in the tongues of mortals and of angels, but do not have love, I am a noisy gong or a clanging cymbal. And if I have prophetic powers, and understand all mysteries and all knowledge, and if I have all faith, so as to remove mountains, but do not have love, I am nothing. If I give away all my possessions, and if I hand over my body so that I may boast, but do not have love, I gain nothing.

Love is patient; love is kind; love is not envious or boastful or arrogant or rude. It does not insist on its own way; it is not irritable or resentful; it does not rejoice in wrongdoing but rejoices in the truth. It bears all things, believes all things, hopes all things, endures all things.

Love never ends. But as for prophecies, they will come to an end; as for tongues, they will cease; as for knowledge, it will come to an end. For we know only in part, and we prophesy only in part; but when the complete comes, the partial will come to an end. When I was a child, I spoke like a child, I thought like a child, I reasoned like a child; when I became an adult, I put an end to childish ways. For now we see in a mirror, dimly,[b] but then we will see face to face. Now I know only in part; then I will know fully, even as I have been fully known. And now faith, hope, and love abide, these three; and the greatest of these is love.

Here are some specific places *hope* is mentioned in the New Testament:

Matthew 12:21   in His name the nations will put their hope (New International Version)

John 3:2-3   hope in Him

Romans 4:18   who against hope, believed in hope

Romans 5:5   hope does not disappoint

Romans 8:24-26   saved in this hope

Romans 15:4   for whatever was written in former days was written for our instruction, so that by steadfastness and by the encouragement of the scriptures we might have hope.

Romans 15:13   May the God of hope fill you with joy and peace in your faith, that by the power of the Holy Spirit your whole life and outlook may be radiant with hope. (J.B. Phillips translation)

Romans 15:43   God of hope fill you with all joy and peace, abound in hope by power of The Holy Spirit.

Ephesians 4:4   called to hope

I Corinthians 9:10 He that plows, should plow in hope.

I Corinthians 13 -   faith, hope and love remain.   (hope offered is also love)

Galations 5:5   wait for hope (this was one that gave me much to consider)

Colossians 1:4-5	love springs from hope
Colossians 1:27	Christ in you, the hope of glory (This is very important)
Hebrews 3:6	hope firm to the end
Hebrews 7:19	the introduction of a better hope
Hebrews 11:1	faith is substance of things hoped for...
I Peter 1:3-5	We have been born anew to a living hope through the resurrection of Jesus Christ from the dead.
Titus 1:2	in the hope of eternal life
Titus 3:4-7	hope of eternal life

As the Bible comes to an end, the author (John of Patmos) describes the greatest vision of hope ever written in Revelation 20:

*Then I saw a **new heaven and a new earth**; for the first heaven and the first earth had passed away, and the sea was no more. And I saw the holy city, the new Jerusalem, coming down out of heaven from God, prepared as a bride adorned for her husband. And I heard a loud voice from the throne saying,*

"See, the home of God is among mortals.
He will dwell[with them;
they will be his peoples,
and God himself will be with them.
He will wipe every tear from their eyes.
Death will be no more;
mourning and crying and pain will be no more,
for the first things have passed away."

And the one who was seated on the throne said, "See, I am making all things new." Also, he said, "Write this, for these words are trustworthy and true." Then he said to me, "It is done! I am the Alpha and the Omega, the beginning, and the end. To the thirsty I will give water as a gift from the spring of the water of life.

So may it be!

We have this hope, a sure
and steadfast
anchor of the soul

Hebrews 6:19

———⊶⊷———

Chapter 5

A trinitarian view of hope

—————⋈—————

Hope is the story we imagine,
Faith is the story we tell,

Love is the story we live.

The Marks of Hope

From the beginning of recorded history, humans have tried to put a name to what many call God. There is a hunger and thirst to label that which is beyond us, the great mystery. The church has centered in on three words: Father, Son and Holy Spirit. This is called "trinity." Interestingly, the word "trinity" is not in the Bible. The church has used this word for centuries to point to God as Father, Son and Holy Spirit. This has been a stumbling block for many people. I have had several to say to me, "I believe in God and Jesus, but not sure about the Holy Spirit. Even the late great preacher/theologian Leslie D. Weatherhead said that "he put the Holy Spirit in a box awaiting further light."[58]

Many theologians have written about the mystery of God in "three persons." The bottom line is that anything that deals with God is holy mystery! Basically, God is not definable. Indeed, everything we know about God falls short of who God is.

Martin Buber used the term "I-Thou"[59] to point to an experience a person has with God or another person or even an inanimate object like a tree. He uses the term "I-It" to point to the ways we strive to describe the I-Thou experience. I like to think of it this way.

I-Thou can occur when a young man is on his first date with a beautiful young woman and after dinner and a movie, he escorts her to the front door. He leans over and kisses her. While he is kissing her, he does not try to describe it. He is simply caught up in the "heavenly" experience of the kiss.

When he drives home, he reflects on the kiss and tries to describe it. The words begin to flow: "I could have stayed there all night. It was great. She has soft lips. I felt so close to her." There are simply no words that do justice in trying to describe or define the experience of that kiss! It is the same with God.

From the beginning of recorded history, humanity has tried to describe God and to name God. The name is so sacred in Judaism that often it is spelled G-d, so that it cannot be pronounced. There are over 100 names for God in the Bible and none of them can possibly "define" who God is!

Interestingly, the more people came to know God, the more names were attached. Elohim means "strong one or creator." Jehovah-jireh means "the Lord will provide." Here are others:

Advocate – 1 John 2:1
Almighty – Revelation 1:8
Alpha – Revelation 1:8
Amen – Revelation 3:14
Angel of the Lord – Genesis 16:7
Anointed One – Psalm 2:2
Apostle – Hebrews 3:1
Author and Perfecter of our Faith – Hebrews 12:2
Beginning – Revelation 21:6
Bishop of Souls – 1 Peter 2:25
Branch – Zechariah 3:8

Bread of Life – John 6:35,48
Bridegroom – Matthew 9:15
Carpenter – Mark 6:3
Chief Shepherd – 1 Peter 5:4
The Christ – Matthew 1:16
Comforter – Jeremiah 8:18
Consolation of Israel – Luke 2:25
Cornerstone – Ephesians 2:20
Dayspring – Luke 1:78
Day Star – 2 Peter 1:19
Deliverer – Romans 11:26
Desire of Nations – Haggai 2:7
Emmanuel – Matthew 1:23
End – Revelation 21:6
Everlasting Father – Isaiah 9:6
Faithful and True Witness – Revelation 3:14
First Fruits – 1 Corinthians 15:23
Foundation – Isaiah 28:16
Fountain – Zechariah 13:1
Friend of Sinners – Matthew 11:19
Gate for the Sheep – John 10:7
Gift of God – 2 Corinthians 9:15
God – John 1:1
Glory of God – Isaiah 60:1
Good Shepherd – John 10:11
Governor – Matthew 2:6
Great Shepherd – Hebrews 13:20
Guide – Psalm 48:14
Head of the Church – Colossians 1:18
High Priest – Hebrews 3:1
Holy One of Israel – Isaiah 41:14
Horn of Salvation – Luke 1:69
I Am – Exodus 3:14

Jehovah – Psalm 83:18
Jesus – Matthew 1:21
King of Israel – Matthew 27:42
King of Kings – 1 Timothy 6:15; Revelation 19:16
Lamb of God – John 1:29
Last Adam – 1 Corinthians 15:45
Life – John 11:25
Light of the World – John 8:12; John 9:5
Lion of the Tribe of Judah – Revelation 5:5
Lord of Lords – 1 Timothy 6:15; Revelation 19:16
Master – Matthew 23:8
Mediator – 1 Timothy 2:5
Messiah – John 1:41
Mighty God – Isaiah 9:6
Morning Star – Revelation 22:16
Nazarene – Matthew 2:23
Omega – Revelation 1:8
Passover Lamb – 1 Corinthians 5:7
Physician – Matthew 9:12
Potentate – 1 Timothy 6:15
Priest – Hebrews 4:15
Prince of Peace – Isaiah 9:6
Prophet – Acts 3:22
Propitiation – I John 2:2
Purifier – Malachi 3:3
Rabbi – John 1:49
Ransom – 1 Timothy 2:6
Redeemer – Isaiah 41:14
Refiner – Malachi 3:2
Refuge – Isaiah 25:4
Resurrection – John 11:25
Righteousness – Jeremiah 23:6
Rock – Deuteronomy 32:4

Root of David – Revelation 22:16
Rose of Sharon – Song of Solomon 2:1
Ruler of God's Creation – Revelation 3:14
Sacrifice – Ephesians 5:2
Savior – 2 Samuel 22:47; Luke 1:47
Second Adam – 1 Corinthians 15:47
Seed of Abraham – Galatians 3:16
Seed of David – 2 Timothy 2:8
Seed of the Woman – Genesis 3:15
Servant – Isaiah 42:1
Shepherd – 1 Peter 2:25
Shiloh – Genesis 49:10
Son of David – Matthew 15:22
Son of God – Luke 1:35
Son of Man – Matthew 18:11
Son of Mary – Mark 6:3
Son of the Most High – Luke 1:32
Stone – Isaiah 28:16
Sun of Righteousness – Malachi 4:2
Teacher – Matthew 26:18
Truth – John 14:6
Way – John 14:6
Wonderful Counselor – Isaiah 9:6
Word – John 1:1
Vine – John 15:1[60]

Names are important. In my family, we all have various "nicknames" for one another. Some of us have many nicknames! The more we are together and know one another, the more names we attach and none of them can possibly enfold all of who we are.

I am a son, brother, husband, father, grandfather, minister, friend, cousin, uncle, great-uncle, clergyperson, teacher... I am not just one of these, but all combined. Sometimes in a funeral I like to suggest that a person's life is like a patchwork quilt and each of us has a piece of that quilt, but none of us have the whole. We are unable to know the entirety of a person.

This is the same with God. Michael W. Smith wrote a song that lists several aspects of God: "You are holy, you are mighty, you are worthy, my prince of peace!"[61] His choice of words points to the indescribable God. God is holy, mighty, worthy, but not contained by any specific one of these but encompasses all.

Basically, the church has summarized all the names for God in "three persons" called "Trinity." God is "Father, Son and Holy Spirit."

Matthew 28:19
Go therefore and make disciples of all nations, baptizing them in the name of the Father and of the Son and of the Holy Spirit,

2 Corinthians 13:14
May the grace of the Lord Jesus Christ, and the love of God, and the fellowship of the Holy Spirit...

I Peter 1:2
Who have been chosen and destined by God the Father and s anctified by the Spirit to be obedient to Jesus Christ.

Paul often began his letters to the churches to whom he wrote saying "The grace of the Lord Jesus Christ and the Love of God and the fellowship of the Holy Spirit be with you all."

When I was active in the church as a pastor, often I would end a worship service with a benediction saying something like "Go with the blessing of God, Creator, Redeemer and Sustainer, knowing that God will be with us right now and forevermore." The words, "creator, redeemer and sustainer" are a different way of expressing the trinity.

Cynthia Bourgeault in her wonderful book <u>The Holy Trinity and the Law of Three</u> suggests other trinitarian formulas in striving to understand God:

Unmanifest/manifesting/ manifested
Hidden ground of love/Wisdom/Word
God/Word/Word made flesh
Mother-Sophia/Jesus-Sophia/Spirit-Sophia
Affirming/denying/reconciling[62]

She goes on to bring more "down-to-earth" trinitarian forms that point to what occurs (arisings) from some triads of life:

Seed/earth/sun =sprout
Flour/water/fire = bread
Plaintiff/defendant/judge = resolution
Sail/keel/helmsperson =course made good[63]

It is the illustration of the last one that intrigues me the most in terms of hope. Bourgearult gives the illustration of a sailboat:

A sailboat, as nearly everyone knows, is driven through the water by the interplay of the wind on its sails (First force) and the resistance of the sea against its keel (second force). The result is that the boat is shot forward through the water, much like a spat-out watermelon seed. But as an any sailor knows, this schoolbook analogy is not complete. A sailboat, left to its own devices, will not shoot forward through the water; it will round up into the wind and come to a stop. For forward movement to occur, a third force must enter the equation, the heading or destination by which the helmsperson determines the proper set of the sail and positioning of the keel. Only if these three are engaged can the desire result emerge, which is the course made good, the actual distance traveled [64]

There are three important insights that emerge from such a simple illustration:

1) What is happening to the sailboat is something that is continuously in process.

2) Water, resistance and the helmsman are essential for a sailboat to serve its purpose

3) Resistance is not the enemy, but the opportunity needed for the helmsman to travel on the water in the first place.

God is always in motion or "process" so to speak. Indeed, God did not simply create the universe, God is still creating, or "at work" in the world. Jesus said that he came to be about the "work" of his Heavenly Father. As the body of Christ in the world today (the church) we are continuing the "work" of God as we worship, share the "good news," nurture, educate and serve to help all in need throughout the world.

Though Sabbath, the day of resting, is vital to our body, mind, and spirit to be refreshed, renewed and restored, our minds never stop thinking or creating new ways for life to bring meaning and purpose to ourselves and others. We are in constant motion!

When I visit with my grandchildren I am constantly amazed at their energy. They wake up ready to play and have fun. All through the day they come up with new things to do. When I tire out, I say to them, let's go sit on the sofa and read. They are bodily still, but their minds are clicking away with new words and what they will do with them. Finally, comes bath, devotion/prayers, and lights out. And though they sleep, their minds are still processing the day through their dreams.

God is always at work seeking us, loving us, and doing all God can (without violating our free will or God's own integrity) to help humanity have abundant life.

However, there are resistances in life to God's work in our life: sin in its multitude of forms that lead to violence, poverty, injustice, stress related diseases, and oppression. The term "life happens" seems to articulate much of the "resistance" that comes to us in life.

I would argue that *hope* is the key that allows the helmsman to guide the sailboat across the resisting waters to achieve the intention of going from point A to point B. Hope allows us to move across the resistances of life that I would also call "anger".

As I write these words, America is suffering from numerous riots and protests concerning police brutality toward minorities. There is great anger about injustice and mistreatment. Anger is *hope* against the resistance to fairness perpetuated by some who are racist and brutal.

Who would ever think of anger as hope!!!

- Note Jesus' anger in the temple – turning over tables and driving out the moneychangers.[65] Why did he do this? In short, in the hope that God's house would be a place of sacredness, prayer and at the forefront of people's lives.

- The anger against slavery, the holocaust, apartheid, lack of civil rights, and the war on terrorism led the way toward hate-laws and in many cases, the end of oppression and tyrant dictatorships, in the hope that the world can live in peace and not just liberty and justice for some.

- A parent's anger at their children's misbehavior (resistance to the rules) results in punishment meant to help them understand what they did wrong in the hope that they will learn and not reenact such actions.

The resistance to ignorance is education.

The resistance to illness is healthcare.

The resistance to injustice is listening and action toward change.

The resistance to poverty and homelessness is shared resources.

The resistance to sin is forgiveness and grace.

The way across the waters of despair is hope.

We can learn from despair and darkness. They are not always the enemy, rather the opportunity to learn and grow. It is rarely comfortable to sit in the darkness of the soul.

In the movie, *O God,* George Burns plays the role of God. One day a little girl named Tracey begins a conversation with him:

Tracey – "God why is there suffering and pain?"

God - "Did you ever see an up without a down?"

Tracey – "No."

God - "did you ever see a front without a back?"

Tracey - "No."

God – "Did you ever see an in without an out?

Tracey – "No."

God - "Well that's why there can't be life without death, pleasure without pain. If I take away sad, happy has to go with it."[66]

Certainly, that is a simplistic way of looking at the great mysteries of life. Though technically these answers have some validity, they fall short of trying to answer the deep resistances of our souls. We do not look into a coffin and view the body of a deceased loved one and simply say, "Well, there can't be life without death." What we might think is "What is going with our deceased loved one right now?" "Is there really a heaven?" "Where is God in my pain and grief." "Why did this have to happen?" "Where is my hope when death comes for me?"

In the midst of the resistances to our once content life, there is an opportunity to move on, to process, through the darkness and deep valleys. God has not left us, and it is the person of God known as Hope that leads us forward.

In Paul's first letter to the church of Corinth, he writes:

And now faith, hope, and love abide, these three;
and the greatest of these is love.

Faith, hope and love remain forever, but the greatest is love. This is a beautiful new way of expressing the trinity: God is Love, Jesus is the Hope of the World, and Faith is the Spirit (the Rurach – or wind) that empowers.

To use the sailboat illustration, I would suggest:

God is the sailboat – Love in action (God is love)

Jesus is the hope that overcomes the resistance of the waters. (the power of the cross is triumph over sin, death and despair that leads to new life, salvation, forgiveness and redemption)

Spirit is the wind (the faith) empowering the sailboat to move at all allowing the helmsman to guide the boat toward a destination. The church empowered by the Holy Spirit is a church on fire to change the world for God's sake.

It takes all three for the sailboat to accomplish its mission. Interestingly, the symbol of the early church was that of a boat! Indeed, many church's sanctuaries are designed to resemble a boat.

Boats are not made to sit in a harbor, they are meant to be out on the waters. Jesus disciples were meant to be together IN the boat, with the mandate to go and make disciples of all nations, baptizing in the name of Father, Son and Holy spirit and teaching all that he had commanded. The boat (Love itself) would not help them to their destination without the wind (spirit) and that which would enable them to resist the blocking forces (hope) in the process. It takes the disciples steering the boat so that it can move the church toward the kingdom of God.

One of the scriptures that I think has been misunderstood for many years is that of Peter asking Jesus to let him walk on water: (Matthew 14:22-33)

> *Immediately Jesus made the disciples get into the boat and go on ahead of him to the other side, while he dismissed the crowd. After he had dismissed them, he went up on a mountainside by himself to pray.*
>
> *Later that night, he was there alone, and the boat was already a considerable distance from land, buffeted by the waves because the wind was against it.*
>
> *Shortly before dawn Jesus went out to them, walking on the lake. When the disciples saw him walking on the lake, they were terrified. "It's a ghost," they said, and cried out in fear.*
>
> *But Jesus immediately said to them: "Take courage! It is I. Don't be afraid."*
>
> *"Lord, if it's you," Peter replied, tell me to come to you on the water."*
>
> *"Come," he said.*
>
> *Then Peter got down out of the boat, walked on the water, and came toward Jesus. But when he saw the wind, he was afraid and, beginning to sink, cried out, "Lord, save me!"*
>
> *Immediately Jesus reached out his hand and caught him. "You of little faith," he said, "why did you doubt?"*
>
> *And when they climbed into the boat, the wind died down. Then those who were in the boat worshiped him, saying, "Truly you are the Son of God."*

Though Jesus invited Peter to walk to him, Peter's fear caused his resistance to achieve the goal. Note that when Jesus reaches out and *catches* Peter, he <u>immediately takes him back to the boat</u>. Perhaps, Jesus is indicating that we are not to leave the *church* (the boat, the body of Christ) and go out into the world that is filled with evil all by ourselves.

We need to work together. We were never designed to walk on water in the first place, but we were designed, indeed called, to be the church (the boat) that goes into the world empowered by the Holy Spirit and full of hope to overcome the resistances to God's great love.

Walter Brueggemann says it this way, "Hope requires a community of faith and action that is open to newness that will be given as a gift, **hope is indeed a communal activity,** *for none can fully hope alone.*"[67]

I love the order Paul puts these terms in when writing the Corinthian Church: *faith, hope and love.* Hope is in the middle between the wind and the boat and rightly so, it is essential to enable the boat to achieve its purpose. These are three strong words to help express the triune God.

LOVE: God is love. This is biblical.[68] Wherever and whenever we experience love, we experience God. I had a friend who told me, years ago, that he did not believe in God. During a discussion about suffering and God, he said to me, "If there is a God, show me the evidence. Show me God." I said to him, "Do you believe in love?" He said, "Of course." I said, "Then if love exists, as you say, show me the evidence. Put love in my hand right now." He was quiet and said, "I can't." I said, "Nevertheless you believe in love because you have experienced love. Your parents have displayed it for you, you have felt love for others and indeed, many girlfriends! Thus, love exists even though you cannot put love in my hand." Then I quoted for him, "God is love" so if you have experienced love, you have experienced God.

The nature of love is to upbuild one another. The apostle Paul says that "love bears all things, believes all things, hopes all things, endures all things. Love never dies."[69] The author of the Song of Solomon says: "love is stronger than death."[70] The whole of Christianity is based on that very thing. The cross is the symbol that love is stronger than death and is the most powerful force in the world!

HOPE: Jesus is hope. Note this in the New Testament:

1 Peter 1:3-6:
Blessed be the God and Father of our Lord Jesus Christ! According to his great mercy, he has caused us to be born again to a living hope through the resurrection of Jesus Christ from the dead, to an inheritance that is imperishable, undefiled, and unfading,

Matthew 12:21:
And in his name the Gentiles will hope.

I Corinthians 15:19:
If in Christ, we have hope in this life

Colossians 1:27
which is Christ in you, the hope of glory.

Jesus not only lived love, but he also embodied hope. His teachings, his preaching, his miracles, his death and resurrection all point to hope for humanity. Notice the hope in these interactions Jesus has with people:

- To the woman he met at a well, he told her about "living water" and treated her as an equal. Her meeting with him gave her the courage to return to her village and proclaim the good news.[71]

- To Zacchaeus, he called him a "son of Abraham" thus restoring dignity to him. Zacchaeus' response to this affirmation was to turn his life around and return to those from whom he had cheated not just what he took, but four-fold![72]

- To the man with evil spirits named Legion, he exorcised them so the man could return to his family and live a healthy life.[73]

- On the night in which he was betrayed, he washed his disciple's feet and served them bread and wine as symbols of his body and blood. They never forgot. Those symbols today come to life when we are in missions to all in need (washing of feet) and participating in the eucharist, as Christ is taken into our body, we are to be the body and life of Christ in the world.[74]

Jesus' parables are parables of hope:

- Prodigal son[75]
- Good Samaritan[76]
- Lost coin[77]
- Lost sheep[78]
- Soil[79]
- Laborers in the vineyard[80]

Notice as you read these and all his parables, how they are intended to help the reader and those who listened to him in person, know God's love and the hope that comes from keeping God central in their lives.

FAITH: Paul says in Romans 10:17, "Faith comes *by hearing* (note that this is an active word!) and how will they hear without a preacher." When a minister stands up to preach, he/she has absolutely no control on what happens when the words from his/her mouth are spoken and how the ear of the receiver digests them. The interaction that can occur when the spoken word permeates into the minds and hearts of the hearers is faith. This holy mystery is the gift of the Holy Spirit or in Paul's theology, *faith*. Faith thus opens the door for God (Love) and Hope to enter.

Though the Holy Spirit is mentioned in the Old Testament, the New Testament gives new meaning: Jesus says that in his leaving, the Spirit will come upon us to bring comfort and power. In the book of Acts we read where Jesus says *you shall receive power to be witnesses in Jerusalem, Judea Samaria and to the ends of the world.* It is the spirit of Jesus himself who comes and surrounds us, giving us peace that the world doesn't know, and gives us power to change the world.

Wind is a word that is synonymous with the Holy Spirit. Wind can be destructive, but it can also be a means of grace. Wind can destroy buildings and kill people. Winds can steer ships, fly kites, power a pipe organ, and sweep away debris. The wind of the Holy Spirit brings hope to the world and empowers the church. What is the difference between a civic organization and the church of Jesus Christ? It is the Spirit of Hope that builds community, a community that lives differently from the world.

The civil rights movement began in the church. It began with the movement of the Holy Spirit empowering the Love of God through Christ, the hope of the world. How else could it be a non-violent movement with a message of loving all people. Those who marched for freedom were led by the ancient words of "the Hope of the World" when he said:

I have come that you may have life, life in all of its fullness. (John 10:10)

We are to love our neighbor as ourselves. (Mark 12:30-31)

If you want to be my follower: die to self, take up a cross, follow me. (Mathew 16:24)

The Great Commission found in Matthew 28 became the mission of the church: *"Go therefore and make disciples of all nations, baptizing them in the name of the Father, and of the Son and of the Holy Spirit, teaching them all that I have commanded you and lo I am with you always, even until the end of the age."*

The trinitarian mark of baptism is the initiation into the church. The waters placed upon us at our baptism "marks" us with the touch of the divine. God never removes the "seal" upon us that names us, blesses us, and calls us into a life of discipleship: loving our neighbors, dying to self, choosing to go to those in the hell of life and bringing "good news" to them. Having faith in God's promise always to be with us ushers us forward into the mission of striving to make this world ready for God's holy kingdom to dwell.

It was the holy trinity at work among God's people, Faith, Hope and Love, that led St. Frances of Assisi to live and work among the people of his day. He is the patron saint of the poor and animals.

It was the holy trinity at work among God's people, that help to destroy Nazism during WWII bringing an end to the torment of the holocaust.

It was the holy trinity at work among God's people, that helped to put an end to Apartheid in South Africa.

It was the holy trinity at work in Dorothy Day that led her into social activism and a political radical.

It is the holy trinity at work among God's people that is standing up against injustice in all of its numerous disguises, welcoming the stranger, clothing the naked, caring for the sick, seeking to help those in prison (bondage), and feeding the hungry.

God, who is faith, hope and love, not only is always with us, but calls us out of ourselves into the world to be agents of change, comfort, and care. Each day I read of people who are creative in helping others with various needs. Men, women and children of various ages, working to ease the pains of those around them, inspiring others to do the same.

During this horrible Covid-19 pandemic, a twenty-year-old from my former church took a gun and shot himself in the head. He was able to call 911 for help, was rushed to the hospital and is now on life-support. Some 300 people have written words of hope and encouragement on the CaringBridge web site that has been set up. Love overflows. Faith in God's presence and ability to bring good out of tragedy permeates almost all of these entries. Together, faith, hope and love, are surrounding this family in ways that are beyond words.

Richard Rohr says, "As Paul says in his great hymn to love, "There are only three things that last, faith, hope, and love" (I Corinthians

13:13). All else passes. Each of these Three Great virtues must always include the other two in order to be authentic: love is always hopeful and faithful, hope is always loving and faithful, and faith is always loving and hopeful. They are the very nature of God."[81]

The Four Candles burned
slowly. Their Ambiance was so
soft you could hear them
speak...

The First Candle said, "I Am
Peace, but these days, nobody
wants to keep me lit." Then
Peace's flame slowly
diminishes and goes out
completely.

The Second Candle said, "I Am
Faith, but these days, I am no
longer indispensable." Then
Faith's flame slowly
diminishes and goes out
completely.

Sadly, The Third Candle Speaks,
"I Am Love and I haven't the
strength to stay lit any
longer. People put me aside
and don't understand my
importance. They even forget
to love those who are nearest
to them." Waiting no longer,
Love goes out completely.

Suddenly...A child enters the room and sees the three candles no longer burning. The child begins to cry, "Why are you not burning? You are supposed to stay lit until the end!"

Then the Fourth Candle speaks gently to the little child, "Don't be afraid, for I Am Hope, and while I still burn, we can re-light the other candles."

With Shining eyes, the child took the Candle of Hope and lit the other three candles.

Never let the Flame of Hope go out of your life. With Hope, no matter how bad things look and are...Peace, Faith and Love can Shine Brightly in our lives.

Chapter 6

Am I responsible for other's hope?

———×———

"One of the most important things you can do on this earth is to let people know they are not alone."

– Shannon L. Alder

Sometimes, when I was growing up, I would ask my parents a question and they would reply "Yes and No." I rarely liked that response! Usually it went like this:

Me: "May I go to my friend's house and play today?"

Parents: "Well, yes and no. Yes, you can do that, but "no", not until you clean your room."

Me: "Do I have to eat my vegetables?"

Parents: "Yes and no. Yes, you must eat them, but no television or dessert until you do."

Are we responsible for other's hope? Yes and No!

In the opening book of the Bible, we do not read far when we come upon the first death, and it was a violent one. It stemmed from one brother being jealous of the other. In a rage, Cain, the older brother, decides to get revenge on his younger brother, Abel, and kills him. Here is how it happened:

> *Cain said to his brother Abel, 'Let us go out to the field.' And when they were in the field, Cain rose up against his brother Abel and killed him. Then the LORD said to Cain, 'Where is your brother Abel?' He said, 'I do not know;* **am I my brother's keeper?'** *And the LORD said, 'What have you done? Listen; your brother's blood is crying out to me from the ground! And now you are cursed from the ground, which has opened its mouth to receive your brother's blood from your hand. When you till the ground, it will no longer yield to you its strength; you will be a fugitive and a wanderer on the earth.' Cain said to the LORD, 'My punishment is greater than I can bear! Today you have driven me away from the soil, and I shall be hidden from your face; I shall be a fugitive and a wanderer on the earth, and anyone who meets me may kill me.' Then the LORD said to him, 'Not so! Whoever kills Cain will suffer a sevenfold vengeance.' And the LORD put a mark on Cain, so that no one who came upon him would kill him. Then Cain went away from the presence of the LORD, and settled in the land of Nod, east of Eden.*[82]

It seems that God is not satisfied with Cain's offerings but was elated over his brother's. In a fit of jealousy, Cain takes his brother out into a field and kills him. God "hears" Abel's blood crying out from the ground. (that is a sermon for another day, but an interesting choice of words. Do we pay attention to those who have died from injustice and with no hope? Can we hear their blood crying out from the ground?) God seeks out Cain and asks him 'Where is your brother?" Cain's remark is his legend! All through history, his words sound loudly *"Am I my brother's keeper?"* That is the question. Are we responsible for our brothers and sisters in general and with hope in particular?

A Rabbi once asked his students, "how do we know when the night has ended, and the day has begun?" Immediately the students thought that they grasped the importance of the question. There are, after all, prayers that can be recited and rituals that can be performed only at night. And there are prayers and rituals that belong only to the day. It is therefore important to know when the night has ended, and day has begun. So, the brightest of the students offered an answer: "When I look out at the fields and I can distinguish between my field and the field of my neighbor's, that's when the night has ended, and day has begun." A second student offered her answer: "When I look from the fields and I see a house and I can tell that it's my house and not the house of my neighbor, that's when the night has ended and the day has begun." A third student offered an answer: "When I can distinguish the animals in the yard – and I can tell a cow from a horse – that's when the night has ended." Each of these answers brought a sadder, more severe frown to the Rabbi's face – until finally he shouted: "No! You don't understand! You only know how to divide! You divide your house from the house of your neighbor, your field from your neighbor's, one animal from another, one color from all the others. Is that all that we can do – divide, separate, split the world into pieces? Isn't the world broken enough - split into enough fragments? No, my dear students, it is not that way at all! Our Torah and Jewish values want more from us. The shocked students looked into the sad face of their Rabbi. One of them ventured, "Then Rabbi, tell us: How do we know that night has ended, and day has begun?" The Rabbi stared back into the faces of his students and with a gentle voice responded: "When you look into the face of the person who is beside you and you can see that that person is your brother or your sister, when you can recognize that person as a friend, then, finally, the night has ended, and the day has begun."[83]

When we can really "see" others and recognize them as "friend" then we begin to understand that we can be nothing other than a "hope-bearer" to them. We know that we are responsible for being a lighthouse to all in need, to all in despair, to all who are lost in whatever way.

Ann Rivers Siddons wrote a book many years ago entitled Heartbreak Hotel. It is the story of young Southern woman of privilege becoming involved in the civil rights movement in Montgomery, Alabama. The young woman is Maggie Deloach, a student at the University of Alabama and a member of the Kappa sorority. She is the last person anyone would think would get involved in the outrage surrounding the entrance of the university's first black student. Why did she get involved? How did it happen?

She happened to be at the jail one evening when an innocent black man was brought in. Beaten and bleeding the man can barely walk and is being drug by two officers. Maggie and the black man's eyes lock on each other. When she is involved in acts of defiance and is questioned why she got involved in the first place, she responded by saying "you have to see the man."[84]

I was only eight years of age when my parents brought my siblings and me into the den of our home (where our only television was located) to watch the "March on Washington." I was mesmerized by the voices of Peter, Paul and Mary as they sang so beautifully Bob Dylan's song *Blowing in the Wind*. Notice these words from it:

How many years can a mountain exist before it is washed to the sea?
How many years can some people exist before they're allowed to be free?
How many times will a man turn his head,
pretending he just doesn't see?

The answer my friend is blowing in the wind,
the answer is blowing in the wind.[85]

I have known parents who were vehemently opposed to homosexuality or abortion, or inter-racial dating only to have one of their children to reveal they were gay or pregnant, or feel they were born in the wrong body, or in love with a person of another race. Unfortunately, a few have turned their children away, but most parents, after getting over the shock, begin to really "see" their children. They begin to learn from them and together they work on the issues. As one father said to me upon learning his son was gay, "I have a lot to learn!" Those were "hope-bearing" words!

In November 2018, raging fires swept through parts of California. A 93-year-old named Margaret Newsum saw the news that the fires were not far from her home and she knew she would have to evacuate. But her caregiver was not around that morning to take her. And when Newsum went to call for help, her electricity shut off and phone service went down.

So, she got her medicine and other vital needs together and walked out of her home in Magalia, California, hoping somebody would come by and help her. Salvation soon came in the form of a garbage truck.

"I was standing there when I looked up and saw this great, big, green monster truck barreling down the street," Newsum told CNN.

Around that time, Dane Ray Cummings, a Waste Management driver, had been told to cut his trash collection route short and head home as the Camp Fire neared. But he wanted to finish his route, and he had a mind to check on some houses with elderly or disabled residents.

Cummings drove up to find Newsum waiting for him. And once he realized she needed to evacuate; he knew what he had to do. "He said you're going with me."

Newsum recently broke her back and uses a walker to get around, which made it tricky to get up into the cab of his garbage truck. Cummings and some neighbors lifted her up and buckled her in, and they strapped her walker to the side of the truck.

With thousands trying to flee at the same time, the trip was slow going.

"He got in the truck and away we went. It was stop, go, stop, go," Newsum said. "We were on the road about 5½ hours. When we started coming down out of the hill, the smoke was so bad, it was like going into the bowels of hell. It was so black. I've never seen smoke that black before. It was frightening."

On the ride, Cummings called up childhood friend and co-worker Brian Harrison, a heavy equipment technician for Waste Management. "He says, 'Brian, you are not gonna believe what I have in my truck.'" They weren't sure what to do with Newsum, but Harrison knew an evacuation center was no place for a 93-year-old.

I said Dane, 'This is a no-brainer. I'm just gonna take her home,' " he said. "It's just the right thing to do." Harrison, a single dad, said his sister and his children have chipped in to help take care of Newsum for the past week -- not that she needs too much help. "She's the most independent 93-year-old you'll ever meet," he said.

For her part, Newsum, who has no family in the area, was incredibly thankful for the care she's received.

"This family has taken me in. I have never felt so wanted and so comfortable and so much brought into making me part of the family," she said. Harrison recently learned it might be a couple of months before Newsum's allowed back into her home, news he said that excited his kids. "They've grown to love her. They just want to keep her," he said. Or as Newsum put it, "I'm like a stray puppy the kids fell in love with."[86]

Dane Ray Cummings was a "hope-bearer." He saw Margaret Newsum more than just a 93-year-old woman, but as a "friend" in need of hope. He put his agenda on hold to rescue her and even took her into his home until she was able to go safely back to her own place to live.

There is a difference between being a *hope-bearer* and a *hope-provider*. All humans, whether they know it or not, have the potential to offer hope to others. However, no human can "provide" hope unless another will receive it.

When I was ordained a clergyperson in the United Methodist Church, a bishop put his hand on my head and said:

Pour out your Holy Spirit upon (my name). Send him now to proclaim the good news of Jesus Christ, to announce the reign of God, and to equip the church for ministry, in the name of the Father, and of the Son, and of the Holy Spirit.[87]

Elders are ordained United Methodist clergy who are ordained to a ministry of Word, Sacrament, Order, and Service. This means elders preach and teach the Word of God, provide pastoral care and counsel, administer the sacraments of Baptism and Holy Communion, and order the life of the church for service in mission and ministry. The servant leadership of the elder takes place both in parish ministry, as well as in extension ministries, like chaplaincy, campus ministry, teaching, missionary work, general agency work and other contexts.

The role of a clergyperson is to be a *hope-bearer* through preaching, teaching, administering the sacraments, and through the whole ministry of the church. Indeed, we are responsible for "living" hope to the congregations we serve.

The laity of the church (all who strive to follow Jesus the Christ) are also called to live in such a way that they are *hope-bearers.* In short, individually and corporately as the church, we are **responsible to be bearers of hope** through the way we live, the way we pray, the way we love and forgive, and the way we teach.

However, we cannot force anyone to receive hope. We cannot force anyone to listen to a sermon or a lesson. A choir director cannot teach someone to sing unless the person is willing to receive the instructions. Parents can prepare a good healthy meal – they cannot make a child eat it. Doctors can write a prescription – they cannot make a patient fill it and take it. Teachers can bring a subject alive – they cannot make a student learn the material.

We cannot "provide" hope as one provides oxygen to a person in an emergency room. Hope cannot be forced upon anyone. It is simply not possible.

Even Jesus, who healed, taught, preached, died, rose from death to bring new life to all the world, cannot make others believe or turn their lives around. Everyone has the choice whether they will allow hope into the heart. Jesus did everything he could to show the amazing, extravagant, and wonderful love of God, but he was powerless to make even his own disciples understand.

On the night in which he was betrayed, he had a meal with his disciples. He washed their feet (taking the role of a servant), he took bread and wine and related them to his body as ritual in which his disciples could remember him. And then he led them to the Garden of Gethsemane to sing and to pray. While there, he was arrested and his disciples in fear, left him to the authorities. For three intensive years, Jesus was with them day and night, sharing the good news of God's radical love for humanity. He was an instrument of hope for all under the oppression of the Roman government. He taught them about the power of God's love than can heal, exorcize demons, and transform lives. And they did not get it!!!! In fact, they felt he had betrayed them when he was arrested! They would have probably said to him, "You gave others hope, but not us! Look at what you've gotten yourself into and how it is affecting us."

It was not until Pentecost that their eyes were opened, and they began to "see" and to know the hope Jesus gave to them. Once this happened, almost all of them went into the world and proclaimed boldly the message of Christ. Most of them died martyr's deaths for their preaching and teaching about the resurrected Christ.

Basically, individually, and corporately as the church, we are always to be hope- bearers. The key is to continue living this way and not be discouraged if others do not respond as we would *hope* they would!

On September 11, 2001, the world watched in horror as planes flew into the World Trade Center towers, the pentagon and one that was headed for the White House crashed in a field in Pennsylvania. Without the ability to get the word out to the community, the church where I was pastor quickly planned a service of hope and healing for that evening. By the time the service began at 7:00pm, the sanctuary was full to overflowing. People came in droves for a message of hope. We were there to offer it. Many were comforted. Many still lived in fear.

Several times, unfortunately, the church had youth who were killed or died from disease or committed suicide. Our youth minister and the clergy of the church were at the church ready to offer hope and healing to those who were deeply hurt and frightened. Many felt comforted and full of hope, some left discouraged and depressed.

When the economy began to crash in 2008, the church offered support groups to those who had to declare bankruptcy, those who lost jobs, and those with depression and fear. Many were helped. Many were not.

Nevertheless, the church must always be a lighthouse of hope. The church must never give up always realizing that every person is responsible for their own actions and their own response to what is being offered.

Nelson Mandela once said, "Our human compassion binds us the one to the other – not in pity or patronizingly, but as human beings who have learnt how to turn our common suffering into hope for the future."[88] It is imperative we offer such hope!

Yes: I am responsible for being an agent of hope to all people, and

No: I am not responsible for making it happen. I cannot force it.

Sunday after Sunday for forty years, I preached. It was my responsibility to study and to work on a sermon in such a way that it might be transformative in the lives of the congregation. As much as I prayed, studied, and prepared, I was powerless to make that happen. I can only be a *hope-bearer* to the best of my abilities and let go and then leave the rest to the work of God. That is true for all.

In essence, my relative was correct in her statement to me "You never *gave* me hope." I was, however, powerless to do so. I am certain that I was a hope-bearer to her. I offered her hope on many levels. Did I fail? Did she fail? I think what is more important is not a black and white answer. Rather, we might all ask ourselves "How intentional is my hope-bearing?" "Do I "see" hope around me?" "Was hope there all along and I missed it?" Hope floods our lives every day, but too often we do not see it or experience it. This is nothing new. There is an old story that shines light on this better than I:

Long ago there lived in the city of Marseilles an old shoemaker, loved and honored by all his neighbors, who affectionately called him "Father Martin."

One Christmas Eve he sat alone in his little shop, reading of the visit of the wise men to the infant Jesus, and of the gifts they brought. He said to himself, "If tomorrow were the first Christmas, and if Jesus were to be born in Marseilles this night, I know what I would give Him!" He arose and took from a shelf two little shoes of softest snow-white leather, with bright silver buckles, "I would give Him these, my finest work. How pleased His mother would be! But I'm a foolish old man," he thought, smiling. "The Master has no need for my poor gifts."

Replacing the shoes, he blew out the candle, and retired to rest. Hardly had he closed his eyes, it seemed, when he heard a voice call his name, "Martin!" Intuitively, he felt aware of the identity of the speaker. "Martin, you have longed to see Me. Tomorrow I shall pass by your window. If you see Me and bid Me enter, I shall be your guest and sit at your table."

He did not sleep that night for joy. Before it was yet dawn, he rose and tidied up his little shop. He spread fresh sand on the floor, and wreathed green bows of fir along the rafters. On the table he placed a loaf of white bread, a jar of honey, and a pitcher of milk; and over the fire he hung a hot drink. His simple preparations were complete.

When all was in readiness, he took up his vigil at the window. He was sure he would know the Master. As he watched the driving sleet and rain in the cold, deserted street, he thought of the joy that would be his when he sat down and broke bread with his Guest.

Presently he saw an old street sweeper pass by, blowing upon his thin, gnarled hands to warm them. "Poor fellow! He must be half-frozen," thought Martin. Opening the door, he called out to him, "Come in, my friend, and warm yourself, and drink something hot." No further urging was needed, and the man gratefully accepted the invitation.

An hour passed, and Martin next saw a poor, miserably clothed woman carrying a baby. She paused, wearily, to rest in the shelter of his doorway. Quickly he flung open the door. "Come in and warm while you rest," he said to her. "You are not well?" he asked.

"I am going to the hospital. I hope they will take me in, and my baby," she explained. "My husband is at sea, and I am ill, without a soul to whom I can go."

"Poor child!" cried the old man. "You must eat something while you are getting warm. Let me give a cup of milk to the little one. Ah! What a bright, pretty little fellow he is! Why, you have no shoes on him!"

"I have no shoes for him," sighed the mother.

"Then he shall have this lovely pair I finished yesterday." And Martin took down the soft little snow-white shoes he had looked at the evening before and slipped them on the child's feet. They fit perfectly. And shortly the young mother went her way full of gratitude, and Martin went back to his post at the window.

Hour after hour went by, and many needy souls shared the meager hospitality of the old cobbler, but the expected Guest did not appear.

At last, when night had fallen, Father Martin retired to his cot with a heavy heart. "It was only a dream," he sighed. "I did hope and believe, but He has not come."

Suddenly, so it seemed to his weary eyes, the room was flooded with a glorious light; and to the cobbler's astonished vision there appeared before him, one by one, the poor street sweeper, the sick mother and her baby, and all the people whom he had aided during the day. Each one smiled at him and asked, "Have you not seen me? Did I not sit at your table?" and vanished.

Then softly out of the silence he heard again the gentle Voice, repeating the old, familiar words: "Whoso shall receive one such little child in my name receives me." "For I was an hungry, and you gave me meat: I was thirsty, and you gave me drink: I was a stranger, and ye took me in." "Verily I say unto you, inasmuch as you have done it unto one of the least of these my brethren, you have done it unto me." (Author unknown)

HOPE

Do you believe, in what you see
do you believe in reality
do you believe in the sun that's bright
do you believe in the stars in the night
Do you believe in the birds that fly
do you believe in clouds and the sky
do you believe in wind that flows
do you believe in moon that glows
do you believe in light
Do you believe the spoken word
do you believe the things you've heard
do you believe in the final answer
do you believe in the swirling dancer
Do you believe in sound and sight
do you believe in moments bright
do you believe in taste and touch
do you believe that much
Do you believe in the soul inside
do you believe in ecstasy and delight
do you believe in glory and god
do you believe in that thought
Do you believe in the sky above
do you believe in love
Do you believe in the heaven and the earth
do you believe in death and birth
do you believe in life
open your eyes with hope within
open the door, let light reach in
if you believe, then you'll win

Siddharth Anand

Chapter 7

What about false hope'

————◇————

Nobody is more full of false
Hope than a Mom who
Places items on the stairs
For her family members to
Carry up.

On Christ the solid Rock I stand
all other ground is sinking sand.

Edward Mote

From the beginning of childhood, we are introduced to "false" hope. Though not meant to be destructive or deceiving, there is much presented that is in fact "false."

Note this Disney song:

When you wish upon a star.

When a star is born
They possess a gift or two
One of them is this
They have the power to make a wish come true

When you wish upon a star
Makes no difference who you are
Anything your heart desires will come to you

If your heart is in your dream
No request is too extreme
When you wish upon a star
As dreamers do
Fate is kind

She brings to those who love
The sweet fulfillment of their secret longing.

Like a bolt out of the blue
Fate steps in and sees you through
When you wish upon a star
Your dreams come true

When you wish upon a star
Makes no difference who you are
Anything your heart desires will come to you
If your heart is in your dream
No request is too extreme
When you wish upon a star
As dreamers do
Fate is kind

She brings to those who love
The sweet fulfillment of their secret longing
Like a bolt out of the blue
Fate steps in and sees you through
When you wish upon a star
Your dreams come true.[89]

Is it really true that we can wish upon a star and our dreams will come true? What about Santa Claus, the Easter bunny and the Tooth Fairy? All of these are "falsehoods" and yet they can make a childhood exciting and fun. What would Christmas be like without the excitement of a child on Santa's lap telling him what they wanted for Christmas? Pulling teeth is far less painful when a reward is discovered under the pillow the next morning. How ingenious to swap a tooth for a coin!!!

And what would childhood be without stories like the three bears, the three little pigs, Mother Goose and the Grinch who Stole Christmas? Stories and myths are essential to teaching our little ones about life. The famous Aesop knew this, and his "fables" have been revered for some 2500 years!!!!

There is a familiar story from Greek mythology found in Hesiod's <u>Works and Days</u>. According to Hesiod, when Prometheus stole fire from heaven, Zeus, the king of the gods, took vengeance by sending Pandora to Premetheus' brother Epimetheus. She was to give him a gift from Zeus but instructed not to open it. Unable to withhold her curiosity, Pandora opened the jar left in her care and the contents that flowed out of it were sickness, death and many other unspecified evils which were then released into the world. Though she hastened to close the container, only one thing was left behind, *hope*.[90]

How often have we thought we were receiving a gift and the gift was more a curse than a blessing? I have witnessed this in those who invested in "get rich" schemes, investing a lot of money and losing everything.

I have known popular boys to call unpopular girls to ask them to go to a dance, only to stand them up and laugh about it. The girl, spending money on a new dress, going to a hair salon to have her hair and nails made to look her best. She tells her best friends and family, and all are excited for her. And then, the huge let-down! I have also known of girls who did this to boys. The false hope was devastating.

What of those who invest in buying a used a car from someone who made the car to look brand new, smell new, and run well. After the purchase, the buyer discovers the automobile is a "lemon." Their hopes were dashed. The same with houses, and other products.

False hope is seen in numerous ways in the world today:

1) False Advertisements

*skin products: take this and it will wipe ten years off of your skin.

* automobiles – drive this and you will be somebody.

* take this vitamin or medicine and it will cure your ailments.

* use this product, it is expensive, but you are worth it.

* buy these clothes and you will be sexier.

* give diamonds, they are a woman's best friend.

2) False religion

The world has witnessed the abuse of numerous "cons" in the world of religion. I will only mention a few:

Jim Jones was an American preacher and faith healer turned cult leader who conspired with his inner circle to direct a mass murder-suicide of his followers in his jungle commune at Jonestown, Guyana. He launched the Peoples Temple in <u>Indiana,</u> during the 1950s. Rev. Jones was ordained in 1957 by the Independent Assemblies of God and in 1964 by the Disciples of Christ. He moved his congregation to California in 1965 and gained notoriety with its activities in San Francisco in the 1970s. He then left the United States, bringing many members to a Guyana jungle commune.

In 1978, media reports surfaced of human rights abuses in the Peoples Temple in Jonestown. U.S. Representative Leo Ryan led a delegation to the commune to investigate. Ryan and others were murdered by gunfire while boarding a return flight with some former cult members who had wished to leave. Jones then ordered and likely coerced a mass suicide and mass murder of 918 commune members, 304 of them children, almost all by cyanide-poisoned Flavor Aid.[91]

David Karush was an American cult leader and musician who played a central role in the Waco siege of 1993. As the head of the Branch Davidians sect, Koresh claimed to be its final prophet.

Koresh fathered multiple children by different women in the group. His House of David doctrine was based on a purported revelation that involved the procreation of 24 children by chosen women in the community. These 24 children were to serve as the ruling elders over the millennium after the return of Christ.

The siege of Mount Carmel Center ended 51 days later on April 19, 1993, when U.S. Attorney General Janet Reno approved recommendations of FBI officials to proceed with a final advance in which the Branch Davidians were to be removed from their building by force. In an attempt to flush Koresh from the stronghold, the FBI resorted to pumping CS gas from a M728 Combat Engineer Vehicle with battering ram into the compound.[30]

During the advance on the compound, the church building caught fire in circumstances that are still disputed. Barricaded inside the building, 79 Branch Davidians perished in the ensuing blaze; 21 of these victims were children under the age of 16. According to the FBI, Steve Schneider, Koresh's right-hand man, who "probably realized he was dealing with a fraud," shot and killed Koresh and then committed suicide with the same gun.[32] A second account gave a totally different story: Koresh, then 33, died of a gunshot wound to the head during the course of the fire. No one knows who killed him or if he killed himself. The medical examiner reported that although federal law enforcement personnel fired no shots that day, 20 people, including five children under the age of 14, had been shot, and a three-year-old.[92]

Jim Baker is an American televangelist, entrepreneur, and convicted fraudster. He hosted the television program *The PTL Club* with his then-wife Tammy Faye from 1974 to 1989. He also developed Heritage USA, a now-defunct Christian theme park in Fort Mill, South Carolina.

In the late 1980s he resigned from the ministry, over a cover-up of hush money to church secretary Jessica Hahn for an alleged rape. Subsequent revelations of accounting fraud brought about felony charges, conviction, imprisonment, and divorce.[93]

Jimmy Swaggart began his evangelistic work in 1955, becoming a radio, revival speaker and a recording artist of gospel music. In the late 1960s, Swaggart founded what was then a small church named the Family Worship Center in Baton Rouge, Louisiana; the church eventually became district-affiliated with the Assemblies of God. Soon, his services were on local television stations. He purchased several radio stations over several years and then selling them, investing instead in for his services to be broadcast over 250 television stations.

IN 1988, Swaggart was implicated in a sex scandal involving a prostitute that resulted initially in his suspension and ultimately being defrocked by the Assemblies of God. Three years later, he was implicated in another scandal involving a prostitute. As a result, his ministry became non-denominational and significantly smaller. He has become known for his now-famous "I have sinned" speech.[94]

Ted Arthur Haggard is an American evangelical pastor. Haggard is the founder and former pastor of New Life Church in Colorado Springs, Colorado and is a founder of the Association of Life-Giving Churches. He served as President of the National Association of Evangelicals (NAE) from 2003 until November 2006.

Haggard made national headlines in November 2006, when a male prostitute and masseur, Mike Jones, alleged that Haggard, who had advocated against the legalization of same-sex marriage, had paid him for sex for three years and had also purchased and used crystal methamphetamine. After initially denying the allegations, Haggard claimed to have purchased methamphetamine and thrown it away without using it. Haggard resigned his post at New Life Church and his other leadership roles shortly after the allegations became public. Later, Haggard admitted to having used drugs, participated in some sexual activity with

Jones, and engaged in an inappropriate relationship with a young man who attended New Life Church.[95]

The Roman Catholic Church for decades has covered up the sexual abuse by numerous priests. To date, the church as paid out over 1.3 billion to victims.[96]

3) Unhealthy theology:

John Wesley often stressed that people should use sanity in their religion. Over the centuries, millions of people have been led astray from those who would use the Bible to manipulate and use people. Adolf Hitler had his soldiers quote scriptures during their marching routines. Numerous preachers exacerbated the cruelty of slavery by lack of understanding of the word "slave" in the Bible. Even today, the issues surrounding the LGBTQ community are often bombarded with scriptures pro and against.

The Bible itself is a library of sixty-six books, written by numerous authors over numerous years. There are many necessary tools to study it. It is a book of faith that presents various ways of God's activity in the world. If it was so simple to read and apply there would not be over 30,000 denominations in the world!

Therefore, it is essential that there are certain criteria for "healthy" theology.

A) "God is spirit and those who worship God, do so in spirit and in truth."[97] God is neither male nor female. Anything that has to do with God has to do with truth and love.

B) "God is love."[98] The "golden rule" applies this "truth" by saying we should treat others the way we wish to be treated."

C) God will always temper justice with mercy. Where we have sinned and fallen short, God expects us to repent (turn around and go a different way). Though we sin, God's grace is greater.

D) God expects us to be good stewards of the earth and all that is in it. (See Genesis 1 and 2)

E) God is at work in the world, always working for the best of humankind. Jesus came to do the work of God, and we are to take up where he left off: feeding the hungry, giving drink to the thirsty, clothing the naked, welcoming the stranger, attending the sick and visiting those in prison. (See Matthew 25)

F) God does not orchestrate disaster or cause disease. If that is the case, why did Jesus go around healing those with infirmities? God has a will, and it is for the best of life.

G) There is too much talk of "hell." I have heard pastors preach that it is all black and white: we either go to heaven or to hell. Jesus rarely talked of "hell" and it was almost always in the context of a person's behavior being "useless" or destructive, but not the person. What does it say about the character of God who would condemn a person for eternity if they don't "love" God? That is like a parent saying to a child, "if you don't love me, I will see that you are tortured forever."

I have heard it said, "just say the words I will tell you to say and you will be saved. It is simple and only takes a minute." What is wrong with this? Salvation is a process. It is a lifetime of walking daily with God. It is not some pill to be taken and all is done, rather it is an on-going relationship. God is always the initiator and acts first. *We love because God first loved us.*[99] Salvation is first and foremost about God's action in our lives, where God is at the center. God's love began from our beginning, not when we decided to love God! We are constantly being born anew!

H) We need to be careful about judging others. I have heard followers of Jesus Christ say things like, "They can't be a Christian if they vote republican or democrat!" "I don't want those folks coming to my church!" "I am going to find another church if the pastor keeps preaching on money or racism, or something I don't like." "I think the marriage is on shaky ground because the wife is a 'loose' woman (or the husband is a 'rounder')."

The word "hypocrite" is used many times to describe "church people." In truth, we are all hypocrites, but hopefully those who attend worship regularly are striving to live less hypocritically and judgmentally. If those "in" the church are constantly arguing and fighting, how can those "outside" of the church want any part of it?

For the church to be a *hope-bearer* it must be a place and a eople of shalom and a house of prayer. Herein lies hope for those who enter. How encouraging and wonderful to walk into a holy place knowing that you are loved no matter what. Together, we can work on our issues that have become stumbling blocks, but first and foremost we are treated and ministered unto as that of the Christ.

Healthy Biblical reading asks the questions:

A) What does the passage say about God?

B) What does the passage say about humanity?

C) What does the passage say about the relationship between God and humanity?

D) Who was talking?

E) What came before the passage we are reading and what came after it?

F) How will apply this to my life?

A healthy theology is always one of hospitality, where our churches, our homes and our lives have open doors, open minds, open hearts, and open arms to those we love and to the strangers in our midst (for by doing so, we are entertaining angels unaware!)

4) **False trust:**

Everything will be ok!
Such a statement should only be used when there is one hundred per-cent certainty that it will.

This won't hurt a bit
How does anyone know how a person will react to pain? I have always appreciated physicians and nurses who have told me that something will hurt. Then I can prepare for it the best way I can.

If you love me, you will have sex with me.
This is nothing but acute manipulation. Love never demands.

I will pay you back.
It is best not to loan money that you know you will never get back! "There are more than one million people who default on their student loans each year. The estimate is 40% of borrowers expected to default on student loans by 2023. Outstanding education debt has tripled over the past three years and totals some 1.5 trillion dollars!"[100]

Just have faith
This is one of the biggest statements of false hope. Just have faith implies that if something does not work out, it is the person's lack of faith that is at fault. I have witnessed this many times where a person is diagnosed with a fatal disease and told to "just have faith" and the person dies. What is said to the family, "they just didn't have enough faith." This is cruel. "Just have faith" is a wonderful thing to say if it means to trust the faith that God has in us!

Trust your money with me!

Bernie Madoff has created a greater fear for those investing large sums of money. Over twenty years, he defrauded his clients of almost 65 billion dollars in the largest Ponzi scheme in history.

Get rich quick schemes are not new, but because of the destruction caused to many, hope in good financial investors can be circumspect.

Justice will prevail

This is not always true. Numerous innocent people have gone to jail for crimes they did not commit. The "Black Lives Matter" campaign has exposed systems of injustice in police brutality and the lack of trust the black community has for "the law." Indeed, there is little "real" justice in the world. Demonstrations all over the world continue to happen over the injustice to George Floyd, Amelia Boynton, Breonna Taylor, and many others. Mention justice to those who have served in federal prisons for decades who have been proven innocent! It is the "hope" of many that one day in the future, there will be justice for all who have been mistreated.

5) False security:

Guns

I grew up with guns in the house. My father had a pistol he kept in his top drawer of his dresser and a shotgun in his closet. He loved to rabbit hunt and often brought home rabbits for my mother to skin and serve at a meal.

Along with my cousins, I would go to the family farm where we would shoot at cans or other targets for the fun of it. In fact, one of my cousins was cremated when he died, and his cremains were put in bullet shells. Some fifty of the relatives shot them over the small pond on the family farm. It was his wish that he be "buried" in this way! My two sons went with me for this occasion, and it was a highlight moment for us.

I have close friends who love to deer hunt, quail hunt, and who simply love to go to shooting ranges. The problem comes when we put our hope for security in weapons.

Following the Sandy Hook Elementary School massacre, a mother in the church where I was serving as pastor at the time, went to the preschool board of directors to offer her insights for better protection for her child who was attending there, and the other children of the school. Her ideas were for the church to hire two police officers to walk the halls during the hours the school was in session, to install locks on all of the room doors, to provide guns for all the teachers and their aides, install bullet proof glass on all the doors, and more alarms and cameras inside and outside of the school.

When we all met together, the clergy, the preschool board, and this woman, the consensus was that the school was safe as it was. No police officers would be hired, no guns given to teachers or their aides, and no bullet proof glass, or alarms. We would install locks on the inside of all preschool room doors. Upon seeing the vote of the group, the mother who had presented these things, stood up and yelled at us that we did not care about children. She said that she was leaving the church and the preschool and going to where people took seriously the safety of children.

In the thirty-three years of the church's history, there have never been any incidences of violence, and I pray there never will be. <u>What this young mother did not seem to realize is that we can never protect our children from harm.</u> We can do our best, but we are incapable of assuring their safety: in buildings, in vehicles, at sports events, in schools, while shopping, or traveling by air, sea, train, bus, or other means of transportation. Certainly, we should do all in our power to help keep all people safe from harm, but no weapon can assure that.

Tom McHale says, "it's far too easy for us to be lulled into a false sense of security by the simple presence of a firearm. "Hey, if something bad happens, I'll just use my gun to extricate myself from trouble." That sounds rational, right up to the point where you start to think through specific scenarios that not only could happen but do happen every single day.

Perhaps the best way to illustrate the dangers of a false sense of security is to consider some self-defense scenarios that you regularly see on the nightly news.

You are sound asleep. Suddenly you wake up to the sound of your front door being destroyed as several guys burst into your hallway. You have got a couple of shotguns locked securely in the gun safe in your closet. Oh, and the ammunition is up on the shelf. How fast can you act?

You are standing in line at a convenience store waiting to pay for a much-needed cup of coffee while checking your smartphone. Suddenly, the man standing behind you draws a gun and tells everyone to put their hands up. You have got a gun in your purse. Did it help you?

You are pumping gas. As you get back into the driver's seat, a guy jumps into the passenger side, points a gun at you, and demands you start driving. Your gun is ready to go – in the glove compartment. Did having a gun help you?

The point of these examples is that the existence of a gun in the vicinity means nothing. Other factors, combined with the presence of a firearm, may or may not make the difference."[101]

Military

Having the largest military budget, largest number of soldiers, airplanes, ships, tanks, and weapons does not assure the United States of security from harm. Since the Japanese attacked the United States at Pearl Harbor on December 7, 1941, for the most part, America has been relatively free from enemy attacks on our own soil. (There have been a few small attacks.) However, September 11, 2001, proved that we are vulnerable to enemy harm once again on our own soil.

What has happened since then is facing the fact that often the "enemy" is invisible with cyber-attacks, chemical attacks, and new forms of espionage at work.

War is costly in lives lost and money spent. (I have listed the wars that have occurred in the United States and the financial costs and loss of lives in each. (See ** in notes from this chapter)

Lottery

Abigail Hess, in an article entitled, *Heres why lottery winners go broke* shares that lottery winners are more likely to declare bankruptcy within three to five years than the average American. What's more, studies have shown that winning the lottery does not necessarily make you happier or healthier."[102]

Jonelle Marte, in writing for *"The Washington Post"* says that "evidence shows that most people who make it to the top one percent of income earners usually don't stay at the top for very long."[103] And economist Jay Zagorsky agrees with this research. He writes: "studies found that instead of getting people out of financial trouble, winning the lottery got people into more trouble, since bankruptcy rate soared for lottery winners three to five years after winning."[104]

Look at Jack Whittaker who won $315 million in a lottery in West Virginia in 2002. In an interview for Time Magazine he said, "I wish that we had torn the ticket up." Since winning, Whittaker's daughter and granddaughter died due to drug overdoses.

Just eight months after winning, he was robbed of $545,000. "I just don't like Jack Whittaker. I don't like the hard heart I've got," he said. "I don't like what I've become."

Some of Whittaker's friends have said, "He's the last person I would have prototyped for going completely crazy, but he did. No question it was because he won the lottery."[105]

The article ends with the author saying, "Many winners struggle with suicide, depression and divorce. 't's the curse of the lottery because it made their lives worse instead of improving them,'"[106]

Another major struggle that winners often face is saying "no" to friends and family who hope to join in on the good fortune. Charles Conrad, senior financial planner at Szarka Financial said "once family and friends learn of the windfall, they have expectations of what they should be entitled to. It is difficult to say 'no.'"[107]

Of course, some lottery winners survive the tumult and go on to thrive. Missouri lottery winner Sandra Hayes has managed to keep her head above water even after splitting a $224 million Powerball jackpot with 12 coworkers. She said, "I had to endure the greed and the need that people have, trying to get you to release your money to them. That caused a lot of emotional pain," she told The Associated Press, "These are people who you've loved deep down, and they're turning into vampires trying to suck the life out of me."[108]

The former social worker has avoided financial misfortune by maintaining her frugal lifestyle even though she no longer lives paycheck to paycheck. "I know a lot of people who won the lottery and are broke today," she said. "If you're not disciplined, you will go broke. I don't care how much money you have."[109]

Fences

Robert Frost began his historic poem *Mending Wall* with the words, "Something there is that doesn't love a wall."[110] Protecting our "walls" ensures thousands of attorneys big incomes every year in this nation! Property disputes are prolific.

Many years ago, a young father (married with two little girls) became enraged over his neighbor's encroachment on his property. Over and over they battled about it. One afternoon, his neighbor was ready for him. He took a gun out and shot him in the head. Fortunately, it did not kill him, but left him disabled where he would never work again.

He was never quite "right" but he became a man of greater patience and kindness. The boundary issue went unsettled because it was no longer important to him.

I preached in a church in a very violent part of Atlanta and some of the members approached me and asked me if I thought it would be a good thing for the property of the church to be enclosed with a chain-link fence. They wanted to keep the "ruffians" off the property. I suggested that instead of fences, they use their gymnasium to host basketball for these "ruffians" and have members of the church there to serve them snacks and colas. Surprisingly, they did just that!

Instead of putting up a fence, they used the money to invest in the community. Though the church had a few break-ins, its very presence in the community has brought much relief, stability and hope!

I think of the great poet Edward Markum who wrote these powerful words:

"He drew a circle that shut me out-
Heretic, rebel, a thing to flout.
But love and I had the wit to win:
We drew a circle and took him in!"[111]

Over the past few years in our nation there has been a debate about the erecting of a wall between the United States and Mexico. The issue is one of those "hot button" issues. No matter what position is held, it is imperative to remember that no materially raised wall will keep all evil out. There are those who will find ways around it, over it, under it and through it. The bottom line, our security is not found in fences. Indeed, fences can bring false hope.

Something there is that doesn't love a wall,
That sends the frozen-ground-swell under it,
And spills the upper boulders in the sun;

And makes gaps even two can pass abreast.
The work of hunters is another thing:
I have come after them and made repair
Where they have left not one stone on a stone,
But they would have the rabbit out of hiding,
To please the yelping dogs. The gaps I mean,
No one has seen them made or heard them made,
But at spring mending-time we find them there.
I let my neighbor know beyond the hill;
And on a day we meet to walk the line
And set the wall between us once again.
We keep the wall between us as we go.
To each the boulders that have fallen to each.
And some are loaves and some so nearly balls
We have to use a spell to make them balance:
'Stay where you are until our backs are turned!'
We wear our fingers rough with handling them.
Oh, just another kind of out-door game,
One on a side. It comes to little more:
There where it is we do not need the wall:
He is all pine and I am apple orchard.
My apple trees will never get across
And eat the cones under his pines, I tell him.
He only says, 'Good fences make good neighbors.'
Spring is the mischief in me, and I wonder
If I could put a notion in his head:
'*Why* do they make good neighbors? Isn't it
Where there are cows? But here there are no cows.
Before I built a wall I'd ask to know
What I was walling in or walling out,
And to whom I was like to give offense.
Something there is that doesn't love a wall,
That wants it down.' I could say 'Elves' to him,
But it's not elves exactly, and I'd rather

145

He said it for himself. I see him there
Bringing a stone grasped firmly by the top
In each hand, like an old-stone savage armed.
He moves in darkness as it seems to me,
Not of woods only and the shade of trees.
He will not go behind his father's saying,
And he likes having thought of it so well
He says again, 'Good fences make good neighbors.'

Technology

Since the age of computers, technology has advanced to incredible levels. The world-wide-web allows us to be in communication almost anywhere in the world at any time. Many keep their data in the Clouds, and a piece of metal the size of a pin can hold worlds of information.

Humans have walked on the moon, spent years in space, descended to the depths of the oceans, cured many diseases, invented new parts for the human body and seen miles beyond the heavens to black holes and even further.

If I need to find a picture of a planet, a rare species of fish or spiders or snakes or birds or what people look like in India, Africa, Asia, Europe or other lands, all my fingers have to do is push a couple of buttons on my computer and instantly these appear.

Today, many do their grocery shopping, their clothing shopping, their Christmas shopping, pay their bills, order their meals, their books, their sporting attire and most anything else they need, on-line. During the Covid-19 pandemic when the need to safe-distance meant staying home, we could simply bring the world to ourselves. Technology is amazing!

On the other hand, we must be very careful about technology. Recently, I sent my son-in-law an email concerning his daughter's on-line learning class. Instead of the email going to him, it went to a friend in my iPhone phone book! I wonder how many times this has happened.

Many a person's identity has been stolen, break-ins happen in large companies where customer's credit card numbers and even bank accounts are stolen.

Technology security is big business. No one is totally safe from technological invasion.

Money

There are those who think that if they just had more money their problems would be solved. Certainly, more money can be helpful, but it is not the answer to life's meaning, purpose, nor stability. Many famous and rich people have led miserable lives.

April Fool's Day, 1997, I was preparing for bed when the phone rang. It was a member of the church telling me that one of their company planes had gone down. They knew that all on board were killed. They could account for the identities of three of the four, but believed their oldest son was the fourth. They were beside themselves with fear. Finally, around four o'clock in the morning, the confirmation came that indeed, it was their son who had burned to death in the crash.

Upon hearing of the news, the parents and I went into the den of their home where we could try to process this information. The father was the sixteenth wealthiest Georgian, a very rich man. What I vividly remember is how he sat on the ottoman of a chair with his head in his hands saying over and over, "I would give everything I have away to have him back."

No amount of money could make that happen. Money cannot bring a person back from the dead. Money cannot buy everything!

Shortly before six that morning, I left their home and made my way back to my house. When I entered, the house was still, dark, quiet. My three children were still asleep. My wife, awake, but still in bed. I slipped in close to her and said, "I learned the difference between rich and wealthy today." I proceeded to tell her about the death of this young man and what his father had said to me. He was rich in money, but I realized that though I did not have much money, I was "wealthy" because my kids were alive, my wife was by my side, we were all healthy, and loved one another. I basked in my wealth then and still today.

Medicine

More and more books are being published each year on the need to learn how to die well. We live as though death is the worst enemy. Certainly, it is natural and healthy to want to live a long and full life, however, we must learn to live with the fact that the mortality rate is 100%. We will die. It is vitally important to keep that fact before us, lest we forget and put our faith and hope in medicines that will keep us alive forever.

It was St. Benedict who said, "to desire eternal life with all the passion of the spirit, to keep death daily before one's eyes."[112] We are to live with eternity in our souls, but never forget that we are mortal.

While I am writing this book, a vaccine has just been released in the fight against Covid-19. In just nine months, scientists have studied and worked to make such a miracle drug a reality. Though sometimes controversial, vaccines have greatly helped to improve the average lifespan considerably.

However, the world has witnessed the deaths of over a million people since this deadly virus came into being. Millions more have been hospitalized and some with permanent disablements. In short, there are not medicines for every sickness nor disease. Because of that, it is imperative that we not put all of our hopes in medicine.

There is a phrase that Jesus used on the cross that is apropos in our thinking of dying and death: "It is finished."[113] Though no one knows for sure if he was talking about his life or his ministry, or both. He said on several occasions that he came "to do the work of his heavenly father."[114] Perhaps that is exactly what he meant. His work was completed.

Wouldn't it be a comfort to feel that way when our time comes to pass from this world! We would come to it not in dread, but in the attitude of completion. Though we may feel that we had another book to write or another sermon to preach, another chance to explore the world or some goal that has been set, instead we take a breath and give thanks for the life that was ours and feast in its completion.

In 2002, doctors diagnosed Pastor Ed Dobson with ALS. They gave him 2 years to live and predicted that he would spend most of that time in a disabled condition.

Shortly after the diagnosis, Ed wanted someone to anoint him with oil and pray for healing. So, he invited a friend, a Pentecostal pastor who had regular healing services, to come over and pray for him. Ed described it as one of the most moving evenings of his life.

The pastor began by telling stories of people he had prayed for who were miraculously healed. He also told stories about people he had prayed for who were not healed and had died, receiving that ultimate and final healing. Before he prayed for Ed, he gave him some advice: "do not become obsessed with getting healed, Ed, if you get obsessed with getting healed you may lose your focus. Get lost in **the wonder** of God and who knows what God will do for you."

Ed lived <u>thirteen more years</u>. He took the pastor's advice and became "lost" in the wonder of God.[115]

The greatest medicine for Ed was not found in a pharmacy, as his disease had no cure, it was found in "losing" himself in the "wonder" of God. It was not the length of time that mattered most to Ed, but the quality of life in the meantime.

Celebrity and Status

False hope is often seen in those who strive to be famous or powerful. What has always been of great concern to me are television shows where there are "celebrities" versus the "common" person. The very title "celebrity" brings the connotation that someone is of greater value than another because they are in movies, television, sports or wealthy financially. The word itself simply means that a person is well-known.

Throughout my life as a pastor, I have had congregants and friends who have tried their hardest to become famous. Some have left their homes, selling everything, to go and live in New York or Hollywood for a chance at "stardom." Not one of them made it!

Sometimes, even pastors seek to be "stars." One time I was sitting with a pastor listening to a sermon by the pastor of the largest United Methodist Church in the world. As the sermon was happening, this pastor turned to me and said, "That is my goal, to be the pastor of the largest church in the world." Before I could bridal my tongue, I said to him, "For their sakes or for yours?" He turned red in the face and seemed to be very offended. Later, he would share with me that he needed to re-evaluate his motives and intentions.

Sadly, there have been many celebrities who have taken their lives: Brian Keith, Freddie Prinze, Marilyn Monroe, Inga Stevens, Robin Williams, Andrew Koening, Kate Spade, Will Rogers, Jr., Kurt Cobain, Anthony Bourdain and numerous others. Being famous did not make these "stars" happy or fulfilled.

The grass is greener on the other side of the fence

In one church where I served as pastor, over thirty men in their mid-thirties, left their wives and family to pursue another younger woman. Almost all of the ones who I talked with felt that life was short, and they wanted to "live it up". They believed they would be "free." What happened? Some of them divorced and remarried which meant they were saddled with alimony and child support payments plus supporting the new wife. Instead of freedom, they were trapped in great financial woes which brought about unrest in the new marriage, usually leading the man to want a divorce and go back to his first wife and kids.

Over and over, I had man after man to come to my office regretting the original decision to leave his home and find "freedom" and "live it up." It provided neither. Indeed, the adage "the grass is greener on the other side of the fence" proved false!

The American Dream

What is the American Dream anyway? Most Americans have been raised to believe that anyone, regardless of any circumstances, can attain success through sacrifice, hard work and desire. Indeed, for many who came to America in the early years of its history, it meant doing better than your parents, owning your own home, and being financially stable.

Certainly, there have been many who have risen from poverty and adverse conditions to achieve "success" through hard work and determination. However, the number of people in prisons, poverty, diseased, and powerless have little hope of seeing the American Dream become a reality in their lives.

Many have risked their lives to come to America because of hearing the phrase *The American dream.* Lives have been lost in the treacherous waters between Cuba and the United States from those seeking freedom from the dictatorship of Castro. Those who have arrived, usually have brought nothing with them and they must begin their lives here completely starting over. Immigration laws make for a life of living in fear of deportation. It is never anyone's dream to live in fear!

This is true for the masses that try to immigrate into this country from Mexico, Central and South America. There is almost no chance of an American dream for them. They usually must take the most menial and lowly of jobs to sustain their existence.

The cycle of poverty and lack of education prohibits many from being able to climb out into a life of stability and financial security.

Just be good

This is a phrase that I often heard in the context of hope. Just "be good" and things will be okay. There are several television shows with the word "good" in them: The Good Doctor, the Good Wife, Good Girls, The Good Fight, The Good Place, and Good Behavior. What does the word "good" mean in them?

Look at some of the movies (over one hundred of them) with the word "good" in the title: As Good As it Gets, The Good, The Bad, and the Ugly, Good Will Hunting, A few Good Men, Good Night and Good Luck, The Good Shepherd, Midnight in the Garden of Good and Evil, The Good German, The Good Girl, Lady be Good, Johnny be Good, One Good Cop, a Good Day to Die Hard, A Good Year, The Good Heart, Good Advice, The Good Lawyer's Wife, In the Good Ole Summertime, In Good Company, The Good Earth, The Good Lie, The Good Thief, Such Good Friends, No Good Deed, Good Morning Vietnam, Good fences, The Good War and one simply entitle Good. Once again, how is the word "good" defined?

For the most part, "good" is usually defined as that which is morally right, the opposite of evil and whose works produce positive outcomes. Jesus used the word "good" in his beautiful image of being the "good" shepherd found in John 10:14 *"I am the good shepherd. The good shepherd lays down his life for the sheep.*

Jesus also uses the word "good" in one of his most famous parables called the "Good Samaritan" found in Luke 10: 25-37:

> *Just then a lawyer stood up to test Jesus. "Teacher," he said, "what must I do to inherit eternal life?" He said to him, "What is written in the law? What do you read there?" He answered, "You shall love the Lord your God with all your heart, and with all your soul, and with all your strength, and with all your mind; and your neighbor as yourself." And he said to him, "You have given the right answer; do this, and you will live."*
>
> *But wanting to justify himself, he asked Jesus, "And who is my neighbor?" Jesus replied, "A man was going down from Jerusalem to Jericho, and fell into the hands of robbers, who stripped him, beat him, and went away, leaving him half dead. Now by chance a priest was going down that road; and when he saw him, he passed by on the other side. So likewise, a Levite, when he came to the place and saw him, passed by on the other side. But a Samaritan*

while traveling came near him; and when he saw him, he was moved with pity. He went to him and bandaged his wounds, having poured oil and wine on them. Then he put him on his own animal, brought him to an inn, and took care of him. The next day he took out two denarii, gave them to the innkeeper, and said, 'Take care of him; and when I come back, I will repay you whatever more you spend.' Which of these three, do you think, was a neighbor to the man who fell into the hands of the robbers?" He said, "The one who showed him mercy." Jesus said to him, "Go and do likewise."

In both of these passages, "goodness" is found in sacrificial giving of oneself without the need for recognition, praise, or compensation. It is goodness for the sake of goodness and nothing else.

Though I believe it is essential that all humans seek to live morally and ethically good lives, that does not mean that our "goodness" will necessarily be appreciated. Indeed, there are many who have performed acts of "goodness" who have not only not been rewarded, but even sued!

Several years ago, I read about a man who stopped on a cold and rainy weekend evening to help a woman who had pulled over on the side of the road with a flat tire. He offered to change it for her, and she was elated.

When he was almost completed, she leaned over to check out his work and the car jack slipped out of his hand and when it landed, it landed on her foot, breaking two of her toes. She sued him for negligence and took him to court. The judge ruled in her favor and he had to pay her medical bills and for emotional trauma!!!

Interestingly, he never let that incidence stop him from helping others in need when he traveled the long stretches of highway for his business. It is this kind of life that truly can be called "good."

The same can be said about Martin Luther, John Wesley, Harriett Tubman, Sojourner Truth, Frederick Douglas, Malcolm X, Rosa Parks,

Martin Luther King, Jr, Jackie Robinson, James Weldon Johnson, e. e. cummings, Desmond Tutu, Nelson Mandela, John Lewis, Abraham Lincoln, Barack Obama, and the unnamed multitudes who were battered, beaten, abused, and still worked for the betterment of humankind. Their "goodness" was not always well-received.

Jesus also said (Mark 10:18), "Why do you call me good? No one is good but God alone." What an interesting thing for Jesus to have said. It seems that if Jesus did not think of himself as "good" then what does that say for us!

Jesus was saying to the man who posed the question, "Do not flatter me." He wanted the person to experience a broader understanding of God than merely flattering him for an answer. (The person asking the question was a rich aristocrat.)

Reinhold Niebuhr is credited to have said, "**More evil is done by good people who do not know they are not good.**" I have seen this far too many times in various people in various settings.

Look at the extreme case of John Wallace who was considered by his community to be a "good" man, indeed a county "kingpin." He was a devout religious man (a United Methodist!) even giving new pews to his church (paid for by illegal gain) He was also a bootlegger and killed a man for stealing some of his cows. His trial was sensational in that it was the first time in Georgia history that a white man was convicted by the testimony of two black men. He would late die in the electric chair. There is a road named for him in his beloved Meriweather County to this day. For some, his imprisonment and death were unjustified, and he should have been released and found innocent! His story can be found in the book *Murder in Coweta County*.

I preached in one church where windows were purposely fit into the doors of the sanctuary for ushers to see out so they could ensure no Blacks would enter. A "good" place and "good" people who did not know they were not "good."

I have already mentioned some religious leaders who preached one thing and did the exact opposite in their person lives, "good people who did not know they were not good."

In our culture today, the meaning of "good" has been distorted. It is imperative we reclaim its true meaning and instill its qualities into every aspect of society but being upfront that "goodness" does not mean that everything will always turn out the way we think it should it.

False Hope Syndrome:

Juli Fraga shares that 25% of those who make New Year's resolutions, will quit them in seven days![116] Basically, it is because we set unrealistic expectations of change for our lives. I have known many to say they will lose weight, quit smoking or drinking or cussing, or not spend money on fast foods, or they will save more each paycheck, or spend more time with their relatives, read the Bible in its entirety, or be regularly in worship and within a few days, the resolutions were broken.

How often do we make promises to ourselves with great intentions and when we veer off the goal, we fill our lives with shame and guilt? We have not learned to begin change in smaller doses.

Signs I have seen along the path of my life concerning false hope:

False hope is worse than despair
Jonathan Kazol

I survived your love, your love didn't break me, it is the hope you gave me
that destroyed me.
I'm tired of getting my hopes up for things that I know will never happen.
The cruelest thing of all is false hope.
Harsh reality is always better than false hope

Julian Fellowes

False hopes are more dangerous than fears.
J.R.R. Tolkien

I am tired of fake people, fake smiles, fake hugs, fake friends
and false hopes.

Returning to the story of Pandora's jar (or box), what remained after all the evil poured out? Hope! Once again, "faith, hope and love remain forever."

Simone Beauvoir, in her book <u>All Said and Done</u>, says it this way: "It is because I reject lies and running away that I am accused of pessimism; but this rejection implies hope- the hope that truth may be of use"[117] or as a quote I clipped from a newspaper said, "Are you holding on to false hope? If so, let go! Hope, in and of itself, is an act of truth and light. Believe the best and hold on, white knuckled, to that version." Indeed, seek the truth and the light will come. Discernment helps enable us to see hope in seemingly hopeless situations and will help plow our way out of false hope into the light of truth.

A Rainbow of Hope

An urgent call
a race down the dark stairs
a flicker of color as I ran outside
an arc, His bow, His promise
shown down on us
standing in awe and wonder
the rich color muted in the city
It curves over the alley
above the tenements, the wires
the clutter, the stresses of life
a timely reminder
in good times and bad
of your faithfulness,
your covenant with your people
a beautiful arc, a shimmering bow
a pleasure to behold
a piece of hope placed
for a moment, a few seconds
unnoticed by so many,
lost in the push and pull
of daily living
shared with those lucky few
who stopped for a moment or two
and looked up

Raymond A. Foss
July 28, 2006
Manchester, NH

Chapter 8

How does the church offer hope?

————◇————

The church is an oasis of hope
in a desert of hopelessness. You
need the church, and the church needs you.

Greg Laurie

Many biblical scholars believe that the church began at creation. Their reasoning is that the Christ spirit (the author of Johns' gospel uses the term "logos") was with God at the beginning of the world's construction. Indeed, we do not read far in Genesis without reading "Let *us* create humankind in *our* image." (Genesis 1:26ff) Some think the reference is to the trinity, others "the heavenly host" and others the maleness and femaleness of God. (The authors of Genesis do not tell us the answer!)

There are others who believe the church came into being at Pentecost when the Holy Spirit descended upon the large gathering of Jews from all parts of the world. (See Acts 1 and 2). Peter preached a powerful sermon, and some three thousand folks began a new movement known as *ecclesia* = the gathering of the faithful, or "church".

Whatever you believe about its origin, the essence of church is and will always be "hope." Everything associated with *church* is about hope.

For this study, let me define church as those who are committed to following the life, death and resurrection of Jesus through corporate and individual worship, spreading the good news of God's love by inviting all to participate in the fellowship, nurturing those who are in need, teaching "all that Christ has commanded" (see Matthew 28) and by sacrificial missional outreach around the world. In short, it means following the "Great Commandment" in Matthew 28:16-20:

> *Now the eleven disciples went to Galilee, to the mountain to which Jesus had directed them. When they saw him, they worshiped him; but some doubted. And Jesus came and said to them, "All authority in heaven and on earth has been given to me. Go therefore and make disciples of all nations, baptizing them in the name of the Father and of the Son and of the Holy Spirit, and teaching them to obey everything that I have commanded you. And remember, I am with you always, to the end of the age."*

The church offers hope through its:

Purpose:

The purpose of the church is to make disciples of Jesus Christ for the transformation of the world. All who profess Jesus Christ as "the way, the truth and the life" are called to not only live out this good news, but to share it in the world. This "good news" is symbolized in the cross where we understand the deeper meaning of forgiveness, redemption, salvation, eternal life.

Theology and doctrines

How do we develop a theology of hope? Throughout the centuries of Christendom, the theology and doctrines of the church emerge from the textbook of the church which is the Bible. Most accredited seminaries teach the study of the Bible through various lenses:

Exegetical theology- that branch of theology which treats of the exposition and interpretation of the Old and New Testaments.

Historical theology refers to the discipline of narrating the development of Christian theology integrating the thoughts of other Christians throughout history.

Systematic theology - is a discipline of Christian theology that formulates an orderly, rational, and coherent account of the doctrines of the Christian faith. It addresses issues such as what the Bible teaches about certain topics or what is true about God and his universe.

Practical theology -the study of the institutional activities of religion (such as preaching, church administration, pastoral care, and liturgics).[118]

Doctrines originate from a distinct sect who come together to propose what is acceptable teachings for their purposes. Some churches use creeds to help articulate their beliefs such as:

The Apostles' Creed

I believe in God, the Father Almighty, Creator of heaven and earth; and in Jesus Christ, His only Son Our Lord, who was conceived by the Holy Spirit, born of the Virgin Mary, suffered under Pontius Pilate, was crucified, died and was buried. He descended into Hell; the third day He rose from the dead; He ascended into Heaven and sitteth at the right hand of God, the Father Almighty; from thence He shall come to judge the quick and the dead. I believe in the Holy Spirit, the holy Catholic church, the communion of saints, the forgiveness of sins, the resurrection of the body and the life everlasting. Amen.[119]

The Modern Creed

Where the Spirit of the Lord is, there is the one true Church, apostolic and universal, whose holy faith let us now declare:

Minister and People:

We believe in God the Father, infinite in wisdom, power and love, whose mercy is over all his works, and whose will is ever directed to his children's good. We believe in Jesus Christ, Son of God and Son of man, the gift of the Father's unfailing grace, the ground of our hope, and the promise of our deliverance from sin and death.

We believe in the Holy Spirit as the divine presence in our lives, whereby we are kept in perpetual remembrance of the truth of Christ and find strength and help in time of need. We believe that this faith should manifest itself in the service of love as set forth in the example of our blessed Lord, to the end that the kingdom of God may come upon the earth.[120]

Or perhaps creeds made to fit a particular church such as the one used during the Hour of Power in California:

"It's not what I do. I'm not what I have. I'm not what people say about me. I am the beloved of God. It's who I am. No one can take it from me. I don't have to worry. I don't have to hurry. I can trust my friend Jesus and share His love with the world."[121]

Since I am a United Methodist, I follow what is called the Discipline of the United Methodist Church. Contained within it is the outline of our beliefs. It is also a book of church law, polity, doctrine, and theology. Such resources like this one give boundaries to help people stay centered in Christ and also to eliminate unhealthy theology.

One Sunday a few years ago, a man came to the church seeking a clergy to visit his wife in the hospital and to offer her a *Stephen minister*.[122] One of the pastors went to the hospital directly after the service and prayed with her and told her he would supply a Stephen minister from the church. She died later that afternoon.

The husband came to the church on Monday morning asking for the same clergy who visited the day before. He wanted to tell him that he would be subpoenaed to court to testify that cremation was Christian. Interesting, the man and his wife were Episcopalians whose children believed cremation was unchristian and wanted their mother bodily buried.

On Wednesday, the hearing began in the Fulton County Courthouse. The judge called on the clergyman to testify. He stood and told the court that he was a United Methodist clergyperson who followed the *Discipline* of the church. He then read:

> *The Bible does not speak about the issue of cremation vs. burial, but usually assumes that bodies will be buried. In the cultures that produced the Hebrew Bible, if a body was burned, it often would have been a sign of disrespect for the person or a punishment for sin (Genesis 38:14; Leviticus 20:14; 21:9; Joshua 7:25). However, it appears cremation may have occurred with no intent to dishonor the dead after a plague or large massacre (Amos 6:9-10).*
>
> *At the time of Jesus, cremation was widely practiced by the Romans, occasionally by the Greeks, but rarely by Jews and Christians. This was because of the belief of both religions in a physical resurrection to come. With the spread of Christianity, cremation disappeared almost entirely as a practice in the West until about 200 years ago. Notable exceptions occurred during times of plague and war when large numbers of the deceased needed to be cared for quickly.*
>
> *Some of those opposing cremation argue the body must not be cremated because at some future date the believer's soul will be reunited with his or her body. Even some who do not hold the soul is separable from the body may express hesitancy to embrace cremation. Still others, whatever their belief about soul and body,*

conclude that since cremation only does rapidly what nature will do also more slowly, cremation is acceptable.

References in our Services of Death and Resurrection to "urn" and "interment of ashes" indicate the practice of cremation is an acceptable means of honoring the deceased.[123].

The judge ruled in favor of the husband. She was sent to the crematory.

I have always been grateful for the quadrilateral written by John Wesley as a guideline for seeking truth. He believed that to get to the heart of truth we must do four-things:

1) Seek out the *Scriptures*.

2) Review our *traditions*.

3) Use our minds to *reason*.

4) Draw upon our own *experiences*.

When I was in college, I was invited to go to a church where the congregation handled poisonous snakes and drank poison. I was gracious to the friend for the invitation, but assertively declined. I knew there was a scriptural basis for these things

And these signs will accompany those who believe: by using my name they will cast out demons; they will speak in new tongues; they will pick up snakes in their hands,[e] and if they drink any deadly thing, it will not hurt them; they will lay their hands on the sick, and they will recover."[124]

But I also knew that my *tradition* did not claim this scripture as literal but claimed it as *truth* in handling the poisonous and deadly of the world. My *reason* told me that I would probably die of a heart attack before entering a place where snakes and poison would be the center of worship, and my own *experiences* have helped me know that having faith in God is better seen in corporate action of feeding the hungry, clothing the naked, welcoming the stranger, caring for the sick and visiting the prisoners.

The church's theology and doctrines help give us hope in the midst of great turmoil and unhealthy situations. There can be great danger of only using the Bible as proof-text for our positions. We need the help of scholars to help us read and study the Bible lest we miss its meaning. There are much greater meanings to such scriptural verses as some like these:

> *"even the hairs of your head are numbered"* [125]

> *"cut off your hand, tear out your eye"* [126]

History:

When I think of the history of the church, my mind immediately thinks of the numerous saints, known and unknown, who lived in such a way that the church was edified and strengthened by their unceasing devotion to bear the good news of Christ wherever they were.

I think of the disciples of Jesus who risked their lives to go into all the world and proclaim the good news of Christ:

Peter was crucified in Rome under the Emperor Nero.

Andrew went to the "land of the man-eaters" in what is now the Soviet Union. Christians there claim him as the first to bring the gospel to their land. He also preached in Asia Minor, modern day Turkey and in Greece, where it is believed he was crucified.

Thomas – probably the most active in the area east of Syria. Tradition has him preaching as far east as India. It is believed that he was pierced with spears of four soldiers.

Philip - possibly had a powerful ministry in Carthage in North Africa and then in Asia Minor, where he converted the wife of a Roman proconsul. In retaliation the proconsul had Philip arrested and cruelly put to death.

Matthew – the tax collector and writer of a Gospel ministered in Persia and Ethiopia. Some of the oldest reports say he was not martyred, while others say he was stabbed to death in Ethiopia.

Bartholomew – had widespread missionary travels attributed to him by tradition: to India with Thomas, back to Armenia, and also to Ethiopia and Southern Arabia. There are various accounts of how he met his death as a martyr for the gospel.

James – the son of Alpheus is one of at least three James referred to in the New Testament. There is some confusion as to which is which, but this James is reckoned to have ministered in Syria. The Jewish historian Josephus reported that he was stoned and then clubbed to death.

I think of the apostle Paul, over one-half of the New Testament is attributed to him.

> *Five times I received from the Jews the forty lashes minus one. Three times I was beaten with rods, once I was pelted with stones, three times I was shipwrecked, I spent a night and a day in the open sea, I have been constantly on the move. I have been in danger from rivers, in danger from bandits, in danger from my fellow Jews, in danger from Gentiles; in danger in the city, in danger in the country, in danger at sea; and in danger from false believers. I have labored and toiled and have often gone without sleep; I have known hunger and thirst and have often gone without food; I have been cold and naked. Besides everything else, I face daily the pressure of my concern for all the churches. Who is weak, and I do not feel weak? Who is led into sin, and I do not inwardly burn? If I must boast, I will boast of the things that show my weakness.*[127]

Stephen a man of great faith in Jesus Christ, who was stoned to death.

Augustine – fourth century bishop of Hippo who was a philosopher, theologian and one of the most important early figures in the development of western Christianity, bringing Christianity to the forefront of the previously pagan Roman Empire. His writings are still influential.

St. Patrick – was born in the late fourth century (c. A.D. 390). would one day become the most successful Christian missionary in Ireland, its patron saint, and the subject of legends.

St. Francis of Assisi – the patron saint of animals, the poor and the environment

St. Clair – founder of the Order of Poor Ladies and the first set of guidelines for a monastic order.

Martin Luther – began the protestant reformation.

John Wesley – saved England from a bloody revolution and gave the world the United Methodist Church

Mother Teresa – the saint of the gutters! She began the Sisters of Charity.

Rosa Parks and Martin Luther King, Jr. – forerunners of the civil rights movement

Followers of Jesus through the centuries who lived for Christ, sacrificed for Christ, and were models of generosity, kindness, love and hope for many, who established hospitals, nursing homes, colleges and universities, orphanages, geriatric facilities, feeding centers for the homeless, and multitudes of ministries to help the needy. Though the history of the church has not always been favorable, at its essence, its core, is the powerful message of grace and hope and peace.

Missions/witness:

The church offers hope through its witness. That can mean with words and it can mean simply by our actions. Being a witness/missionary means living close to Christ every day. It means loving the unlovely, going to the needy, helping those we may not like, and it can mean suffering.

Corrie Ten Boom was a follower of Jesus Christ. Her way of being a witness during World War II was to hide Jews in a special "hiding place" in her home. She and her family were able to save the lives of many, yet many were caught and put to death. Indeed, her father and sister died in German concentration camps. She was able to be freed from captivity and she spent her life traveling the world sharing the Good News of Christ.

The United Methodist Church offers hope through its Board of Global Ministries where the church:

* provides training and sending missionaries all over the world.
* provides children's homes.
* provides geriatric facilities.
* provides hospitals and medical centers.
* provides colleges and universities.
* provides seminaries for the training of clergy.
* provides feeding centers for the homeless
* established a ministry of relief (UMCOR) that can be anywhere in the world in four hours' time bringing relief in times of tragedy and crisis.
* provides camping and retreat ministries for children, youth and adults.
* and provides multitudes of local ministries.

The founder of Methodism, John Wesley, said "I consider all the world to be my parish."[128] The UMC is a world church. Whenever I put a dollar in the offering plate, I know that it will be split in numerous ways to spread the love of Christ, literally, around the world.

The United Methodist Church has more than 350 missionaries who serve in more than 65 countries around the world. One of the missional organizations is the United Methodist Committee on Relief (Atlanta, GA) This is one of my favorite ministries of the church. The UMC can be anywhere in the world in four hours' time bringing relief to those in crisis or tragedy. 100% of the money that is used by this organization goes directly for missional relief.

There are over 100 United Methodist affiliated colleges and universities in the USA! There are many more around the world!

There are facilities for the elderly, homes for children in peril, and camping and retreat centers. One of them is very close to my heart:

Nestled in the North Georgia mountains, there is quiet and peaceful sense of God's presence as one drives through the gates. The beautiful Cane Creek Falls is a place where hundreds have gone to pray and meditate and give their lives to God's service in the world. As a child through my senior year in high school, each summer I spent in camp where I learned more of God's love for me and how to live that love in the world for others. Friendships were made for life.

Today, I serve on the board of this great camp. All of my siblings went there and two later became counselors. All of my children attended camp there and two of mine became counselors. Now, my grandchildren go there. It is the focal point of their summer.

Interestingly, when my daughter was in the ninth grade, she spent two weeks in Europe on a youth church choir tour. Though the trip was impactful in multitudes of ways, she could not wait to get home and have us drive her to Camp Glisson early the next morning. (Camp began on Sunday and she did not arrive back in the States until Sunday evening. She wanted us to take her from the airport to camp, but we needed one evening with her before doing so!)

Each of my daughter's children were baptized in the chapel at Camp Glisson. I have performed weddings there. It is a place that offers great hope with just its presence.

I have been blessed to be a chaplain through the UMC at Children's Hospital of Atlanta, Emory University Hospital, Grady Hospital Emergency Room, Georgia Mental Health, Wesley Woods Center for the Again, and Atlanta Medical Center. It was the church that "sent" me to these places to be in ministry.

The church provides chaplains all over world at colleges, universities, children's homes, and to the Armed Forces of America.

Architecture

The very structure of a church in many cases offers hope by its presence. I cannot fathom a person seeing the great cathedrals of Europe and around the world and not feel a sense of hope. The world was glued to the weddings of Prince Charles and Lady Diana Spencer, and their children William and Harry all in beautiful London cathedrals. When Princess Diana was killed, the world watched in shock and grief as she was memorialized in the historical and lovely Westminster Abbey.

Though it is technically not a cathedral, millions flock each year to Vatican City to walk in St. Peter's Basilica or other chapels of the Apostolic Palace there. Certainly, the Sistine Chapel is one of the most famous places because of the monumentally incredible paintings of Michelangelo.

Visiting New York City, the architectural structures of the Riverside Church, The Cathedral of St. John the Divine, The Church of All Nations, and Marble Collegiate Churches reflect the deep faith and financial commitment of the masses over the years who built and maintained these institutions as symbols of hope. In Washington, D.C., the National Cathedral also symbolizes to those who pass by, the importance of faith in our politics.

There is great beauty and a sense of peace in passing by a white-framed country church in a rural area, and facilities of worship by the ocean or a lake. Simply seeing such architecture can stir the soul and draw us closer to God.

Not only can the outside of a church offer hope, but also the interior. The church is far more than just a facility, it is a "mirror" which reflects the divine, and also the body of God: the abside (or front of the church) is the head, the nave is the body, the transept the open arms, and the altar is the heart of Christ.[129]

The pulpit symbolizes and reminds us of the mountain where God spoke to Moses and handed down the Ten Commandments. Jesus preached his greatest sermon on the "mount."

The candles on the altar symbolize the divinity and humanity of Jesus. Acolytes process in with the light reminding all that Jesus, the light of the world, is with us. We gather to worship and when the service ends, we follow the light out into the world to be as Jesus (light) wherever there is darkness.

Many churches have stained glass windows that symbolize the biblical stories as well as saints throughout church history. I have seen such windows that depict Abraham, Moses, King David, the prophets, Ruth, the nativity, the baptism of Jesus, crucifixion, resurrection and even those with Augustine, Luther, Wesley and symbols of various denominations. I was in one church where the largest stained glass was of Jesus as a shepherd and he had six toes on each foot!!!!!

Worship

No two churches worship alike! Even to use the words "traditional" or "modern" or "Contemporary" or "Taize" or "Blended" fall short of the meaning of worship. Some worship with pipe organs, electronic keyboards, guitars, drums, orchestras, piano, and some worship with no musical instruments at all. Some worship with an "order of worship" and some worship as "the spirit leads them." Some churches have ordained clergy and others do not believe in ordination, rather let whoever is led by the spirit to speak.

I was raised in a "traditional" United Methodist Church where there were two kinds of worship experiences each Sunday. On Sunday morning, we attended worship wearing our "Sunday best" and the music was very formal, and the choir sang glorious anthems. On Sunday evening, we wore our casual clothing, no choir, and the music was informal. Often people would call out their favorite hymn and it would be sung by the congregation.

One of the things I loved about Sunday evening worship was the time set aside for the congregation to spend time at the altar in prayer. Usually, the altar rail would fill with people on their knees bowing in prayer. The lights would be lowered, and the music would be soothing and comforting. There was a tremendous feeling of "family" and inclusion. I do not know about others, but that time brought me great hope for the week ahead.

As I think back on my years as a pastor, I realize that every aspect of worship was an offering of hope. Let me explain with a typical order of worship for a Sunday service:

Prelude - usually soft music played for the congregation to prepare for worship by praying, reading scripture or by simply being quiet and viewing all the symbols in the sanctuary – letting them "speak" as they would.

Hymns or praise music - more people seem to remember the words to hymns and praise music than scripture and the points of a sermon. Such hymns travel with us through our lives inside the church and outside in the secular world. Often when I visited the sick in the hospital or hospice places, we would sing and almost always the first song was *Amazing Grace*. It is the number one hymn in America because of its offering of hope.

Standing at the grave of young person, a baby, or a beloved grandparent and hearing the words of *Amazing Grace*, stirs the heart to a greater meaning and purpose that death will never defeat.

Billy Graham almost always closed his crusades with the hymn *"Just As I Am"* because of its powerful message that God loves us just as we are, but is never content to leave us there if sin is blocking us from eternal living.

When one of my cousins died at the age of twenty-eight, he left behind a wife and two children. He lacked six months completing his internship as a physician when he was diagnosed with leukemia. When my wife and I went to the funeral home to visit with his family, his father (my uncle) came up to me with tears in his eyes and said, "You will play the organ at his funeral won't you." I was not expecting such a request, but how could I say "no?" Then he turned to me and said, "play anything you want, but when we enter the church, please play *A Mighty Fortress is Our God* and pull out all the stops, and at the end of the service as we are leaving, please play Handel's *Hallelujah*. With both of those played, I know I can get through the service."

The great hymns and great praise music through the years offer tremendous hope in times of joy and celebration as well as in times of dying, darkness, and death.

Affirmation of faith -some churches use creeds as a synopsis of their beliefs. Though none that have been written to date are complete, they can offer a broader, yet concise way of explaining the Christian faith.

Gloria Patra and Doxologies – these are simply praise songs used on a consistent basis to ingrain in our hearts and minds the need to pause and thank God for all that is ours.

Baptism Whether a person is "dunked" or "sprinkled" or had water "poured" on his head, baptism is a symbolic act that "marks" a person as a child of God. Sometimes when Martin Luther would get overwhelmed or feel tempted to sin in some way, he would remind himself that "I am baptized." He knew he belonged to God and that honor would override anything detrimental he would seek to do. What great hope is offered to humanity through this glorious act!

Offering This part of worship is far more than just throwing a few dollars into an offering plate. Taken seriously, the money we "offer" symbolizes our very lives. Try to visualize putting your whole body in the offering plate!!!! The action itself suggests that we give our entire life to God: body, mind, emotions, spirit, and material possessions. What we put into the "plate" reflects the seriousness in which we understand this vital part of worship.

Anthem or solo or praise song - is usually a sermon in song and often reflects the scripture and sermon that will take place. Many times, before I got up to preach, the choir would sing an anthem that would almost literally take my breath away, not only for its beauty in singing but for the powerful message of the words. One such anthem that stirred my soul when I was going through great pain and facing critical surgery was O God Beyond All Praising. The last stanza stood out to me offering me a renewed hope and peace beyond words:

> *Then hear, O gracious Savior,*
> *accept the love we bring,*
> *that we who know your favor*
> *may serve you as our king;*
> *and whether our tomorrows*
> *be filled with good or ill,*
> *we'll triumph through our sorrows*
> *and rise to bless you still:*
> *to marvel at your beauty*
> *and glory in your ways,*
> *and make a joyful duty*
> *our sacrifice of praise.*[130]

I felt like standing up after hearing those powerful words and saying a benediction and going home. I had heard God's holy Word and it was healing and hope filled.

Pastoral Prayer and The Lord's Prayer

One of the special moments in worship is to name our personal and corporate prayer concerns before the congregation and then take them to God in prayer. Prayer is one way of putting our hope in God's eternal love for humanity.

Perhaps one of the most impactful prayers I have ever heard was in a college gathering to remember a professor on campus who had committed suicide. He was dearly loved by all who knew him. His death at thirty-eight years of age was shocking. It seemed like a black cloud hovered over the campus.

Shortly after the words of greeting and opening hymn, one of the professors stood and invited us to bow in prayer. His words penetrated into my soul and gradually lifted me out of my despair. When he said "Amen" I felt as if I had received healing. I looked around me and the expressions on the faces of the students were as mine. After the service ended and many of walked to lunch, we all commented on the prayer as the center of the service.

I was so taken by the prayer that I went to the professor's office to ask for a copy of it. He told me that he had spent most of the night preparing for that prayer but that no words came to him. Finally, he said he slept, and trusted God to work through him. He then confessed that he did not know what he had even said! To this day, it was one of the most powerful and life-changing prayers of my life!

Scripture

It is the church that gave the world the Bible, not the other way around. Throughout the centuries, the church has preserved this sacred library of sixty-six texts. Millions have died over it. Wars fought over it. Some countries have banned it. And even though it is misused time and time again, it is still a best-seller, the mostly wide read resource in the world and provides the essentials for eternal living. It is the greatest book on hope ever written.

When I feel like God is silent and my prayers are hitting the ceiling, I often turn to Psalm 139 to remember and to be reassured that the presence of God is in my life and will always be. The great theologian and minister to the chapel of Boston University, Howard Thurman would read this psalm every day and pray through it. Notice the power of Psalm 139:1-18:

> *O Lord, you have searched me and known me.*
> *You know when I sit down and when I rise up;*
> *you discern my thoughts from far away.*
> *You search out my path and my lying down,*
> *and are acquainted with all my ways.*
> *Even before a word is on my tongue,*
> *O Lord, you know it completely.*
> *You hem me in, behind and before,*
> *and lay your hand upon me.*
> *Such knowledge is too wonderful for me;*
> *it is so high that I cannot attain it.*
> *Where can I go from your spirit?*
> *Or where can I flee from your presence?*
> *If I ascend to heaven, you are there;*
> *if I make my bed in Sheol, you are there.*
> *If I take the wings of the morning*
> *and settle at the farthest limits of the sea,*
> *even there your hand shall lead me,*
> *and your right hand shall hold me fast.*
> *If I say, "Surely the darkness shall cover me,*
> *and the light around me become night,"*

even the darkness is not dark to you;
the night is as bright as the day,
for darkness is as light to you.
For it was you who formed my inward parts;
you knit me together in my mother's womb.
I praise you, for I am fearfully and wonderfully made.
Wonderful are your works;
that I know very well.
My frame was not hidden from you,
when I was being made in secret,
intricately woven in the depths of the earth.
Your eyes beheld my unformed substance.
In your book were written
all the days that were formed for me,
when none of them as yet existed.
How weighty to me are your thoughts, O God!
How vast is the sum of them!
I try to count them—they are more than the sand;
I come to the end—I am still with you.

The Bible is a living document for when it is read and studied, it continues to offer life in new and vibrant ways. It offers the way to eternal living and is truly a light unto our paths.

Sermon

Critical to worship is the sermon. Why? The apostle Paul said it best when he wrote "faith comes by hearing and how will they hear without a preacher?"[131] More than ever before, the world is in need of the prophetic voice that cuts to the reality of sin and destruction yet is an instrument offering the greatest hope to the world.

One of my seminary professors once said to us, "in every sermon, say something to those who are hurting." He was suggesting that in our preaching, we throw a "hope-rope" to all in attendance.

The Lord's supper

Often there are those who are helped more by participating in the breaking of bread and receiving the cup of "salvation" than any other part of the service. It is at the table of Christ, who is the host, that we are reminded that we are One people, with One faith, One Lord, and One baptism. Here we are neither rich nor poor, male nor female, American nor other nationality, gay nor straight, old nor young, but One people in Jesus Christ. When we partake of the elements of holy Communion we are taking Christ within us and we leave the table to be as Christ to the world.

Invitation to Discipleship

Usually at the end of the service, the pastor invites any who will to come and join the body of Christ known as the church. When people do so, the church is strengthened and able to be a more vibrant force for goodness in the world.

The pledge of membership:

In the United Methodist Church, when a person(s) comes to the front of the church to "join", the pastor asks them to take the "pledge" of membership. The question is this: "Will you be loyal to the United Methodist Church and uphold it with your prayers, presence, gifts, service and witness?" What does this mean? The person(s) saying "I will" is pledging that they will pray daily for the church in general, the local church in particular and its clergy, leaders, congregants, and missions.

They pledge that they will be "present" in worship regularly. Unfortunately, I have known people to join a church to get their child in the preschool or to have a wedding there or even for the pastor to write a letter of recommendation for a college or university. Once those things are accomplished, they are rarely seen again.

It has been documented in scientific studies that those who attend worship regularly live longer and have better health.

Being involved in the whole worship experience lifts us beyond ourselves to unite with others in a common cause, the betterment of humanity in God's name.

The pledge also asks that "gifts" be used to enhance the worship of God and further the mission of the church. These "gifts" include giving monetarily and sharing talents. Most churches ask that whoever joins set aside the first tenth of their income to give to God through the ministry of the church. In Biblical terminology this is called "tithing."

Such financial gurus as Financial Peace says that when one receives a paycheck that the first tenth should go to God, the next ten percent go to savings and live on eighty percent! Those who strive to do this find themselves in better financial shape and have hope for a more a stable life.

The fourth part of the "pledge" is "service." When I was a pastor, I would remind the congregation from time-to-time that the whole congregation is on the evangelism committee, the education committee, the missions committee and the worship committee. Everyone is responsible for reaching out to others through paths of service. Some can teach a class, some are better at singing in the choir, others are better at keeping the nursery, and still others at working at a soup kitchen or painting a room at a children's home. Nevertheless, all are expected to serve in some capacity.

The last part of the pledge is to be a "witness" for Jesus Christ. Perhaps this is one of the most difficult. Being a witness is, in short, a lifestyle! To witness is not simply performing a few acts of kindness each day but living kindness each day. A witness is one who stives to live a Christ-like, Christ-centered life in their speech and conduct. Their motives are pure. Their actions are genuine.

I have known some who are always eagerly ready to give a "witness" in church or other places telling of their love for Jesus but live the exact opposite.

One minister friend began his own ministry. He named it for himself. He went all over the country professing the love of God until he was arrested on sixteen counts of child molestation. He was found guilty, went to prison, disgraced his family, and died while there. He did not "walk his talk." Witnesses are those who do their best to live what they say they believe about God's love.

The blessing/benediction

I read about a man who lived about five miles from the church where he attended. One Sunday, he awoke to a heavy snow. He could not get his car to work and so he bundled up and began to walk to church. He had to take it slowly as the roads were icy and slick.

By the time he arrived, the pastor was beginning to offer a benediction. Following this, the organist began to play a postlude and the service was over. As people began to file out of the church some said to him, "Bet you feel cheated getting here just in time for the benediction and missing the whole service." The man replied, "It was worth my walk to hear the pastor say:

> The Lord bless you and keep you
> The Lord make his face to shine upon you
> And be gracious to you
> The Lord lift up his countenance upon you

And give you peace
In the name of God who is
Father, son and Holy Spirit.
Amen."

He said, "That benediction will last me a lifetime!" Benedictions are meant to send the congregation back into the world with hope and peace.

Old Irish blessing

One of the traditions of churches where I have served is the singing of the Old Irish Blessing. Sometimes, the congregation would hold hands, stretching across the aisles, and sing it as a prayer to one another:

May the road rise to meet you.
May the wind blow at your back.
May the sun shine warmly on your face
May the rains fall softly on your fields.
And until we meet again,
Until we meet again,
May God hold you in the palm of His hands.

Often, I would witness tears streaming down the faces of those who sang it, because it meant so much to them. I have officiated in weddings where it was sung and in funerals where it brought great hope and peace to the grieving. Truly, it is a prayer of hope.

Weddings

Today, many weddings are held in barns or wedding venues instead of inside a church facility. There is nothing wrong with that. However, I do miss being inside a sanctuary where there is an organ playing, the pulpit, the baptismal font, and the Bible on the Bible stand are visible.

I miss having an altar table in the center of the chancel area. And I miss the candles that represent the life of Christ on either side of the altar.

Nevertheless, weddings held in other places can have great inspiration and meaning. I have officiated weddings in front of lakes, the ocean, on top of a mountain, at horse farms, beside swimming pools, backyards of someone's homes, and in venues with small outdoor chapels. To see a bride and groom come together for marriage (at any age) symbolizes hope for the future.

Funerals

At the time of death, more than ever there is a need for hope. Where do we find it? Once again, I turn us toward the church, who has the greatest message of hope in the world.

An order for a "celebration of life" service or as some call it, a funeral, is hope-filled. Notice how the liturgy for a United Methodist Service of Celebrating the Life of an individual begins with words of great hope:

THE WORD OF GRACE

Jesus said, I am the resurrection and I am life.
Those who believe in me, even though they die, yet shall they live,
and whoever lives and believes in me shall never die.
I am Alpha and Omega, the beginning and the end,
the first and the last.
I died, and behold I am alive for evermore,
Because I live, you shall live also.

GREETING

Friends, we have gathered here to praise God
and to witness to our faith as we celebrate the life of Name.
We come together in grief, acknowledging our human loss.
May God grant us grace, that in pain we may find comfort,
in sorrow *hope*, in death resurrection.

PRAYER:

Eternal God,
we praise you for the great company of all those
who have finished their course in faith
and now rest from their labor.
We praise you for those dear to us
whom we name in our hearts before you.
Especially we praise you for *Name,*
whom you have graciously received into your presence.
To all of these, grant your peace.
Let perpetual light shine upon them;
and help us so to believe where we have not seen,
that your presence may lead us through our years,
and bring us at last with them
into the joy of your home
not made with hands but eternal in the heavens;
through Jesus Christ our Lord. Amen.

SCRIPTURE READINGS such as:

John 14: selected verses
[Jesus said,] "Do not let your hearts be troubled.
Believe in God, believe also in me.
In my Father's house there are many dwelling places.
If it were not so,
would I have told you that I go to prepare a place for you?
And if I go and prepare a place for you,
I will come again and will take you to myself,
so that where I am, there you may be also.
Peace I leave with you; my peace I give to you.
I do not give to you as the world gives.
Do not let your hearts be troubled, and do not let them be afraid."

2 Timothy 4:7-8
I have fought the good fight, I have finished the race, I have kept the faith.

Revelation 21:1-7
And I saw the holy city, the new Jerusalem,
coming down out of heaven from God,
prepared as a bride adorned for her husband.
And I heard a loud voice from the throne saying,
"See, the home of God is among mortals.
He will dwell with them as their God;
they will be his peoples, and God himself will be with them;
he will wipe away every tear from their eyes.
Death will be no more;
mourning and crying and pain will be no more,
for the first things have passed away."
And the one who was seated on the throne said,
"See, I am making all things new."
Also he said, "Write this, for these words are trustworthy and true."
Then he said to me,
"It is done! I am the Alpha and the Omega, the beginning and the end.
To the thirsty I will give water
as a gift from the spring of the water of life.
Those who conquer will inherit these things,
and I will be their God and they will be my children."

Eulogy

Usually, a eulogy has two parts to it. The first is an assurance of God's love and care for all of humanity and that God is with us in life, death, and life beyond death.

The second is a time to quicken our appreciation for the life of the deceased. Sometimes there are humorous stories that are shared along with achievements that highlighted the life. All of this is done in the context that a person may die, but who they are lives forever in the hearts of all who knew them and the seeds of love and goodness they spread in life, will continue to grow for generations to come.

Lastly, and most importantly, the church offers the world:

EASTER!

It is the greatest day of the Christian year! More people attend services on Easter Sunday than any other time! A church that normally is only partially filled on "normal" Sundays, will be filled to overflowing on Easter. Why?

Perhaps it is to answer the questions, "Is it true?" "Did Jesus really overcome death?" "Because Jesus rose from death, will we as well?"

Perhaps it is to find reassurance that our lives have meaning not only now, but after we are gone.

Perhaps it is to blend in with the masses so that we don't feel so alone in our questioning about death and beyond.

Perhaps it is to find peace and hope in the midst of great suffering.

Easter is the great reminder that pain, death, and the losses of our lives do not get the last word. God always has the last word, and it is LIFE!

Jim Wallis aptly put it when he wrote:

"the news from the women at the tomb was the greatest hope that the world has ever known. And yet what did the male disciples first call it? Nonsense! Hope unbelieved is always considered nonsense. But hope believed is history in the process of being changed. The nonsense of the resurrection became the hope that shook the Roman Empire and established the Jesus Movement. The nonsense of slave songs in Egypt and Mississippi became the hope that let the oppressed go free.

The nonsense of a confessing church stood up to the state religion of the Nazi regime. The nonsense of prayer in East Germany helped bring down the Berlin Wall. The nonsense of another confessing church in South Africa helped end apartheid. The nonsense of a bus boycott in Montgomery, Alabama, became the hope that transformed a nation, and the nonsense of saying 'Black Lives Matter' defends and continues that transformation today.[132]

He goes on to say that:

> "Hope is the very dynamic history.
> Hope is the engine of change
> Hope is the energy of transformation.
> Hope is the door from one reality to another."[133]

The church of the Risen Christ, was conceived in hope, exists in hope and points to the eternal consummation of human history in hope. Indeed, a theology of hope has a foundation in the life, teachings, preaching, healings, suffering, death and resurrection of Jesus. Through his resurrection we are bound together in Him with the promise of eternal life that begins even now and will continue until the end of the age. This is where hope has "power."

The book of Acts begins with the apostles gathering in Jerusalem for instructions from the resurrected Jesus. Here his words to them from Acts 1:6-8:

> *So when they had come together, they asked him, "Lord, is this the time when you will restore the kingdom to Israel?" He replied, "It is not for you to know the times or periods that the Father has set by his own authority. But you will **receive power** when the Holy Spirit has come upon you; and you will be my witnesses in Jerusalem, in all Judea and Samaria, and to the ends of the earth."*

Not only our hope but hope for the world is found when we receive the spirit of the risen Christ and live as witnesses in our homes (Jerusalem) our neighborhoods (Judea) our region including our enemies (Samaria) and to all the world. This is the essence of "church." This is our mission. Empowered by the Holy Spirit of Jesus Christ, we believe we can make a difference in the world and we go forth to do so. Thus, the church becomes an offering of hope to all.

Hope is invented
every day

James Baldwin

———⧓———

Chapter 9

Where have I offered hope, or so I thought!

———✕———

Remember, Hope is a good thing,
Maybe the best of things,
And no good thing ever dies.

Stephen King

As I licked my wounds from my relative's words to me that I had never given her hope, I found myself a quiet place to sit down and think about how I have offered hope or tried to offer hope to her and to others. Interestingly, my first thoughts were to two situations where I did <u>not</u> bring hope at all in my best efforts to do so!

The first was when I was a student chaplain on the "terminal" cancer floor of Emory University Hospital. My first day on the job I was to visit three men dying of cancer. Two of them were twenty-four years of age and one was twenty. I spent time with the first two men and when I entered the room of the third, the man in the bed looked at my name tag that said, "Chaplain." He pointed his finger at me and said, "Get out!" "Get out!" I hate God for what I am going through! I am dying! How dare you come in here and attempt to say anything good about God!' He died with great anger toward God, the church, and the medical communities lack of wisdom to heal him. Interestingly, I only said "Hello" before he saw my name tag and began to rant. I felt a tremendous sense of failure that he was in such pain and thought God was the cause.

The second occurred several years later when a man in the church where I was serving, suffered a seizure on a Sunday morning. Normally, he and his wife would be in their usual places in worship. When I received word that he was in the hospital, I left worship and drove to visit him. He was in the emergency room resting in a bed when I arrived. He looked up at me and said, "You are the last person I want to see today! (He was serious.) Am I dying? Is that why you are here? I am in too much pain to hear anything about God." I left the room feeling like a failure. My very presence brought anxiety and fear rather than calmness and peace as I had so greatly desired.

One of the things I learned early in life is that I choose how and what I will do for others. <u>I do not do it expecting anything in return because that always sets up for disappointment.</u> I choose to enjoy giving my time and efforts to others. If I do not receive a thank you note or any praises, I am not disappointed. If I became sad over such things, I would be the problem.

There are probably a million other ways that I did not give hope along my journey in life. For those, I can only give a blanket apology. Ministry for me has always been in lifting others up, edifying the church (congregation), striving to offer God's healing to the broken, light in darkness, and hope in despair.

Instead of concentrating on the negative, I began to make a list of ways I *hoped* I had offered *hope* to others. It is not complete, nor do I assume any of these offered people *hope*. Nevertheless, here goes:

1) through preaching (literally thousands of sermons)
2) visiting the sick
3) being with the dying

4) visiting the elderly

5) officiating at funerals

6) officiating at weddings

7) performing baptisms

8) serving the Lord's Supper

9) visiting those in jail

10) being available to those with issues

11) welcoming newcomers

12) writing letters, texts and emails in times of crisis

13) listening

14) praying for those in need

15) giving monetarily to the church

16) giving monetarily to charities

17) giving monetarily to colleges and universities

18) Attending church and participating in its rituals

19) Teaching

20) Offering a smile to a stranger and to those in crisis or need

21) Recycling

22) Sending Christmas cards

23) Attending events for charitable causes

24) Inviting people to a meal

25) Giving gifts

26) Writing books

27) Taking someone to lunch

28) Intentional acts of kindness

29) Stopping at a youth car wash

30) Phoning people on my prayer list

31) Taking care of my grandchildren when they are ill

32) Spending quality time with my grandchildren

33) Taking care of my children's pets

34) Taking youth on mission retreats

35) Helping clear the street where I live after a storm

36) Striving to love my enemies (or those to whom I disagree)

37) Paying taxes (without complaint as much as possible!)

38) Writing recommendations for high school seniors toward college

39) Keeping my yard clean

40) Keeping my house clean

41) Driving the speed limit

42) Offering compliments to those who rarely get them

43) Sending flowers to my wife

44) Writing homilies for weddings I perform

45) Sending encouraging notes to our pastors at church

46) Refraining from singing too loud!

47) Practicing gratitude

48) Carpooling when possible

49) Striving for truth

50) Laughing and smiling

51) Taking a child to a hospice center

52) Telling inspirational stories

53) Trying to love those who are difficult to love

54) Voting

55) Calling our restaurant "servers" by name

56) Letting someone go ahead of me in the check-out line

57) Dressing modestly

58) Weekly visits to help my grandkids with their on-line school

59) Asking for forgiveness

60) Working in a soup kitchen

61) Loving the "under-dog"

62) Striving to 'bite my tongue" when I feel a need to criticize or correct

63) Conserving water when brushing my teeth and washing dishes

64) Taking my faith in God seriously day by day as I journey through life

I had hoped to have at least one hundred items on this page but could not get more than these. Perhaps, in time, I will recognize more and add them to my list. It is never arrogant to acknowledge things we might have done well in our prayer life. If we confess our sins, by the same token, we should confess to God our strengths so that we can offer thanks and praise and to ask God's blessings to continue to use them and build on them.

Let me encourage us all to take some time to make a list of ways we can be hope-bearers in the world around us. One of the beneficial things that has come from my relative's words to me is how I am acutely sensitive about being a hope-bearer. The process of sitting down and writing such a list has helped me see some of the ways I have tried. It has also prodded me to find more ways.

Recently, I preached at a church near our home. After the service an older woman came up to me and said, "When I came into church this morning I was down in the dumps, but I am leaving with joy. What a great service we had today." What made the difference? I believe she received hope through the beautiful hymns, the duet by two young women, the scripture, (I pray, the sermon), prayers, and the passing of the peace, the fellowship of kindred spirits. In short, "hope" comes to us in multitudes of ways. I am still trying to understand where I have offered it along the path of my life.

The very least you can do in your
Life is figure out what you hope for.
And the most you can do
Is live inside that hope.
Not admire it from a distance
But live right under it,
under its roof.

Barbara Kingsolver
Animal Dreams

———————⋈———————

Chapter 10

Who have offered me hope?

———————✕———————

Hope begins in the dark, the stubborn hope
that if you just show up and try to do the
right thing, the dawn will come. You
wait and watch and work:
You don't give up.

Anne Lamott

When I sat down to put pen to paper and think about who have offered me hope, I quickly wrote: parents, teachers, professors, coaches, Sunday school instructors, pastors, scout leaders, my spouse, my children, my grandchildren, financial planners, physicians, nurses, dentists, cooks, friends, postal workers who bring my mail each day, grocery stores that provide food, car washes, police, firefighters, institutions for those with chemical dependency, the automobile industry, clothing industry, aviation transportation, animals, blue skies, stars, sun, moon, weddings, golf courses, cathedrals, hospitals, sports arenas, and the beautiful faces of innocent children. There are many more, but I am just getting started!

I am much more aware of the world around me since being told I had never given hope. When I am driving in my neighborhood, I usually see several deer, squirrels, rabbits, birds, occasionally a fox, opossum, and woodchucks. They have become more than just "scenery" for me, rather instruments of keeping the world in its rhythm, a great offering of hope.

The first book of the Bible takes the time to express the creation of each day of the week and what was created in the day. Nature itself offers hope beyond hope! Indeed, there are countless ways nature offers hope to the world. Let me name some:

Fishing
>whether in the ocean, a lake, a creek, a pond, or a river

Hunting
>Bird watching out your window or as you take a walk outside
>Going to the ocean and observe the fish, dolphins, sharks, whales and play in the sand!

Pets – all kinds of them!
>Horses

Barnyard animals.
>Cows, pigs, sheep, lambs, ducks, chickens, goats, turkeys

Zoo animals:
>lions, tigers, giraffes, monkeys, elephants, rhinoceros, hippopotamus, polar bears, seals, snakes, leopards, cougars, buffalo, deer, rabbits, flamingos, peacocks, zebras, frogs and turtles, and marine life

Many are filled with hope when working directly in the soil through planting vegetable gardens, or flower beds, raking leaves, cutting grass.

How long has it been since you took a blanket into the yard at evening and counted the stars, pointed out the big and little dipper and the North star? Or during the day, watched the clouds, danced in the rain, snow skied down a mountain, watched the sun come up and the sun set? Do we take the time to smell the flowers around us, pick a bouquet and give to someone in need? What about driving to places in early autumn and see the leaves changing their colors to look like a patchwork quilt?

The world is a miraculous place with millions of different species and people! All around us nature is throwing us a "hope-rope" in multitudes of ways. How can we look at all these creations and not believe in hope? Even winds and storms, thunder and lightning, hurricanes, tornadoes, tsunamis, earthquakes, and snow and sleet and fire and floods, turn our minds and hearts toward the One who doesn't send them, but is with us and constantly striving to transform any damage into means of grace.

Nature itself, points us toward hope. Fortunately, where I live, four distinct seasons rotate faithfully each year. Cold winters melt into the beautiful kaleidoscopic colors of springtime and warmer weather. Then summer appears riding spring's coattails bringing the opportunity for outdoor living at its best: water skiing, swimming, fishing, gardening, golf, baseball, bicycling, long trail walks, picnics, watermelons, ice cream cones, grilling hamburgers and hotdogs, and watching late night outdoor movies. Finally, as summer tires, autumn sweeps in with school beginning again, football season, Halloween, turkeys and pumpkins, sweet potato casserole, cranberries, and tailgating! Each season, though one to enjoy as it comes to us, also offers hope that the next one will arrive soon enough bringing fresh new possibilities for the fulfillment of life.

And then there are human beings! They come in all shapes and sizes, backgrounds, cultures, ages, colors, and languages. We cannot live without them! Some seem to crush our hope at times where others offer it in ways we do not always see or understand. Nevertheless, I am deeply thankful for those who have offered me hope, especially during trying times of my life.

When I completed the ninth grade, my father was transferred to a large church in a small town. There was only one high school, a Dairy Queen, and very few restaurants. It seemed that everyone knew everything about everyone. I was not used to this, having been raised thus far in larger cities.

My first day of high school, I found my geometry class and sat near the front of the room. The teacher was new. After introducing himself, he asked us to get out a piece of paper and a pencil to take a test. I was stunned! It was the first day of class! Here are some of the questions I remember:

1) What is the number of this classroom?
2) How far is it from our town to another town?
3) How far is it to the moon?
4) How much does a medium-priced Chevrolet cost?
5) What is the largest business in this town?
6) How many students go to school here?

There were ten questions, but these are the only ones I remember. I did not know the answers to any of them. I make an F. He counted it in our grades. I was off to a horrible start.

To make matters worse, he used standardized tests which did not cover the cover the material we were taught. I continually made C's. After about a month of this, I begged my parents to get me some help. They thought I was just being lazy and not studying enough, but nevertheless, sought out a tutor.

I will never forget going into her home. Dad took me to the simple, white-framed house with a screened in front porch. She had a fire going in the fireplace. Her husband was sitting in the kitchen hooked up to a breathing machine. She welcomed us in, told us her husband was suffering from emphysema and that she had to quit teaching in the high school to care for him.

Then she looked at me and said, "who is your geometry teacher?" I told her his name. She looked at my father and said, "He is a kook!" I wanted to hug her right then on the spot. She told Dad and me that she had numerous complaints about him and that he could not teach his way out of a paper bag. I loved her!

All through the year, I suffered from this teacher's crazy tests. The wonderful outcome was becoming a student of Virginia Harlow. She was a devout Christian woman. She had great patience. She was a tremendous teacher. I made the highest grade on the final exam of all the geometry students in the school. But I never learned one thing from the teacher. He was fired after that year. Ms. Harlow was my real teacher and she inspired me to major in mathematics in college. I also became a math tutor for the college because I knew how much college math could be scary.

She lived into her mid-90's and I visited her often and wrote to her periodically over the years. She was hope made flesh! She invested her time in my studies and made geometry come alive and exciting. I always wanted to become an architect, and geometry is vitally important to that process. Though I obtained my degree in math, I went straight to seminary and became a pastor. In some ways, I had "my cake and ate it too" because in forty years of active ministry, I was involved in the building of four major facilities: two sanctuaries, and two educational facilities. For me, there is nothing quite like sitting down and discussing what is needed, drawing a few sketches, and then letting the architects do their work and seeing the wonders of blueprints that make possible the construction of a building. Her time with me in my formative years helped me to assist the congregation in more ways than just leading a financial campaign. Reading financial reports, setting financial goals and being able to read architectural plans and designs came in handy.

Fast forward to the year that videos began to come into being. I was in seminary at Emory University. There was a new class that was all the rave called "preaching on video television." It was the first of its kind and I thought it would be fascinating. I signed up and made the class roll.

The class was instructed to work on a sermon and each week, two students would preach. Each sermon would be recorded and afterward, the class would look at it and critique. I had never seen anything like this before!

The second week of class, the professor said, "the first person who will preach a sermon for us is Dee Shelnutt." I was caught off guard and suddenly extremely nervous. The class had some thirty students in it and I only knew a hand full.

I went to the lectern and preached my sermon. When I finished, the professor said, "let's run the tape back, show it and critique it." When the tape reversed to the beginning, it was blank. I was not on the tape! The professor said, "Oh no! I forgot to turn this button on that records, so Mr. Shelnutt, you will have to preach your sermon again." I was horrified!

Once again, I went to the lectern and preached my sermon over again. This time, when the tape was reversed, I appeared on the screen. As I looked at myself and heard my voice, the tears welled-up in my face. I could barely understand my southern accent! I despised my voice. I felt humiliated having to listen and look at myself while the class critiqued. Fortunately, I managed to get through the class without breaking down in tears, but I was weeping inside. I decided right then and there that I was leaving seminary and finding something else to do.

When the class ended, I asked the professor if I could meet him in his office. He agreed. When I went in and closed the door, the tears came down in sheets. I told him I was leaving the ministry. If I could not understand me, how on earth could others? I thought the whole experience was a disaster.

He let me express all of my emotions and then he said, "Mr. Shelnutt, did it ever occur to you that Moses could not speak well? And God used him!" He paused and then he said, "You keep on in the ministry and give your voice to God and let God determine how it will be used, not you. Sure, you are southern, but that is not a handicap. You must work on your voice by not speaking so slowly and enunciating better. There is nothing wrong with your voice." He came around from his desk, put his arm around my shoulder and said, "Let me pray for you." And though I do not remember the words, I remember feeling affirmed, loved, healed. I stayed in seminary and in ministry for forty years. I still do not like to hear my voice on tape, but I have quit whining over it. My professor offered me the hope I needed to accept myself and my limitations as an offering to God. I have preached over 2500 sermons in over 100 churches, performed over 400 funerals and 300+ weddings, spoken before 200,000 people (in my largest experience) prayed at two Peach Bowls with over 66,000 in attendance, as well as many other sporting and church events. I work my hardest on the material I use in all circumstances but pray before speaking that God will use my voice and not let it be a hindrance. I never take anything for granted. I am aware of my limitations, but also the power of God to use even the worst speaking voices as a means of grace!

My fourth-grade schoolteacher told my father one day when he came to pick me up from school that "I was not college material!" I had made two C's on my report card. In my family, that was the same as making an F. He went to see her to inquire about his straight A son making his first two C's. Her response, "Some kids are just not college material." Talk about not giving someone hope!!!!

I could not help but think of her the day I graduated with honors from Emory University with my Doctor of Ministry Degree. Though she had little *hope* in me, I was surrounded by folks who thought otherwise. Too many to name, but numerous teachers and professors who invested their time and interest in me made learning deeply satisfying.

Just one little word can cause a person to give up.
Just one angry expression can cause a person to turn away.
Just one little word can make the difference between life and death.

When my wife and I were appointed to begin a brand-new church, I was 28 years of age and only been in the ministry for seven years. I knew next-to-nothing about beginning a church. The bishop of North Georgia told me in February that I would be assigned in June to be the founding pastor of new United Methodist church. I was excited. I was scared. I would be put in a place where I had no church members, no keys to any buildings, not budgets, indeed, nothing. Since there was no church, there was no parsonage for my wife, my little girl or me to live. We would have to buy a house. Just one little problem with that, I had no way of paying for one.

I went to my parents and told them the exciting news as well as confessing that I needed their help. At this point in my parent's life, they had relatively little savings. Nevertheless, they agreed to loan me the down payment. I signed a loan with them that I would pay back the money within three years.

My wife and I had purchased a lot on lake West Point a year before knowing anything about a move to begin a new church. Immediately we put up the place for sale. It sold within a few months and one-half of the amount to my folks was repaid. Then we sold my wife's car and bought a less expensive one. Now, we were within $8000 of paying it all off with a year to go. We lived very meagerly and paid the last penny a couple of months before the loan came due.

Without the sacrifice of my parents, we would never have been able to buy a house. We lived there ten years and when we moved, we rented it for six years. The money we made on it helped to send our children to college. When we sold the house, we invested in the retirement home where we live today.

My parents put their hope and trust in me to begin a church. It was a tremendous risk to them. It was a great sacrifice as well.

Perhaps one of the greatest experiences of hope in my life came during my first summer in the church where my children had moved for the first time. All they had ever known was Fayette County and my parents being with them in worship alongside my wife. Now, they were in a new city, new church and about to begin a new school year where they would be the new kids in town.

On Sunday morning (before they were to begin school the next day) the children came downstairs to breakfast and said to me, "Dad, will you come straight home after church and be with us today? We just want to be with you and mom the whole day until we have to start school tomorrow." My heart ached for them. I knew all too well what it was like to be the new kid in town. I was the new kid in first grade, second grade, sixth grade, seventh grade, ninth grade and tenth grade! I knew the butterflies in my stomach that made me nauseous and fearful. How true it is that a parent would rather suffer than see their children hurt.

We went to church, came home, and ate a great lunch around the table. Then we played outdoor games and rested by reading and later watching a movie. Following supper, we headed upstairs for baths and devotional time. Reluctantly, each child nestled in their beds and prepared as best as they could for the new day in their new school.

My wife and walked downstairs with tears in our eyes. And then the doorbell rang. We opened it and on our front lawn, on a warm August evening, were twenty plus teenagers from our church singing Christmas hymns!!!! Naturally, all three of our children rushed down to see what was going on. The young people sang some other songs and then they shouted: "WE LOVE YOU!" "WE LOVE YOU!" They rushed up and hugged us, including each child, and then they ran, got back in the church vans and took off back to the church.

As we waved them good-bye, we turned to the children and said, "Time to get back to bed." They stood in awe. Then our daughter said, "Is it true? Do they really love us?" I said, "Well, you heard them, and drove nine miles to tell us that today." The kids turned and they ran back upstairs, we heard them say, "I'm excited about tomorrow. It's going to be great!'

Those teenagers will never know what hope they brought to my family and me in that one act of kindness. Indeed, it was life changing. The four years we spent in that place were four of our best.

I know firsthand that when others bring hope to our children, they bring hope to us, the parents. That is one reason I can know for certain, that though my relative said that "I brought hope to her child, but not to her" could never be true.

When the coach selects your child, it brings hope to
the child and to the parent.
When the teacher praises the child, it brings hope to
the child and to the parent.
When a student receives a "care-package" from the church during
their final exams, it brings hope to the student and to the parent.
When a student receives a scholarship to a college either academically
and in sports, it brings hope to the student and to the parent.
When a person offers hope to a child,
the parent receives hope whether they
know it or not.

Perhaps more than any "one" person, I have received the greatest hope from the church. Let me be more specific, The United Methodist Church. I was born at Emory University Hospital on the campus of Emory University. That is a campus owned by The United Methodist Church. It has one of the greatest medical centers in the world.

My father was a United Methodist pastor and when I left the hospital as a baby, I was carried into the home where my family lived, a parsonage owned by Sandy Springs UMC. The congregation of the church brought food and gifts and flowers to celebrate my arrival. The UMC provides homes for all of their clergy at no cost to the family.

The insurance provided by the UMC paid for my birth and hospital stay. The church paid my father's salary so we could have all the needs of a family in that day.

I was baptized into the church. The water marks on my head symbolized that I belonged to God and God's universal church. Wherever I went in the world, I was a member of the family of God, and not just in Methodism, but any church.

The colleges I have attended were affiliated with the UMC. I received Methodist scholarships to college, seminary and when I worked on my doctorate.

When I was hospitalized, I had no bills because of the grace of good insurance provided through the UMC and the Stiles Bradley Fund established by Mr. Bradley to assist all UM clergy with bills beyond what insurance could not pay. This continues today and has brought much financial relief.

All my adult life, I have worked through the UMC. It has put food on the table, clothes on my family, educated us, provided great medical care, embodied us in congregations with wonderful people, and when I retired, provided a pensions program that enables my wife and I to live comfortably. When ordained as a um clergy, the church provides a "guaranteed" appointment. This gives a minister the freedom to preach God's Word without fear of being case of the church. I never had to find a church; the church SENT me to pastor.

Because the UMC is a "connectional" church, I grew up moving around to various cities. Thus, I know people from all over place. Having been a delegate to World UM events, my eyes have been opened to the UMC activities all over the world.

The church is, and always will be, the greatest source of hope in the world.

Not in militaries, not in money, not in status, not in power, not in things, but I find my greatest hope in the One who lived and emphasized the greatest commandment:

> *You shall love the Lord your God*
> *With all of your heart, soul, mind and strength,*
> *And your neighbor as yourself.*

Though no religion, denomination or church is perfect, I am proud to be a member of the church. The hope it has given me has led me thus far in my life, and I lean on it to continue to offer hope with every breath I take.

Lord save us all from
...a hope tree that
Has lost the faculty
Of putting out
Blossoms

Mark Twain

————————⋈————————

Chapter 11

Famous Folks, Famous Quotes

———————⋉———————

Hope shines brightest in
The darkest moments.
Never give up!

Tranquil Waters

    <u>Maxime Lagacé</u> started collecting quotes in 2004, after he lost his girlfriend in a car accident. In search of meaning, he dived in the self-improvement world, psychology and trail running. His goal was to understand his pain, his depression, his fears, his lack of motivation and inspiration. Books, blogs, quotes, and nature became his guide. The ones listed here are exceptional. Take the time to read each one and think about them:

Once you choose hope, anything's possible.
Christopher Reeve

We must accept finite disappointment, but never lose infinite hope.
Martin Luther King Jr.

Everything that is done in this world is done by hope.
Martin Luther

I dwell in possibility.
Emily Dickinson

May your choices reflect your hopes, not your fears.
Nelson Mandela

It is because of hope that you suffer. It is through hope
that you'll change things.

Maxime Lagacae

If we will be quiet and ready enough, we shall find
compensation in every disappointment.
Henry David Thoreau.

Hope is being able to see that there is light despite all of the darkness.
Desmond Tutu

Every cloud has a silver lining.
John Milson

While there's life, there's hope.
Marcus Tullius Cicero

The darkest hours are just before dawn.
English proverb

I don't think of all the misery, but of the beauty that still remains.
Anne Frank

Our greatest glory is not in never falling,
but in rising every time we fall.
Confucius

Only in the darkness can you see the stars.
Martin Luther King Jr

In all things it is better to hope than to despair.
Johann Wolfgang von Goethe

Walk on with hope in your heart, and you'll never walk alone.
Shah Rukh Khan

There is nothing like a dream to create the future.
Victor Hugo

Carve a tunnel of hope through the dark mountain
of disappointment.
Martin Luther King Jr.

Hope never abandons you, you abandon it.
George Weinberg

Most of the important things in the world have been accomplished
by people who have kept on trying when there seemed to
be no hope at all.
Dale Carnegie

However bad life may seem, there is always something you can do
and succeed at. Where there's life, there's hope.
Stephen Hawkins

Hope is a good thing, maybe even the best of things, and
good things never die.
Andy Dufresne (Shawshank Redemption)

Hope means hoping when things are hopeless, or it is no virtue at all... As long as matters are really hopeful, hope is mere flattery or platitude; it is only when everything is hopeless that hope begins to be a strength.
G.K. Chesterton

In the unlikely story that is America, there has never been anything false about hope
Barack Obama

Hope is but the <u>dream</u> of those who wake.
Matthew Prior

I find hope in the darkest of days and focus in the brightest. I do not judge the universe.
Dalai Lama

I am prepared for the worst but hope for the best.
Benjamin Disraeli

Far away there in the sunshine are my highest aspirations. I may not reach them but I can look up and see their beauty, believe in them, and try to follow them.
Louisa May Alcott

Find the seed at the bottom of your heart and bring forth a flower.
Shigenori Kameoka

Hang on to your hat. Hang on to your hope. And wind the clock, for tomorrow is another day.
E.B. White

Where there is no vision, there is no hope.
George Washington Carver

Hope is passion for what is possible.
Søren Kierkegaard

Hope is an embrace of the unknown.
Rebecca Solnit

Hope is outreaching desire with expectancy of good. It is a
characteristic of all living beings.
Edward S. Ame

Hope is a renewable option: If you run out of it at the end of the day,
you get to start over in the morning.
Barbara Kingsolver

Hope is the power of being cheerful in circumstances
that we know to be desperate.
G.K. Chesterton

Hope is one of the principal springs that keep mankind in motion.
Thomas Fuller

Keep your face to the sun and you will never see the shadows.
Helen Keller

You must not lose faith in humanity. Humanity is an ocean; if a few
drops of the ocean are dirty, the ocean does not become dirty.
Mahatma Gandhi

You will face many defeats in your life, but never let
yourself be defeated.
Maya Angelou

Shoot for the moon. Even if you miss, you'll land among the stars.
Norman Vincent Peale

Hope is the poor man's bread.
Gary Herbert

Hope is a waking dream.
Aristotle

To live without hope is to cease to live
Fyodor Dostoyevsky

There is a saying in Tibetan,
"Tragedy should be utilized as a source of strength". No matter what
sort of difficulties, how painful experience is, if we lose our hope,
that's our real disaster.
Dalai Lama

When you're at the end of your rope, tie a knot and hold on.
Theodore Roosevelt

All the interests of my reason, speculative as well as practical, combine
in the three following questions: 1. What can I know? 2. What ought
I to do? 3. What may I hope?
Immanuel Kant

This new day is too dear, with its hopes and invitations,
to waste a moment on the yesterdays.
Ralph Waldo Emerson

The pessimist sees difficulty in every opportunity.
The optimist sees the opportunity in every difficulty.
Winston Churchill

In the end, that's what this election is about. Do we participate in a
politics of cynicism or a politics of hope?
Barack Obama

The best way to not feel hopeless is to get up and do something. Don't wait for good things to happen to you. If you go out and make some good things happen, you will fill the world with hope, you will fill yourself with hope.
Barack Obama

If you lose hope, somehow you lose the vitality that keeps moving, you lose that courage to be, that quality that helps you go on in spite of it all. And so today I still have a dream.
Martin Luther King Jr

Hope is such a beautiful word, but it often seems very fragile. Life is still being needlessly hurt and destroyed
Michael Jackson

The miserable have no other medicine, but only hope.
William Shakespeare

Learn from yesterday, live for today, hope for tomorrow. The important thing is not to stop questioning.
Albert Einstein

Success is not final, failure is not fatal: it is the courage to continue that counts.
Winston Churchill

If you are going through hell, keep going.
Winston Churchill

For every dark night there's a brighter day.
Tupac

Hope is the last thing ever lost.
Italian proverb

A leader is a dealer in hope.
Napoleon Bonaparte

Hope and change are hard-fought things.
Michelle Obama

Hope springs eternal in the human breast.
Alexander Pope

Oft hope is born when all is forlorn.
J.R.R. Tolkien

Hope is medicine for a soul that's sick and tired.
Eric Swensson

Hope can get you through anything.
Jamie Ford

We must pass through the darkness, to reach the light.
Albert Pike

Hope is a passion for the possible.
Søren Kierkegaard

Hope costs nothing.
Colette

Hope is a verb with its shirtsleeves rolled up.
David Orr

Hope keeps you alive.
Lauren Olive

I inhale hope with every breath I take.
Sharon Kay Penman

However long the night, the dawn will break.
African proverb

Let your hopes, not your hurts, shape your future.
Robert H. Schuller

Hope is the only universal liar who never loses his
reputation for veracity.
Robert G. Ingersoll

Hope is that thing inside us that insists, despite all the evidence to the
contrary, that something better awaits us if we have the courage to
reach for it and to work for it and to fight for it.
Barack Obama

Hope is important because it can make the present moment less
difficult to bear. If we believe that tomorrow will be better, we can
bear a hardship today.
Thich Nhat Hanh

Hope itself is like a star – not to be seen in the sunshine of prosperity,
and only to be discovered in the night of adversity.
Charles Haddon Spurgeon

Hope is the companion of power, and mother of success; for who so
hopes strongly has within him the gift of miracles.
Samuel Smiles

The best we can hope for in this life is a knothole peek at the shining
realities ahead. Yet a glimpse is enough. It's enough to convince our
hearts that whatever sufferings and sorrows currently assail us aren't
worthy of comparison to that which waits over the horizon.
Joni Eareckson Tada

Lord, make me an instrument of your peace; where there is hatred, let me sow love; where there is injury, pardon; where there is doubt, faith; where there is despair, hope; where there is darkness, light; and where there is sadness, joy.
Francis of Assisi

You are full of unshaped dreams... You are laden with beginnings... There is hope in you...
Lola Ridge

Children are the world's most valuable resource and its best hope for the future.
John F. Kennedy

A person can do incredible things if he or she has enough hope.
Shannon K. Butcher

Hope has a cost. Hope is not comfortable or easy. Hope requires personal risk. It is not about the right attitude. Hope is not about peace of mind. Hope is action. Hope is doing something. The more futile, the more useless, the more irrelevant and incomprehensible an act of rebellion is, the vaster and more potent hope becomes.
Chris Hedges

I believe that imagination is stronger than knowledge. That myth is more potent than history. That dreams are more powerful than facts. That hope always triumphs over experience. That laughter is the only cure for grief. And I believe that love is stronger than death.
Robert Fulghum

It is difficult to say what is impossible, for the dream of yesterday is the hope of today and the reality of tomorrow.
Robert H. Goddard

We need never be hopeless because we can never be irreparably broken.
John Green

A strong mind always hopes and has always cause to hope.
Thomas Carlyle

If winter comes, can spring be far behind?
Percy Bysshe Shelley

Hope and reality lie in inverse proportions.
Jodi Picoult

The best bridge between despair and hope is a good night's sleep.
E. Joseph Cossman

To hear the phrase "our only hope" always makes one anxious, because
it means that if the only hope doesn't work, there is nothing left.

Lemony Snicket

Fairy tales do not tell children the dragons exist. Children already
know that dragons exist. Fairy tales tell children the
dragons can be killed.
G.K. Chesterton

People without hope not only don't write novels, but what is more to
the point, they don't read them.
Flannery O'Connor

Got no check books, got no banks. Still I'd like to express my thanks –
I got the sun in the morning and the moon at night.
Irving Berlin

Think left and think right and think low and think high. Oh, the
things you can think up if only you try!
Dr. Seuss

Fear grows in darkness; if you think there's a bogeyman around,
turn on the light.
Dorothy Thompson

To plant a garden is to believe in tomorrow.
Audrey Hepburn

Look at how a single candle can both defy and define the darkness.
Anne Frank

In the midst of winter, I found there was, within me,
an invincible summer.
Albert Camus

A man devoid of hope and conscious of being so has ceased
to belong to the future.
Albert Camus

Hope is like the sun, which, as we journey toward it, casts the
shadow of our burden behind us.
Samuel Smiles

What oxygen is to the lungs, such is hope to the meaning of life.
Emil Brunner

Sanity may be madness but the maddest of all is to see life as it is
and not as it should be.
Don Quixote

There is no medicine like hope, no incentive so great, and no tonic
so powerful as expectation of something tomorrow.
O. S. Marden

Hope is definitely not the same thing as optimism. It is not the
conviction that something will turn out well, but the certainty that
something makes sense, regardless of how it turns out.
Vaclav Havel

Hope is like a road in the country; there was never a road, but when
many people walk on it, the road comes into existence.
Lin Yutang

Of all ills that one endures, hope is a cheap and universal cure.
Abraham Cowley

He who has never hoped can never despair.
George Bernard Shaw

Hope rises like a phoenix from the ashes of shattered dreams.
S.A. Sachs

Hope is the only bee that makes honey without flowers.
Robert Ingersoll

To eat bread without hope is still slowly to starve to death.
Pearl S. Buck

We promise according to our hopes and perform
according to our fears.
François de La Rochefoucauld

The oil of hope makes life's machinery run smoothly.
James Lendall Basford

In the hopes of reaching the moon men fail to see the flowers
that blossom at their feet.
Albert Schweitzer

Without hope, there is no despair. There is only meaningless suffering.
D. Morgenstern

Faith goes up the stairs that love has built and looks out the
windows which hope has opened.
Charles Haddon Spurgeon

By perseverance the snail reached the ark.
Charles Haddon Spurgeon

In an age of hope, men looked up at the night sky and saw "the
heavens." In an age of hopelessness, they call it simply "space".
Peter Kreeft

You'll stop hurting when you stop hoping.
Guillaume Musso

It is the first purpose of hope to make hopelessness bearable.
Robert Brault

What seems to us as bitter trials are often blessings in disguise.
Oscar Wilde

Hope is not an emotion; it's a way of thinking or a cognitive process.
Brené Brown

Hope is important because it can make the present moment less
difficult to bear. If we believe that tomorrow will be better, we can
bear a hardship today.
Thich Nhat Hanh

Critical thinking without hope is cynicism. Hope without critical
thinking is naïveté.
Maria Popova

Hope is not a strategy. Luck is not a factor. <u>Fear</u> is not an option.
James Cameron

When you stop hoping you start settling.
Valorie Burton

Do not spoil what you have by desiring what you have not;
remember that what you now have was once among the
things you only hoped for.
Epicurus

The natural flights of the human mind are not from pleasure to
pleasure but from hope to hope
Samuel Johnson

He who has <u>health</u> has hope, and he who has hope has everything.
Proverb

The very existence of libraries affords the best evidence that we may
yet have hope for the future of man.
T.S. Eliot

Consult not your fears but your hopes and dreams. Think not about
your frustrations, but about your unfulfilled potential. Concern
yourself not with what you tried and failed in, but with what is still
possible for you to do.
Pope John XXIII

Hope itself is a species of happiness, and, perhaps, the chief happiness which this world affords; but, like all other pleasures immoderately enjoyed, the excesses of hope must be expiated by pain.
Samuel Johnson

A lesson for all of us is that for every loss, there is victory, for every sadness, there is joy, and when you think you've lost everything, there is hope.
Geraldine Solon

The difference between hope and despair is a different way of telling stories from the same facts.
Alain de Botton

To wish was to hope, and to hope was to expect.
Jane Austen

Live, then, and be happy, beloved children of my heart, and never forget, that until the day God will deign to reveal the future to man, all human wisdom is contained in these two words, "Wait and Hope".
Alexandre Dumas

Scared and sacred are spelled with the same letters. Awful proceeds from the same root word as awesome. Terrify and terrific. Every negative experience holds the seed of transformation.
Alan Cohen

All the great spiritual leaders in history were people of hope. Abraham, Moses, Ruth, Mary, Jesus, Rumi, Gandhi, and Dorothy Day all lived with a promise in their hearts that guided them toward the future without the need to know exactly what it would look like.
Henri Nouwen

Hope arouses, as nothing else can arouse, a passion for the possible.
William Sloane Coffin

Never give out while there is hope; but hope not beyond reason,
for that shows more desire than judgment.
William Penn

There is no hope unmingled with fear, and no fear
unmingled with hope.
Baruch Spinoza

Things start out as hopes and end up as habits.
Lillian Hellman

If it were not for hope, the heart would break.
Thomas Fuller

Rock bottom became the solid foundation on which I rebuilt my life.
J.K. Rowling

Never give up. Expect only the best from life and take action to get it.
Catherine Pulsifer

As long as we have hope, we have direction, the energy to move, and
the map to move by.
Lao Tzu

To sit patiently with a yearning that has not yet been fulfilled, and to
trust that, that fulfillment will come, is quite possibly one of the most
powerful 'magic skills' that human beings are capable of. It has been
noted by almost every ancient wisdom tradition.
Elizabeth Gilbert

All human wisdom is summed up in two words; wait and hope.
Alexandre Dumas

When you get into a tight place and everything goes against you, till it seems as though you could not hang on a minute longer, never give up then, for that is just the place and time that the tide will turn.
Harriet Beecher Stowe

What you need is to recognize the possibilities and challenges offered by the present moment, and to embrace them with courage, faith, and hope.
Thomas Merton

Character consists of what you do on the third and fourth tries.
James A. Michener

I knew life began where I stood in the dark, looking out into the light.
Yusef Komunyakaa

Not to give up under any circumstances should be the motto of our life: we shall try again and again, and we are bound to succeed. There will be obstacles, but we have to defy them. [...] The goal is ahead of you. If you do not give up, you are bound to reach your destined goal.
Sri Chinmoy

Courage, it would seem, is nothing less than the power to overcome danger, misfortune, fear, injustice, while continuing to affirm inwardly that life with all its sorrows is good; that everything is meaningful even if in a sense beyond our understanding; and that there is always tomorrow.
Dorothy Thompson

We are made to persist. That's how we find out who we are.
Tobias Wolff

There are far, far better things ahead than anything we leave behind.
C. S. Lewis

Never deprive someone of hope; it may be all they have.
H. Jackson Brown Jr

When the world says, "give up", hope whispers try it one more time.
Unknown

Prayer is man's greatest power!
W. Clement Stone

Whether you've seen angels floating around your bedroom or just
found a ray of hope at a lonely moment, choosing to believe that
something unseen is caring for you can be a life-shifting exercise.
Martha Beck

Religion is the resolute following of the star of hope through
triumphs and tragedies of time.
A. Eustace Haydon

Life is meaningless only if we allow it to be. Each of us has the power
to give life meaning, to make our time and our bodies and our words
into instruments of love and hope.
Tom Head

Many things are possible for the person who has hope. Even more is
possible for the person who has faith. And still more is possible for
the person who knows how to love. But everything is possible for the
person who practices all three virtues.
Brother Lawrence

Hope sees the invisible, feels the intangible,
and achieves the impossible.
Helen Keller

The word hope I take for faith; and indeed, hope is nothing else
but the constancy of faith.
John Calvin

Is prayer your steering wheel or your spare tire?
Corrie ten Boom

A baby is God's opinion that the world should go on.
Carl Sandburg

Hope is some extraordinary spiritual grace that God gives us to
control our fears, not to oust them.
Vincent McNabb

Christ showed us hope transformed into sacrificial love
Chuck Colson

Hope is the word which God has written on the brow of every man.
Victor Hugo

We should ask God to increase our hope when it is small, awaken it
when it is dormant, confirm it when it is wavering, strengthen it when
it is weak, and raise it up when it is overthrown.
John Calvin

Never be afraid to trust an unknown future to a known God.
Corrie ten Boom

For I know the thoughts that I think toward you, says the Lord,
thoughts of peace and not of evil, to give you a future and a hope.
Jeremiah 29:11

So now faith, hope, and love abide, these three;
but the greatest of these is love.
1 Corinthians 13:13

Having hope will give you courage. You will be protected
and will rest in safety.
Job 11:18

Life without idealism is empty indeed. We just hope or
starve to death.
Pearl S. Buck

Courage is like love; it must have hope for nourishment.
Napoleon Bonaparte

Sometimes our light goes out but is blown again into instant flame by
an encounter with another human being.
Albert Schweitzer

We always kept in our hearts the most noble, beautiful feeling that
sets human beings apart: hope.
Manel Loureiro

We live by hope. We do not always get all we want when we want it.
But we have to believe that someday, somehow, some way, it will be
better and that we can make it so.
Hubert H. Humphrey

It was stupid to hope, she knew. But sometimes hope was all you had.
Cassandra Clare

The hope you feel when you are in love is not necessarily for anything
in particular. Love brings something inside you to life. Perhaps it is
just the full dimensionality of your own capacity to feel that returns.
Susan Griffin

They say a person needs just three things to be truly happy in this
world: someone to love, something to do, and something to hope for.
Tom Bodett

The very least you can do in your life is figure out what you hope for.
And the most you can do is live inside that hope. Not admire it from a
distance but live right in it, under its roof.
Barbara Kingsolver

Hope is both the earliest and the most indispensable virtue inherent
in the state of being alive. If life is to be sustained hope must remain,
even where confidence is wounded, trust impaired.
Erik H. Erikson

Love without hope will not survive. Love without faith changes
nothing. Love gives power to hope and faith.
Toba Beta

In joined hands there is still some token of hope,
in the clinched fist none.
Victor Hugo

If you can love someone with your whole heart, even one person,
then there's salvation in life. Even if you can't get together
with that person.
Haruki Murakami

The capacity for hope is the most significant fact of life. It provides
human beings with a sense of destination and the energy to
get started.
Norman Cousins

In each family a story is playing itself out, and each family's story
embodies its hope and despair.
Auguste Napier

My great hope is to laugh as much as I cry; to get my work done
and try to love somebody and have the courage to
accept the love in return.
Maya Angelou

It is hope that gives life meaning. And hope is based on the
prospect of being able one day to turn the actual world into a
possible one that looks better.
François Jacob

How far would you go to keep the hope of love alive?
Nicholas Sparks

One lives in the hope of becoming a memory.
Antonio Porchia

While the heart beats, hope lingers.
Alison Croggon

Hopeful, we are halfway to where we want to go; hopeless,
we are lost forever.
Lao Tzu

Keep a little fire burning; however small, however hidden.
Cormac McCarthy

Never lose hope. Storms make people stronger and never last forever.
Roy T. Bennett

When you have lost hope, you have lost everything. And when you
think all is lost, when all is dire and bleak, there is always hope.
Pittacus Lore

That was all a man needed: hope. It was lack of hope
that discouraged a man.
Charles Bukowski

We dream to give ourselves hope. To stop dreaming –
well, that's like saying you can never change your fate.
Amy Tan

<u>Hope can be a powerful force</u>. Maybe there's no actual magic in it, but
when you know what you hope for most and hold it like a light within
you, you can make things happen, almost like magic.
Laini Taylor

I have learned two lessons in my life: first, there are no sufficient
literary, psychological, or historical answers to human tragedy, only
moral ones. Second, just as despair can come to one another
only from other human beings, hope, too, can be given to one
only by other human beings.
Elie Wiesel

The value of another's experience is to give us hope, not to tell us how
or whether to proceed.
Peter Block

Strange as it may seem, I still hope for the best, even though the best,
like an interesting piece of mail, so rarely arrives, and even when it
does it can be lost so easily.
Lemony Snicket

Even in the mud and scum of things, something always, always sings.
Ralph Waldo Emerson

Never talk defeat. Use words like hope, belief, faith, victory.
Norman Vincent Peale

It's the possibility that keeps me going, not the guarantee.
Nicholas Sparks

Where there is no hope, it is incumbent on us to invent it.
Albert Camus

Faith has to do with things that are not seen and hope with things
that are not at hand.
Thomas Aquinas

Hope begins in the dark, the stubborn hope that if you just show up
and try to do the right thing, the dawn will come.
Anne Lamott

Hope is sweet-minded and sweet-eyed. It draws pictures;
it weaves fancies; it fills the future with delight.
Henry Ward Beecher

As long as there is one upright man, as long as there is one
compassionate woman, the contagion may spread, and the scene is not
desolate. Hope is the thing that is left to us, in a bad time.
E.B. White

If you have made mistakes, there is always another chance for you.
You may have a fresh start any moment you choose, for this thing we
call "failure" is not the falling down, but the staying down.
Mary Pickford

Optimism is the faith that leads to achievement.
Nothing can be done without hope and confidence
Helen Keller

Optimism is an expectation of the future, but hope is a way of experiencing the present. Optimism argues with the predictions of cynicism and bitterness, and is often proved wrong. Hope rejects cynicism and bitterness as unhelpful, and is perennially proved right.
Doug Muder

Hope is a force of nature. Don't let anyone tell you different.
Jim Butcher

Plant seeds of happiness, hope, success, and love; it will all come back to you in abundance. This is the law of nature.
Steve Maraboli

The inability to open up to hope is what blocks trust, and blocked trust is the reason for blighted dreams.
Elizabeth Gilbert

Believe in yourself and all that you are. Know that there is something inside you that is greater than any obstacle.
Christian D. Larson

Where hope would otherwise become hopelessness, it becomes faith.
Robert Brault

Each time a person stands up for an ideal, or acts to improve the lot of others, or strikes out against injustice, he sends forth a tiny ripple of hope, and crossing each other from a million different centers of energy and daring, these ripples build a current that can sweep down the mightiest walls of oppression and resistance.
Robert F. Kennedy

It's important to emphasize that hope is only a beginning; it's not a substitute for action, only a basis for it.
Rebecca Solnit

None who have always been free can understand the terrible
fascinating power of the hope of freedom to those who are not free.
Pearl S. Buck

The past is made out of facts... I guess the future is just hope.
Isaac Marion

Hope – hope in the face of difficulty. Hope in the face of uncertainty.
The audacity of hope.
Barack Obama

Hope is what led a band of colonists to rise up against an empire;

what led the greatest of generations to free a continent and
heal a nation;

what led young women and young men to sit at lunch counters and
brave fire hoses and march through Selma and Montgomery for
freedom's cause.

Hope is what led me here today – with a father from Kenya, a mother
from Kansas;

and a story that could only happen in the United States of America.

Hope is the bedrock of this nation; the belief that our destiny will not
be written for us, but by us;

by all those men and women who are not content to settle for the
world as it is;

who have courage to remake the world as it should be.
Barack Obama

To be hopeful in bad times is based on the fact that human
history is not only of cruelty, but also of compassion, sacrifice,
courage, kindness.
If we see only the worst, it destroys our capacity to do something.
If we remember those times and places where people have behaved
magnificently, this gives us the energy to act.

And if we do act, in however small a way, we don't have to wait for
some grand Utopian future.

The future is an infinite succession of presents, and to live now as we
think human beings should live, in defiance of all that is bad around
us, is itself a marvelous victory.

Howard Zinn

Nothing worth doing is completed in our lifetime, therefore, we are
saved by hope.
Nothing true or beautiful or good makes complete sense in any
immediate context of history;
Therefore, we are saved by faith.
Nothing we do, however virtuous, can be accomplished alone.
Therefore, we are saved by love.
No virtuous act is quite a virtuous from the standpoint of our friend
or foe as from our own;
Therefore, we are saved by the final form of love which is forgiveness.
Reinhold Niebuhr

Listen to the exhortation of the dawn!
Look to this day!
For it is life, the very life of life.
In its brief course lie all the
Verities and realities of your existence.
The bliss of growth,
The glory of action,
The splendor of beauty;

For yesterday is but a dream,
And to-morrow is only a vision;
But to-day well lived makes
Every yesterday a dream of happiness,
And every tomorrow a vision of hope.
Look well therefore to this day!
Such is the salutation of the dawn!
Kalidasa

For what it's worth... it's never too late, or in my case too early, to be whoever you want to be.
There's no time limit.
Start whenever you want.
You can change or stay the same.
There are no rules to this thing.
We can make the best or the worst of it.
I hope you make the best of it.
I hope you see things that startle you.
I hope you feel things you've never felt before.
I hope you meet people who have a different point of view.
I hope you live a life you're proud of, and if you're not, I hope you have the courage to start over again.
F. Scott Fitzgerald

To love means loving the unlovable. To forgive means pardoning the unpardonable. Faith means believing the unbelievable. Hope means hoping when everything seems hopeless.
G.K. Chesterson[134]

When the world
Says, "give up."
Hope whispers
Try it one more time.

Michelle Bengtson
"Hope Prevails"

———————————⟨✕⟩———————————

The right to hope is the
most powerful human
motivation I know.
Hope will guide us
Through.

Aga Khan
49th spiritual leader of the Shia Ismaili Muslims

———————————⟨✕⟩———————————

Chapter 12

The Sounds of Hope

———————◇———————

Hope is hearing the music of the future.

Faith is to dance to it.

Ruben Alves

Throughout my life I have heard that "music is the language of the soul." Truly, music speaks to people of all ages. There are times when I feel stressed or a bit "down in the dumps" and I can go to the piano and practice, or turn on music by Alfie Boe and hear his brilliant soprano voice singing "Bring him home" from Les Miserable, or the Mormon Tabernacle choir singing hymns of the faith, or listen to the organ music of the late Virgil Fox, or an old Beatle's song, or Garth Brooks and Tricia Yearwood singing duet, or Lady Gaga singing anything and the stress will begin to dissipate, and the "blues" will slowly ease away.

Kevin Kniestedt tells the true story of Naomi Wachira who was born and raised in Kenya, studied broadcasting in Chicago, then theology in Seattle. While she always had an impressive singing voice, she sang in choirs since she was five, becoming a professional musician wasn't truly on the radar until 2013, after her father, a pastor in Kenya, passed away.

"He followed his calling; he followed his life passion which was helping people and believing in people. And I think for me it made me realize that when my time is done here on earth, I want to be able to have done something worthwhile and something that would have helped a person here or there, and I knew it was through music."

Six months after her father's passing, she quit her job and dove into music full time. She wants her music to have a positive lasting impact, especially when it comes to dealing with tragedy.[135] Basically, Naomi wanted her music to be an offering of hope to others.

Many years ago, a parishioner in the church where I was serving, was diagnosed with Alzheimer's at the young age of fifty-four. Within five years she was in a nursing home where she stayed in her bed in a fetal position. She was unable to communicate as her mind was almost completely gone.

One day, a new medicine was being tested and she was one selected to be in the trial study. When she took the medicine the first time, she came out of the fetal position and sat up in her bed. Then she stood up and walked out into the hallway into the main gathering room on her floor. She walked to the piano and sat down and began to play a song she had learned in childhood. She could not remember all of it, but enough for the family and medical team to know what it was. When she finished, she walked back to her bed, assumed the fetal position, and remained like that until her death eighteen months later.

Music therapy can offer hope for people with various forms of dementia. CBS News carried an article in their December 2012, issue entitled "Patients with cognitive impairment benefit from singing." In that article it says, "There's growing evidence that music can help people struggling with disorders of the mind, like autism, dementia, and Parkinson's.

Frank Russo, a cognitive scientist doing research at Ryerson University in Toronto, is using new technology to probe the link between sound and the parts of the brain that control movement.

Music therapy can help Parkinson's patients walk and people with Alzheimer's remember, with song lyrics surfacing in the brain even among people who have lost the ability to recognize their own relatives.

Russo is hoping to develop a clearer picture of how music can rehabilitate damaged circuitry and hopes to apply that research to conditions ranging from autism to stroke.[136]

Perhaps you have seen commercials advertising new medicines for those

suffering from psoriasis. One of the people that speaks on the products behalf is Cindi Lauper. She has suffered for many years with the chronic inflammatory condition herself.

In 2019, Cindi released "Hope," her first new single since 2016. She said, "I'm so excited to finally release 'Hope' as a single," Lauper says in a statement. "The song doesn't really have too many words. I wanted everyone to get the message through the feeling of it. With all the craziness going on in the world, we might not agree on much, but I think we can all agree that the world could use a little hope right now. I hope that people get that from the song."

She went on to say, "I swore I wouldn't write a song called 'Hope,'" she told CBS Philly last year. "As soon as I started writing, that's what came out. And I thought to myself, *Well, you lughead, just do it.* People need hope. Everybody needs hope."[137]

As a little boy, I especially loved Sunday night worship. It was "laid-back" where folks dressed down and we sang out of the old Cokesbury Hymnal. One of my favorites went like this:

Like the faint dawn of the morning,
Like the sweet freshness of dew,
Comes the dear whisper of Jesus,
Comforting, tender and true.
Darkness gives way to the sunlight,
While His voice falls on my ear;
Seasons of heaven's refreshing
Call to new gladness and cheer.
(and then the refrain)

Whispering hope, like the song of the angels,
Jesus, Thy love is sweet music to me.
Hope is an anchor to keep us,
Holding both steadfast and sure;
Hope brings a wonderful cleansing,
Thro' His blood, making us pure.
Whispering hope of His coming,
How my heart thrills at His Word!
O to be watching and wating,
Ready to welcome the Lord![138]

The old hymn, "We Shall Overcome" has been a treasured song for those who suffer from racism. Its very words offer a vision of hope where one day we shall be free of hate and injustice. Notice, not only the power in the words, but the overall sense of hope:

We shall overcome,
We shall overcome,
We shall overcome, some day.

Oh, deep in my heart,
I do believe
We shall overcome, some day.

We'll walk hand in hand,
We'll walk hand in hand,
We'll walk hand in hand, some day.

Oh, deep in my heart,
We shall live in peace,
We shall live in peace,
We shall live in peace, some day.

Oh, deep in my heart,
We shall all be free,
We shall all be free,
We shall all be free, some day.

Oh, deep in my heart,
We are not afraid,
We are not afraid,
We are not afraid, TODAY[139]

During my teenage years, Bob Dillon along with Peter, Paul and Mary, sang many "protests" songs during the Vietnam War. I remember seeing and hearing Peter, Paul and Mary singing at the March on Washington, when Martin Luther King, Jr., gave his "I have a dream" speech. One of the most beautiful and hope-filled ones was this one:

How many roads must a man walk down
Before you call him a man?
How many seas must a white dove sail
Before she sleeps in the sand?
How many times must the cannon balls fly
Before they're forever banned?
The answer, my friend, is blowin' in the wind
The answer is blowin' in the wind

How many years can a mountain exist
Before it's washed to the sea?
How many years must some people exist
Before they're allowed to be free?
And how many times can a man turn his head
And pretend that he just doesn't see - the answer
The answer, my friend, is blowin' in the wind
The answer is blowin' in the wind

How many times can a man look up
Before he sees the sky?
How many ears must one person have
Before he can hear people cry?
And how many deaths will it take 'till he knows
That too many people have died?
The answer, my friends, is blowin' in the wind
The answer is blowin' in the wind
Oh, the answer, my friends, is blowin' in the wind
The answer is blowin' in the wind[140]

The hated slave owner, John Newton, left his slave-trading business and became a passionate pastor who preached against the evils of slavery. During his ministry he would write what is known as America's favorite hymn, *Amazing Grace*. Perhaps it is so well-loved because of the hope it offers through God's "amazing" love. Feel the power of hope in each word of this outstanding hymn:

> *Amazing grace! How sweet the sound*
> *That saved a wretch like me!*
> *I once was lost, but now am found;*
> *Was blind, but now I see.*
>
> *'Twas grace that taught my heart to fear,*
> *And grace my fears relieved;*
> *How precious did that grace appear*
> *The hour I first believed!*
>
> *Through many dangers, toils and snares,*
> *I have already come;*
> *'Tis grace hath brought me safe thus far,*
> *And grace will lead me home.*
>
> *The Lord has promised good to me,*
> *His Word my hope secures;*
> *He will my Shield and Portion be,*
> *As long as life endures.*
>
> *Yea, when this flesh and heart shall fail,*
> *And mortal life shall cease,*
> *I shall possess, within the veil,*
> *A life of joy and peace.*
>
> *The earth shall soon dissolve like snow,*
> *The sun forbear to shine;*

But God, Who called me here below,
Will be forever mine.

When we've been there ten thousand years,
Bright shining as the sun,
We've no less days to sing God's praise
Than when we'd first begun. Words:[141]

For centuries, the Jewish people have endured the hatred and injustice of many. Nazism alone exterminated over six million Jews during World War II. In the history of the world, many times that amount have perished from the prejudices of hate-filled people.

One of the things that has sustained them is their faith in the God of Abraham, the Torah, and their music. One of the most stunningly powerful hymns that comes from the hymnody of Judaism is entitled "Hope." It is filled with great pain and yet points to their hope. Notice its passion:

I saw how many they went, too many of them did not return
friends separated, houses broken, tears of families spilled
buds of people flowers that didn't flower
the hope in our heads, the love in our hearts, the dream in our spirits so
wecontinue in our path.

The silence has disappeared for it, again sounds of war
another soldier returns, wrapped in what? In the flag of the country,
blood and tears absorbed by the land and
another shocked mother is left with just a picture
the hope is locked in the heart, the strong nation will not fold over,
'cuz the s.o.b. that can stop Israel hasn't been born.
Give me the hope to accept what there isn't
the strength to change what there is.
Let's continue, our life is in front of us
it's not late because tomorrow is a new day
the dream will perish if we lose the hope
so reach out to love.

You promised a dove, in the sky there's a hawk
brother, poisonous twig pricks, this is not an olive branch
living in a dream, everybody talks about peace
but they shoot, oppress, pull, squeeze the trigger
in a world of suicide attacks, the people are still talking'

living in an illusion of righteousness,
they widen the rift in the nation.
I go through madness every day in order to survive
don't want to live in order to fight,
sub fights in order to live
plant hope, sends out roots
shield in my body for the dream
so it won't be shattered to splinters
enough, enough with the hurt, enough with the tears
a year that the land bleeds not sleeping and why?

Give me the hope to accept what there isn't
the strength to change what there is.
Let's continue, our life is in front of us
it's not late because tomorrow is a new day
the dream will perish if we lose the hope
so reach out to love

G-d, give me the hope to accept what there isn't
give me the courage to try to fix the world.
Let's continue, our life is in front of us
it's not late because tomorrow is a new day
the dream will perish if we lose the hope
so reach out to love

G-d, give me the hope to accept what there isn't
Give me the strength to change what is
Give me the courage to try to fix the world.

Let's continue, our life is in front of us
It's not late because tomorrow is a new day
The dream will perish if we lose the hope
So reach out to love.[142]

There are hymns of hope in most religions. And there are songs of hope in almost every genre of music. Whether the background music is an organ, piano, guitars and drums, symphony, or simply a person singing acapella, hope can be found.

Other sounds can be instruments of hope besides music. It is said that a baby can distinguish the sound of the mother's voice above all other voices. Her voice can bring hope to the baby crying or in distress. Numerous times I have witnessed a baby screaming in the crib (at home or at the church nursery) and when the mother comes in the room speaking softly, the child will begin to stop crying and when the mother puts the child in her arms and whispers in the ear, the cries stop and the child is at peace.

In my own life, when the phone rings and I hear the familiar voice of a friend or a member of the family, I will often feel a sense of peace and hope. This was especially true of my parents. When they were living, we talked almost daily, and I eagerly anticipated hearing their voices to know that they were feeling well. Since I lived the closest to them of their four children, I looked after them throughout their retirement years. I cherished their wisdom and their deep love for all of their offspring. Their voices brought a sense of stability and security to my life.

Other sounds that can offer hope:

> Sound of an ice cream truck
> Sound of birds chirping from a nest
> Sound of waves crashing against the shore
> Sound of people clapping
> Sound of people partying and having fun
> Sound of the doorbell knowing a friend is coming to visit
> Sound of a movie beginning in a cinema
> Sound of water: waterfalls, shower water, ocean, and rain
> Sound of children playing on the playground or sporting event

Sound of dinner being prepared

Sound of wind chimes

Sound of a washing machine or dryer or dishwasher

Sound of a tractor tilling up the soil in preparation for planting seeds

Sound of a boat as it lifts a skier up on the water

Sound of church bells

Sound of wind howling through the trees

Sound of a person whistling as they walk down the street

Sound of a book being open by a youth

Sound of school bells

Sound of the newspaper being opened on Sunday morning

Sound of a police whistler signaling our turn to go forward

Sound of tailgaters before a big football game

Sound of cheering on the team

Sound of letters being opened from friends

Sound of packages being opened

Sound of lights being turned on in a dark house

Sound of a parent's voice

Sound of Aretha Franklin and Diana Ross

Sound of James Earl Jones' voice

Sound of my car cranking up

Sound of an umbrella opening

Sound of my phone telling me I have mail

Sound of ducks quacking and geese flying

Sound of silence

Sound of hearing someone saying my name

Sound of a soda can being opened

Sound of "Alexia" telling me what the weather will be like today

Sound of a British accent

Sound of a child's laughter when tickling them

Sound of baby's cooing while holding them

Sound of Andy Griffith's voice
Sound of wood crackling in a roaring fire
Sound of bacon sizzling
Sound of fireworks on Fourth of July
Sound of a cork popping
Sound of a train's whistle
Sound of a violin
Sound of a grandfather clock ticking
Sound of a kettle boiling
Sound of a lawn mower in the summer
Sound of crickets chirping
Sound of popcorn popping
sound of the ocean in a seashell
Sound of a clock being wound
Sound of the clicking of a camera
Sound of my favorite song on the radio
Sound of "I love you!"
Sound of tap dancing
Sound of tennis balls being hit back and forth
Sound of a golf club hitting a golf ball
Sound of my children's footsteps while learning to walk
Sound of the "wave" at a Braves game
Sound of the national anthem
Sound of the lamp turning off and sleep is on the way
Sound of taps and reveille playing at a burial
Sound of trumpets on Easter morning

What sounds offer you hope? Most likely, more than you know!

It's always something, to know
You've done the most you could.
But, don't leave off hoping,
Or it's of no use doing anything.
Hope, hope to the last!

Charles Dickens

———————✕———————

Chapter 13

The smell of hope

———◇———

Hope feels like the smell of freshly baked bread.

Sahana Nagaraja

When I was a little boy, I loved to walk up on the front porch of my grandparent's home, open the door that led directly into the kitchen and smell the scent of my grandmother's cooking. In the morning would be the smell of biscuits, bacon, and coffee; in the afternoon it would be the smell of vegetables cooking in lard; and in the evening it would be the smell of roast beef or fried chicken. These smells gave me a sense of feeling *home, safe,* and that *all was right in the world.* I knew that when I sat down at the table in her kitchen, the food would be extraordinarily delicious, cooked with great love and care.

For my grandmother, food was a priority. It was her way of expressing love. The smells that flowed like incense throughout the house, gave me a blessed feeling of hope that I would always be welcomed there, that nourishment would be provided, and that love would always abound. Just the thought of going to their home gave me immense hope. I anticipated being swallowed up in the arms of my grandmother's hugs as the smells from her kitchen enveloped me with assurance that I would be well-fed. I knew I was loved.

My wife, Kandy, learned to make homemade bread from her aunts Florrie and Ellagene. The bread was not made in a machine, rather it was a process that took several days to produce. When the time came for it to be baked in the oven, the smell filled our home with the most wonderful aroma.

Her bread not only had an exquisite taste, but its smell filled my lungs with joy. She referred to baking this bread as a ministry. She would take it to the sick, the grieving, to newcomers, and to anyone she knew in need. There were times when the mission area of the church asked her to bake several loaves to be sold at their "silent" auction. Amazingly, people paid as much as $35.00 a loaf! People called it "Kandy-bread!"

After twenty-five years of baking the bread, she decided to take a year off to help plan our daughter's wedding. After the year off, she had gotten used to not making it and decided to take more time off until I came home and told her about a visit I had made one afternoon to a parish member who was dying.

Jerry was a giant in the church. He was one of the most respected men in both church and community. He was diagnosed with inoperable cancer and sent home to die. When I made the first visit to his home, he was in a chair in the den wrapped in blankets. He was emaciated and in great pain. Before I left, I asked him what I (and the church) could do for him. Without a moment's hesitation he said, "you can pray for me and then go home and tell you wife that I would love some of her homemade bread."

Once the words were out of my mouth, my wife went into the kitchen and began the whole process of preparing the "starter" so that in a few days the bread could be baked. She would go the "second mile" to give a dying man his final wish.

When I walked into his home to take the bread, I was barely in the door when he spoke from the den. He said, "Honey, that must be our pastor, I can smell the bread." Hope was in the air!!! His eyes lit up like the sun and a huge smile was on his face. His wife immediately took the bread into the kitchen and cut him a piece and took it to him. He devoured it. As he ate it, I could see tears gathering in his eyes. Then the tears fell down his cheeks. I went to him and hugged his neck and he told me what this act of kindness meant to him. I told him there would be more coming. Bread, in its amazingly wonderful smell and taste, became a sense of hope for him.

Each Wednesday for many years in the church where I was pastor for eighteen years, I looked forward to the kitchen "angels" making their way into the kitchen and begin cooking the food that would serve our congregation for dinner that evening. The first thing they did was to make cinnamon rolls. The scent from the kitchen permeated the entire facility. The smell drew people together as we anticipated someone from the kitchen to burst through the doors with a cart ready to serve all the staff and clergy. As we were served, we laughed, told stories, and shared thoughts about ministry. Each Wednesday, the smells from the church kitchen gave us a hope that soon we would be together in community.

There are many smells that can offer hope:

- The antiseptic smell of a hospital or doctor's office
- Approaching rain
- Honeysuckle, gardenias, roses
- Movie popcorn
- Classroom chalk
- Polished church pews
- Pizza
- Bbq
- Candles
- New car
- Coffee
- Victory
- Freshly cut grass
- A new book
- Garlic
- Spearmint
- Peppermint
- Christmas trees
- New shoes
- Bakery
- Lavender
- Barn
- Citrus
- Forest
- Crayons
- Elmer's glue

- Polished brass
- Lilies
- Vanilla flavoring
- Pine trees
- Fresh cut wood
- Sea breeze
- Mint
- Oranges
- Coconut
- Chocolate
- Baby powder
- Baby lotion
- Hair after being washed
- Old Spice
- Puppies
- Fresh money
- Pipe
- Beer
- Tobacco
- Swimming pool chlorine
- Hardware stores
- Wine
- Horses
- Fried chicken
- Nail polish
- Fireplace
- Your own home
- Your spouse's cologne or perfume
- Fresh laundry
- Old baseball gloves
- Fresh paper
- The Bible
- Carnivals
- Magazines
- New Band-aids
- Butterscotch
- Sunscreen
- Art rooms
- Playdough
- Saunas
- Leather
- Warm cookies
- Pancakes
- shampoo
- Bacon
- Clothes from the cleaners
- Hay
- Antiques
- Newspapers
- Mouthwash
- Dirt
- Apple cider
- Pumpkin pie
- Soaps
- British Sterling
- Hamburgers cooking on the grill
- Watermelon

If any of these smells bring a sense of hope, it is usually because they bring back special memories.

My father wore a leather jacket that still has his scent. He died in 2005, and I cherish that coat. Often, I will go to it just to smell it and feel close to him. As I am filled with the scent of him, I also am filled with the hope of all he brought into my life and that maybe one day, I will be remembered with such affection and admiration.

Good people smell of closeness, hugs and affection. We tend to be more open because we feel close to them and they make us feel at home.

Throughout my life, one of the best places where true inclusivity exists is at a barbeque at a fairground. It is not uncommon to see older folks, youth, and children gather to eat. Also, there are Christians and Jews, Muslims and atheists; republicans and democrats and libertarians and independents; gays, straights, men and women, rich, poor, happy and sad; red and yellow, black and white, thin and obese, educated and uneducated, even vegetarians...gathered together under the delicious smell of smoke from the fires sustaining good food! When viewed from a distance, the scene is a foretaste of the kingdom of God, where we are gathered at the banquet of heaven and seated at the table of life!

**Hope is the
Only thing
Stronger
Than fear**

———————∝———————

Chapter 14

The Taste of hope

———————✕———————

To love is to believe, to hope,
To know; tis an essay,
A taste of heaven below!

Copied

When I was a child, Sunday lunch was the best meal of the week. My mother would get up early on Sunday morning and fry chicken. The wonderful smell filled our home with expectation and a bit of drooling. I could not get to church fast enough to have Sunday school and worship so I could get home and get to my place at the dining room table. We ate in our Sunday clothes and were expected to sit up straight and have the best of table manners.

Along with the huge plate of fried chicken, mother prepared rice and gravy, green beans, (in the summertime, lots of homegrown vegetables), bread and dessert. My older sisters and I fought over who got to eat the "pully-bone" or "wish-bone" and who we would share it with after the meal to see whose wish would come true!

My dad's stepmother (his mother died when he was young) would always prepare fried apple pies when we ate at her house. I cannot remember anything else she put on our plates, but I will never forget those pies!

Eating is especially important throughout the Bible. Lauren Winner, in her wonderful book *Wearing God*, says that,

"it would not be an exaggeration to say that the Bible is a culinary manual, concerned from start to finish about how to eat, what to eat, when to eat. Food is the first way the Bible shows that God intends to provide for humanity: all those seed-bearing plants and trees with fruit in the garden of Eden given to Adam and Eve to eat."[143]

During the Exodus (that lasted forty years) we read that God provided for the Israelites enough food for each day. It was called "manna." Without it, the wandering people of God would have died of starvation.[144]

The beautiful twenty-third Psalm says ""you prepare a table before me in the presence of mine enemies."[145] It is important to God that we never shy away from those who do not like us or consider us an enemy. We are to even eat with them!

Notice the words in Isaiah about the expectation of the Great Feast on the "Last Day" and the importance of food:

> *"On this mountain the LORD Almighty will prepare*
> ***a feast of rich food for all peoples,***
> *a banquet of aged wine—*
> *the best of meats and the finest of wines.*
> *On this mountain he will destroy*
> *the shroud that enfolds all peoples,*
> *the sheet that covers all nations;*
> *he will swallow up death forever.*
> *The Sovereign LORD will wipe away the tears*
> *from all faces;*
> *he will remove the disgrace of his people*
> *from all the earth."[146] (Isaiah 25:6-8)*

There are echoes of this prophecy being fulfilled in the last book of the bible (Revelation) with the *Marriage Supper of the Lamb*[147] and the "new heavens and the new earth."[148]

Jesus was one who talked frequently about food. Notice the following passages:

- *"What sign are you going to give us then…our ancestors ate the manna…give me the bread so I will never be hungry again.*[149]

- *"I tell you I will not drink of this fruit of the vine from now on **until that day when I drink it anew with you in my Father's kingdom**."*[150]

- *"When the hour came, Jesus and his apostles reclined at the table. And he said to them, 'I have eagerly desired **to eat this Passover** with you before I suffer. For I tell you, I will not eat it again until it finds fulfillment in the kingdom of God.' After taking the cup, he gave thanks and said, 'Take this and divide it among you. For I tell you I will not drink again of the fruit of the vine until the kingdom of God comes.'*[151] (Luke 22:16-18)

- *Blessed is the man who will eat at the **feast** in the kingdom of God"*[152]

- *"And I confer on you a kingdom, just as my Father conferred one on me, so that you may **eat and drink at my table** in my kingdom and sit on thrones, judging the twelve tribes of Israel."*[153]

- *"People will come from east and west and north and south and will take their places at the **feast** in the kingdom of God."*[154]

- *"It will be good for those servants whose master finds them watching when he comes. I tell you the truth, he will dress himself to serve, will have them recline at the table and will come and wait on them."*[155]

- *"And while they went to buy, the bridegroom came, and those who were ready went in with him to the marriage feast; and the door was shut."*[156]

- *"My flesh is real food, and my blood is real drink:*[157]

- In John 21:1-12, Jesus cooks breakfast for his disciples following the resurrection.[158]

- In the Emmaus Road story, Jesus is known in the "breaking of bread."[159]

- Jesus refers to himself as "The bread of life."[160]

Notice the importance of the bread and cup in Paul's writings:

Because there is one bread, we who are many are one body, for we all partake of the one bread.[161]

*"For whenever you eat this bread and drink this cup, you proclaim the Lord's death **until he comes**."*[162]

In each of the Synoptic Gospels and in 1 Corinthians 11, the Words for the Institution of the Lord's Supper look forward to a fulfillment in the future. A key element in our own celebration of the Lord's Supper is future looking as well.

The Book of Revelation also refers to *the Great Banquet*. In a promise to overcomers in his letter to the churches, Jesus says:

*"He who has an ear, let him hear what the Spirit says to the churches. To him who overcomes, I will give the right **to eat from the tree of life**, which is in the paradise of God."*[163]

Revelation culminates with the Marriage Supper of the Lamb:

"Then I heard what sounded like a great multitude, like the roar of rushing waters and like loud peals of thunder, shouting:

'Hallelujah!
For our Lord God Almighty reigns.
Let us rejoice and be glad
and give him glory!

For the wedding of the Lamb has come,
and his bride has made herself ready.
Fine linen, bright and clean,
was given her to wear.'

Then the angel said to me, 'Write: "Blessed are those who are
*invited to **the wedding supper of the Lamb!"'** And he added,*
'These are the true words of God."'[164]

When he said, "I am the bread of life," He must have meant he was scattering bits of himself Like a trail of crumbs leading us to speak and act and Scatter forgiveness in his name to the ends of the earth.

Susan Springer

Bread and wine are important throughout the bible. John Calvin once said, "Wine is God's special drink. The purpose of good wine is to inspire us to a livelier sense of gratitude to God.[165] Wine is a symbol of God's grace.

The book of Acts tells that at Pentecost, bystanders thought the disciples were drunk at 9:00 in the morning. Instead of being drunk on wine, they were filled with the Holy Spirit, acting differently than they normally did.[166]

Even the beautiful Psalm 23 mentions "my cup runneth over." When experiencing the love of God, our lives are filled to overflowing with new life, joy and fulfillment. However, the "overuse" of alcohol can result in disease, destruction, and death. There are Biblical passages that speak against getting drunk on alcohol.[167]

To be invited to a meal is an offering of hope. Inclusion almost always brings hope and affirmation.

JoAnna Gaines' magazines and books are about preparing the home to look its best and the center of the home is the kitchen where the food is prepared. She goes to great length to ensure the table is set properly and beautifully. Her specialty is not only in her ability to decorate houses, but also her fabulous and delicious recipes. Her cookbooks are filled with multitudes of tasteful delights that are easy to prepare. These are not only for family, but for friends and other guests to the home.

Last year, our family Christmas celebration ended with the whole family driving to our local fire station and delivering a meal to the firefighters. We did this to try to set an example to our grandchildren that Christmas is not all about them and their receiving of gifts, but the importance of helping others, thanking others, and taking the time to give of our resources.

The grandchildren made small gifts for each of the firefighters and helped to make the cookies and cake for their desserts. We enjoyed a few tastes of each as we prepared for them. The taste of hope is always delicious!

Because of the Covid-19 pandemic, my wife and I are not able to invite all the people we normally have to our home at thanksgiving. So, we have decided to prepare special desserts to take to their homes instead. It is our intention that we are offering hope to them as they taste, not only the food prepared, but the special ingredient of love that is mixed with the food when delivered.

Life may not be the party
we hoped for,
But while we're here
We should
Dance.

Unknown

—————⋈—————

Chapter 15

The feeling of Hope

————————⟨✕⟩————————

People hope to touch the sky.
I dream of kissing it.

Krista Ritchie

From the moment we are born, touch is vitally important. We have learned that babies who do not have sufficient touch in the first year of life will develop "Child Attachment Disorder." When a mother does not connect with her baby in the first year of life the following can happen:

- The baby cries inconsolably.
- The mother or caregiver does not seem to react to the baby when the child is distressed.
- The mother or carer does not respond to the baby's needs - for example, hunger or needing a nappy change.
- The mother or carer does not seem to smile at the baby or have any eye contact.
- Later, once attachment disorder has developed, signs might include:
- The baby or child does not turn to his/her mother or main caregiver when upset.
- The baby or child avoids being touched or comforted.

265

- The baby or child does not smile or respond when interacting with an adult.
- The child does not show any affection towards his/her parent or caregiver.
- The baby or child does not seem to be upset in situations where you might expect them to be upset.
- The child does not play with toys or engage in interactive games with others.
- The child has difficult, aggressive behavior towards other children or adults.
- The child is very withdrawn and does not interact with other children or adults.
- The child is anxious, fearful, or depressed.
- The child is unable to control his/her temper or anger.
- The child is not getting on very well at school.
- By the time the child is a teenager, they may be more likely to be in trouble with the police. They may have anxiety, depression or phobias.

Or:

- The child is inappropriately friendly to children or adults they don't know.
- The child may hug people they don't know, or in inappropriate situations (a doctor or teacher for example).
- The child has no wariness of strangers and may go off with somebody they do not know without checking with their parents or caregiver.[168]

When I was a little boy, I had numerous earaches and even had one of my eardrums to break requiring surgery (mastoid). Then I had to have tonsils and adenoids removed. Often, I would run a fever and my mother would take a washcloth and let cold water pour over it and she would then put it on my forehead. I can still remember the way she would pat my head and my cheeks with that soothing touch of the cold cloth. Though not cognizant of it, that action offered me hope, a hope that I would be well.

There were also times she would rub *Vick's Vapor Rub* on my chest. Once again, her touch brought relief.

As a pastor, I have often been with the sick and held their hands as I prayed for them. Sometimes, I would take oil and put it on my thumb and make the sign of the cross on their forehead. On confirmation Sundays, I would put my hand on the heads of the confirmands (in the tradition of the early church which is called "the laying on of hands.") and say to them:

> *"(the name of the person), the Lord defend you with his heavenly grace and by his Spirit confirm you in the faith and fellowship of all true disciples of Jesus Christ.*[169]

In Baptism, I would dip my hand in the baptismal fount and put water on the head of the person(s) being baptized and say to them:

> *"I baptize you in the name of the Father, the Son and Holy Spirit. You are marked with God's eternal love."*

The gift of touch can be a tremendous means to hope. A simple handshake, a hug, a kiss on the cheek, the pat on the back, the holding of a loved one's hands, can all be agents offering hope.

In 1990, I felt like I was having a stroke. I told my wife to get me to the doctor quickly. When I arrived, all the doctor did was to put his hand on my chest and asked me to touch his hand with my chin. I could not move my neck. He said, "you have to get to the emergency room right now" and he put me in his car and drove me there. (My wife brought me with our three children, and she had to take them back home and get my parents to watch them so she could come to the hospital) On the way, he said, "You are either having a stroke, meningitis or encephalitis." I told him I wanted more choices!

When we arrived, he immediately took spinal fluid from my back, and then I was carted off to have a cat scan. While in the cat scan, he stood at my feet and gently patted them. He spoke words that meant the world to me, "I will be beside you through this." He was.

When the technicians brought in the results of the spinal tap and the cat scan, he said, "You have encephalitis. You will be quarantined. You have a 50-50 chance of survival." He rode with me up the elevator to my room and stayed with me until my wife could make it.

To this day, I remember his care for me. His touch brought me a hope that sustained me through the whole ordeal.

Several years later, this doctor's daughter was killed in a car wreck. She was a beautiful young woman in her sophomore year of college where she was studying to be a physician. I immediately went to his home. After we talked about funeral arrangements and her memorial service, he walked me outside to my car. There, the tears streamed down his face, and I put my arms around him and held him. I had no words. All I could do was embrace him in such a way that he would have hope and peace during this great darkness. As he had cared for me, so I wanted to care for him.

In the mid-1980's, there were six men in the church where I was serving at the time who were diagnosed with AIDS. All were hospitalized (and all died within the same year.) and as their pastor, I knew I needed to go and be with them. I was very afraid of the disease since at that time, no one knew how it was contracted.

When I arrived for the first visit, I was put in a gown and face mask. I walked over to the bed and saw the look of fear in the eyes of the young man lying there. He knew he was going to die. Seeing that the gown he was wearing covered his shoulder and upper arm, I put my hand on him and told him that the church was praying for him, that as his pastor, I was there for him. I continually patted his shoulder and held his arm while I prayed. I would repeat this with all the others dying from the same disease.

The whole time I was dealing with those who suffered from AIDS, I thought of Jesus who touched lepers. His touch brought healing and hope to them. He touched the dying, touched the dead and brought them to life, and he healed with his gentle and loving hands on a person's head.

Jesus even washed the feet of his disciples, a job that was only performed by the housekeeper or a slave. No rabbi would ever do such a thing, but Jesus knew the importance of touch. It is amazingly endearing to picture him squatting down on his knees, removing the shoes of each disciple, taking a cloth and dipping it into a bowl of water, and tenderly washing each foot from all of its dust and dirt. Afterwards, he takes a towel and dries them.

When Jesus completed the process, he stood up and said to them, "As I have done for you, you must do for others. I have set an example before you."[170] Jesus literally meant for all who follow him to serve one another. When we follow that commandment, we bring hope into the world.

Perhaps one of the most beautiful illustrations of touch I have ever heard was when the father of James Dobson died, he brought his mother to the funeral home to see her husband's body. He said that his mother simply stood for several minutes looking at him from the top of his head to the tips of his feet. And then slowly, but tenderly, she went to his face, took it in her hands and kissed his forehead, then his cheeks and then his lips. She drank in the face that she had loved for many decades. And then she patted his chest, arms, stomach, the pelvic area, his legs and then wrapped her hands around his feet. After several minutes, she let go and walked out of the room. Her need to say good-bye to her beloved lover was best done with touch instead of words.

Many of the services of the church deal with touch: I have mentioned baptism already, but also, when I pull a piece of bread from the loaf during the sacrament of the Lord's supper, I put it in the hands of the congregant, purposely touching them with my hand and I say, "This is the body of Christ given for you." My touch, I pray, is felt as the hand of Christ offering them his great love.

During the Ash Wednesday service, the beginning of the liturgical season of Lent, I would put my thumb into the "bowl" holding the ashes and I would put the sign of the cross on the foreheads of all who would receive them.

At weddings, during the pronouncement of marriage, I have the couple holding both of their hand together and I put my hand on top of theirs as I say, "I announce that you are husband and wife together, in the name of the Father, Son and Holy Spirit."

After worship, I would always stand at the door to the sanctuary and shake hands with people, often hugging them. This was a great way of bonding with the congregation as well as bringing touch to some who never received it during the week.

When anyone united with the church through membership, they were offered "the right hand of fellowship." Then they would recess with the clergy to the front of the church where the congregation could greet them with hugs and handshakes.

When completing the committal at the grave of a loved one, I go to each family member and enfold my hands around theirs and offer words of hope. I have always believed that the touch was far more important at that time than any words I could possibly say.

Every first Sunday of October, the church celebrates the "blessing of animals." This is done in memory of Saint Francis of Assisi. People come to the church and bring their pets: dogs, cats, rabbits, iguanas, birds, snakes, turtles, horses, tarantulas, frogs, and other living creatures, and I would put my hands on them (except the tarantulas) and bless them. Often, people would want me to hold their pets in my arms and love on them. Fortunately, I am a "pet-person" so it was never an inconvenience nor a problem.

Once a quarter, the church had "healing" services. These were beautiful services where we offered prayers for all who were suffering from physical, mental, emotional, or spiritual "disease." Usually near the end of the service, there was an invitation to come to the altar to kneel and I would put my hands on their heads and have a prayer for healing. For those who wanted it, I would anoint them with oil, putting the sign of the cross on their foreheads with my thumb.

When I was a child, my father was good about picking me up and holding me. Often, I sat in his lap and hugged him. He would hold my hand when crossing the street. But when I was in the fifth grade, I began to notice a difference. Though he was always loving, instead of hugging me, he shook my hand. It was obvious he was uncomfortable with any other kind of touching. For the most part, men in his generation did not show physical affection to their sons.

I never saw my dad hug another man. He was incredibly careful with hugging women and mainly just shook hands. As a pastor and a husband, he never wanted to be in a position that would cause any doubt in the minds of his parishioners that his intentions were anything but the highest of morals and ethics.

When I married, I told my wife that when we had children, I would always hug them no matter their ages. To this day, I still hug my sons and kiss them on the cheek when we gather. I have no problem hugging my male friends and am thankful we can do that. I love to hug period. For me, it is healing.

The youth minister of the church, where I spent the last years of ministry as a pastor, would end each Sunday evening time with all the young people by having them gather in a huge circle and they would sing a song, have a prayer and then he would shout "hug ten people before you leave here." It was amazing to see teenage boys hugging one another, teenage girls hugging one another and teenage boys and girls hugging. They became close-knit by such actions.

We still live in somewhat of a "homophobic" world, particularly with men. Women seem to be comfortable holding hands and kissing one another on the cheek without a thought to being misunderstood as a homosexual advance. Men are not quite that comfortable although I have had a few men to kiss my cheek at a wedding, funeral or after a sermon. None of them were "sexual advances" or could be mistaken for anything but a loving gesture of affirmation. I am grateful that men (in general) are more and more able to express outward expressions of affection without feeling paranoid about their sexuality.

I have been impressed with some celebrity father-son relationships where pictures of them expressing their love for one another has been photographed and printed in national magazines and newspapers. Such photographs can offer hope to men who have been afraid to physically express their love to their own fathers or important men in their lives. Some include Michael Douglas kissing his father, Blake Shelton kissing Gwen Stefani's father, Tony Danza hugging his son, and Chris Pine embracing his father.

Notice the male-bonding in sports. Men often jump into each other's arms, chest-bump, hug, and slap each other on the buttocks. These reactions seem to come naturally bringing a greater closeness to each other.

Tiffany Field, director of the Touch Research Institute at the University of Miami School of Medicine, says that "touch is the first, and perhaps most profound, language we learn when we're very young. It might have a more immediate impact than words because it is physical and leads to a chain of bioelectric and chemical changes that basically relax the nervous system."[171]

She goes on to say that "touch has been found, among other things, to reduce stress, heart rate and blood pressure. Touch has even been found to lower the level of cortisol in the body (especially in women) which, when elevated, impedes our working memory and, most critically, the immune system's resiliency.

It should be great news that something free, widely available and lacking in harmful side effects is so good for us, but it gets ignored in a touch-averse culture like ours. According to Jay Skidmore, former chairman of the psychology department of Seattle Pacific University, 'social-cultural trends in America have focused for decades on reducing touch.'

Of course, it would not be surprising if recent allegations of sexual assault by public figures make people even more skittish about initiating or receiving physical contact. Indeed, many men self-police their hands around each other. In younger men this manifests itself in the ubiquitous "No homo!" response if they accidentally touch another guy, and in older men it translates into the same awkward discomfort (read: fear) that many men, experience when faced with reaching out to another male, even an intimate. Yet these reactions are a relatively modern phenomenon. Men shared the same bed with strangers in early American taverns, and scholarship is unearthing letters — including ones from Abraham Lincoln — revealing how men sometimes nurtured same-sex friendships that were more emotionally and physically intimate in nonsexual ways than the relationships they shared with women. Some 19th-century tintypes, such as those collected in the book "Bosom Buddies: A Photo History of Male Affection," illustrate this.

The fear that girds the lack of platonic touch among American men also fuels the destructive force of their hands, a *2002 study in the journal Adolescence* found. Dr. Field was the lead author of the study, which looked at 49 cultures. "The cultures that exhibited minimal physical affection toward their young children had significantly higher rates of adult violence," she said. But "those cultures that showed significant amounts of physical affection toward their young children had virtually no adult violence."

Perhaps it's not surprising, then, that *a 2011 study from the Kinsey Institute* at Indiana University, published in the Archives of Sexual Behavior, found that among more than 1,000 heterosexual middle-aged and older married couples in five countries, hugging and kissing were more central to the happiness of men than they were to women."[172]

David Linden, renowned neuroscientist suggests:

- Newborns that are given nurturing touch grow faster and have more improved mental and motor skill development.
- Children raised with more physical interaction tended to be less aggressive and violent.
- Partners who cuddle have been shown to have lower stress levels and blood pressure and improved immune function.
- Elderly people who receive the soothing, affirming experience of touch have been shown to better handle the process of aging and passing with dignity.
- From the moment we are born to the final days of our lives, touch acts as a central aspect of the human experience — impacting our physical, mental and emotional health, and quite literally shaping the way we go through our lives.[173]

Linden's insights on our technological means of communication are also worth noting: "Humans have lived in social groups now for hundreds of thousands of years. And so, we're extraordinarily good at reading other people's facial expressions, tone of voice, body language. We're extremely well-adapted for that. **But when we communicate via email, text or social media, all of those unspoken signals are impoverished.** It's the difference between sending a sad emoji and actually reaching out and touching someone to console them. It's the difference between hugging someone and just texting them that you are thinking of them. So, there is this missing component of the human experience. There is no real substitute for touch. The bond it creates, the trust it conveys – it's part of our evolutionary background. I really can't stress the power of touch enough and the massive benefits it has for yourself and for others."[174]

Following the resurrection of Jesus, one of the disciples, Thomas, missed the first appearance of Jesus when he revealed himself to the others. When told of their experience of the "risen" Christ, Thomas said to them, "I will not believe until I can touch him."[175]

Though attributed to the great Saint Teresa of Avila, the following poem is not found in any of her writings:

"Christ has no body now but yours. No hands, no feet on earth but yours. Yours are the eyes through which he looks compassion on this world. Yours are the feet with which he walks to do good. Yours are the hands through which he blesses all the world. Yours are the hands, yours are the feet, yours are the eyes, you are his body. Christ has no body now on earth but yours."

Go forth to be the body of Christ in this world starving for love.

A sunrise
And
A sunset
Reminds us of
New beginnings
And the hope of
A better tomorrow

Richard Krawczyk

———————∝———————

Chapter 16

The Humor of Hope

———————◇———————

"Laughter is a symbol of hope,
and it becomes one of our greatest needs of life,
right up there with toilet paper."

Erica Rhodes

Numerous times during my years as a pastor, I would have days where I was emotionally, physically, and even spiritually exhausted. Members would be in several hospitals all over the Atlanta area, deaths occurred, trouble with teens, and those with marital unrest would fill my calendar. Though I love people and love ministry, sometimes I felt like the old commercial "Calgon, take me away!" I dreamed of being in a large bathtub filled with warm water, bubbles surrounding me and soft music playing in the room. I could relax and fill re-created and renewed.

First of all, I did not have such a room. Secondly, we did not use Calgon. Lastly, there was not always time for such a dream to come true!

When life became a bit too much, I would go home and turn on a comedy or maybe go to a funny movie. Just to see Steve Martin put a smile on my face. Robin Williams could make me "belly-laugh." One of his movies I could see over and over and never tire: Mrs. Doubtfire. He was masterful in it.

Other stars like Goldie Hawn, Chris Rock and Eddie Murphy send me into fits of laughter. Saturday Night Live can be enormously funny. I enjoy the humor of Steven Colbert, James Corden, Jimmy Kimmell, Trevor Noah, and John Oliver.

Who can forget Carol Burnett's show where she dressed up Scarlett O'Hara in a green dress made from curtain still on the rod? Or Tim Conway as the dentist who accidently gives Novocain to himself instead of Harvey Korman!

What about the humor from shows like Friends, I Love Lucy, Seinfeld, Cheers, Frazier, All in the Family, Good Times, Sanford and Son, Roseann, Andy Griffith, and Dick Van Dyke? We crave them!

Movies that bring great laughter: Blazing Saddles, The Jerk, Coming to America, National Lampoon's Vacation, Monty Python's Life of Brian, Planes, Trains and Automobiles. Meet the Parents, Barbershop, My Big Fat Greek Wedding, and others.

Humor is healing balm to a suffering soul. Humor allows us to know it is okay not to take life so seriously. Even in the midst of great tragedy, crisis, and sadness, humor points us to something greater than our issues. Humor allows us to reconnect to our humanness. Indeed,

Wherever there is laughter, there is hope.

Abraham Lincoln was often told that he was not a pleasant looking person. One day he responded this way: "If I were two-faced, would I be wearing this one?"[176]

Let me share a few that have brought a smile to my face every time I read them:

- I don't' need google, my wife knows everything!
- This year instead of giving gifts, I'm giving my opinion.
- If you see me talking to myself, I'm getting expert advice.
- Went to an antique show and people began bidding on me.

- We are too broke to buy anything.
- We know who we are voting for.
- We have found Jesus.
- Seriously, unless you are giving away beer,
- Please go away!
- Silence is golden unless you have children, then silence is suspicious.
- Love cooking with wine, sometimes I even put it in the food.
- I named my dog "5-miles" so I can tell people I walk five miles a day.
- After the rapture, can I have your car.
- The new can crusher I bought broke; it was soda pressing.

True story: One of my distant cousins has kept up with her best friend from high school through the years. They are both 74 years of age. The best friend went to visit her daughter who lived several hours away and fell and broke her hip the first day there.

After she was released from the hospital and put in a rehabilitation center, she had a filling to fall out of one of her teeth. Her daughter took her to a dentist close to the facility and as she was pushing her mother in a wheelchair toward the dentist' front office, her mother noticed the name. She turned to her daughter and said, "I went to high school with a man by the same name. I wonder if it is him."

When her named was called to be taken to the operatory, the mother got a glance at the dentist. She immediately thought the man was too old to have been in her class in high school. She decided not to say anything.

When the dentist came into the room, she studied his face and decided to risk asking him and she said, "Did you go to Hapeville High School in the Atlanta area?" He said, "I sure did." She said, "I think you were in my class." He turned and looked at her and said, "Oh really, what did you teach?"

My cousin called me and told me what had happened, and we laughed and laughed. Why? because we usually think we look better or younger than others! It was healthy to look at ourselves and be able to laugh.

In an article from Texas A&M University, a researcher said, *"Laughter might be the best medicine for transforming the faintest of glimmers of hope into an eternal spring. Humor may significantly increase a person's level of hope."*[177]

Dr. Rosen goes on to say: "The experience of humor can positively influence a person's state of hopefulness. As part of the study, which appeared in the International Journal of Humor Research, select participants viewed a 15-minute comedy video. Those that viewed the video had statistically significant increases in their scores for hopefulness after watching it as compared with those that did not view the video, Rosen notes.

The finding, he says, is important because it underscores how humor can be a legitimate strategy for relieving stress and maintaining a general sense of well-being while increasing a person's hope. Previous studies have found that as high as 94 percent of people deem lightheartedness as a necessary factor in dealing with difficulties associated with stressful life events, he says.

Rosen says humor may competitively inhibit negative thoughts with positive ones, and in so doing, foster hope in people. Positive emotions, such as those arising from experiencing humor, can stimulate thought and prompt people to discard automatic behavioral responses and pursue more creative paths of thought and action, he explains.

Such a process, Rosen says, could lead to a person experiencing a greater sense of self-worth when dealing with specific problems or stressful events. He says these positive emotions could, in turn, lead to an increase in a person's ability to develop a "plan of attack" for a specific problem as well as increase a person's perceived ability to overcome obstacles in dealing with that problem - two aspects that psychologists believe comprise hope.

A good, hearty laugh relieves physical tension and **stress**, leaving your muscles relaxed for up to 45 minutes after. Laughter boosts the immune system. Laughter decreases **stress** hormones and increases immune cells and infection-fighting antibodies, thus improving your resistance to disease."[178]

Laughter is The best medicine!

Laughter reduces pain, increases job performance, connects people emotionally, and improves the flow of oxygen to the heart and brain.[179]

You can't deny laughter;
when it comes, it plops down in your
favorite chair
and stays as long as it wants."

Stephen King

The Corona Virus Covid-19 pandemic continues to spread across the world. The news is full of the hardships caused by this deadly disease. Thousands have been hospitalized and thousands have died. There is a dark cloud of fear that engulfs us. We wear masks, we wash our hands, and we stay at least six feet away from people in public. Every little cough is a sudden scare that the virus just might be in us. Even worse is when we are notified that a friend or loved one has it.

One of my closest friends has twelve relatives in another state where four have died and eight are in the hospital with Covid-19. He is unable to attend the funerals or visit any in the hospital. His grief is profound.

Interestingly, even during this horror that has rocked the world, many have found relief and hope in those who can find humor and help us laugh at ourselves. Let me share a few that continue to cause me to laugh and reduce stress.

1. Why did the chicken cross the road? Because the chicken behind it didn't know how to socially distance properly.

2. Two grandmothers were bragging about their precious darlings. One of them says to the other, "Mine are so good at social distancing, they won't even call me."

3. Whose idea was it to sing "Happy Birthday" while washing your hands? Now every time I go to the bathroom, my kids expect me to walk out with a cake.

4. My husband purchased a world map and then gave me a dart and said, "Throw this and wherever it lands—that's where I'm taking you when this pandemic ends." Turns out, we're spending two weeks behind the fridge.

5. Ran out of toilet paper and started using lettuce leaves. Today was just the tip of the iceberg, tomorrow *romaines* to be seen.

6. My mom always told me I wouldn't accomplish anything by lying in bed all day. But look at me now, ma! I'm saving the world!

7. Every few days try your jeans on just to make sure they fit. Pajamas will have you believe all is well in the kingdom.

8. I never thought the comment "I wouldn't touch them with a 6-foot pole" would become a national policy, but here we are!

9. The World Health Organization announced that dogs cannot contract COVID-19. Dogs previously held in quarantine can now be released. To be clear, WHO let the dogs out.

Today is one of my daughters-in-law's thirtieth birthday. Since we are quarantined, we are unable to be with her or my son or the rest of the family to celebrate this great milestone and entry into a new decade of her life. I am sending her this quote from a man named Jonny Sun who is also celebrating his thirtieth birthday:

"My 30th birthday is today but I just want everyone to know that I will be postponing it indefinitely due to the coronavirus, and I will be turning 30 at a later date. Thank you!

We need humor especially in tough times.

When my brother-in-law died suddenly one morning, people began to come to his home. He was a beloved lawyer in town and one who lived life to the fullest. He woke up, as usual, and went into the bathroom to take a shower before heading to work and simply died. It was a massive heart attack.

We were all stunned. We were deeply and profoundly bereaved. My wife and I immediately went to the house to be with his wife (my wife's sister) and her children. Soon the yard and house filled with people who loved him, coming to bring food and hugs and expressions of sympathy. Within minutes of people arriving, the sound of laughter filled the outside and inside of his home.

Throughout the whole day, laughter and tears seemed to be the constant emotions. My brother-in-law was one of the funniest men I have ever known. Everyone had a story to tell about him. As we cried and laughed together, we knew that we would get through our sadness. The laughter was healing. The stories became like medicine to our souls, and hope was building within us, the kind of hope that assures us that his life will forever be in our hearts. As Jesus said "though he is dead, yet shall he live." (John 14?) My brother-in-law was gone, but acutely present. He was dead, but vibrantly alive.

It is imperative that humor shares a big space in our lives. We need to be able to laugh at ourselves. When we are troubled and life becomes too serious, watch a funny TV show or movie, or read a funny book. Look for humor in the seriousness of life. And by all means, help others see humor in themselves.

Many years ago, I was in the room with a woman who was dying. She was one of my favorite members of the church. She had suffered from cancer for several years and the family had gathered. We knew that this would be her last day on earth.

When I went into the bedroom where she was resting, her two daughters were by her side. Tears streamed down their faces. The mother was quiet, resting with her eyes closed.

The daughters began to talk about their mother and how wonderful she was. They told stories about her. As they remembered, they began to laugh at some of the things she had done.

Though I do not' remember the details of what led me to share this story, I told them about an aunt that I loved dearly. Like their mother, she had cancer for many years eventually claiming her life. We adored her.

One day, my aunt gave us a sofa that had been in her home. It was beautiful but it was made of wool. Whenever we sat on it, we began to itch. For fun, we would invite guests to sit on that sofa so we could see if they itched and began to scratch. Every time, and I mean every time someone would sit on that couch, they would begin to itch and start scratching. We named it "Itchy couch."

When I said those words, the woman who was dying began laughing. Not just a petite little laugh, but loud belly-laughing. Tears began to roll down her cheeks. Her daughters began to laugh. We laughed so much, and so loud, other family looked in on us and began laughing even though they did not know what was funny.

We finally calmed down and the mother took her last breath. The daughters held her hands and said, "what a gift that she died laughing." We knew this would be difficult for us, but her joy as she died is strengthening us. Then the daughters hugged and then left the room with smiles in the midst of tears, to share the news that their mother had died, peacefully and with joy. They had a renewed hope and strength that surprised them. The service that celebrated their mother's life had a wonderful balance of sharing stories about her life. It was so uplifting that people left the sanctuary inspired and hopeful that one day when their own time came to leave this world, their service would be the same for those who would attend. I know that's my prayer!

"The note of hope is the only note
that can help us or save us
from falling to the bottom of the
heap of evolution because,
largely, about all a human being is,
anyway, is just a hoping machine."

Guthrie

———————⟨⟩———————

The Hymn of Promise

In the bulb there is a flower;
In the seed, an apple tree;
In cocoons, a hidden promise: butterflies will soon be free!
In the cold and snow of winter
There's a spring that waits to be,
Unrevealed until its season,
Something God alone can see.

There's a song in every silence,
Seeking word and melody;
There's a dawn in every darkness, bringing hope to you and me.
From the past will come the future; what it holds, a mystery,
Unrevealed until its season,
Something God alone can see.

In our end is our beginning;
In our time, infinity;
In our doubt there is believing;
In our life, eternity,
In our death, a resurrection;
At the last, a victory,
Unrevealed until its season,
Something God alone can see.

Nancy Allen

Chapter 17

A future and A hope

——————⟨✕⟩——————

Practice hope. As hopefulness becomes a habit,
you can achieve a permanently happy spirit.
Norman Vincent Peale

Hope is the deeply religious conviction that God has not quit.
Walter Brueggemann

We must accept finite disappointment, but never lose infinite hope.
Martin Luther King, Jr.

"Our hope rests not merely in what happened in the past,
but in what God will do today and in the future."[180]

The Christian faith is centered in the life of Jesus of Nazareth: his teachings, his preaching, his healings, his miracles, his suffering, death, and resurrection. His whole life on earth was enveloped in love and offering people God's holy kingdom "on earth as it is in heaven." The very word "Jesus" is synonymous with the words hope, *love, peace, joy, eternal life, forgiveness, redemption. light, salvation, and goodness.* He is, as stated earlier, "the hope of the world."

We have a great future ahead of us when Jesus is at the center of our lives. Focusing on Him, we can walk the path of life with confidence and strength. We are not easily blown away by what the world does to us. One of the great hymns of Christianity emphasizes this:

> My life flows on in endless song;
> Above earth's lamentation,
> I hear the sweet, though far-off hymn
> That hails a new creation
>
> Through all the tumult and the strife,
> I hear that music ringing
> It finds an echo in my soul
> How can I keep from singing?
>
> What though my joys and comforts die?
> I know my Savior liveth
> What though the darkness gather round?
> Songs in the night he giveth
>
> No storm can shake my inmost calm
> While to that refuge clinging
> Since Christ is Lord of heaven and earth
> How can I keep from singing?[181]

The cross is the focal point of human history. It points us to God who can take the negative and tragic in our lives and transform them into a means of grace and salvation. In its essence, the cross is the symbol of hope.

When I was in college, I had 6 friends to die in six different ways. I was so bereaved I did not think I could go on with college, so I took myself to a psychiatrist. After I poured out my heart, he said to me, "What are you going to do with your grief and pain? Will you let it cause you to quit school and do nothing. Will you let it eat up your joy and life? Will you let it instead lead you to take it and do something transformative with it? He then invited me to read a little book called The Will of God by Leslie Weatherhead. I would encourage you to obtain a copy and read it, reread it and reread it again. He helped me understand that God does not send suffering. God's will is for life and health and peace.

God's intention is for humanity to live long, healthy, and good lives. Unfortunately, sometimes LIFE HAPPENS. Circumstances beyond our control cause tragedy, crisis and suffering. But God does not sit on a throne somewhere dictating that one person will get cancer, another hurt in an accident, or murdered. I could not be a minister of the good news of God's love if I believed that. Jesus said that God is like the good parent and no good parent would ever cause their children harm.

But ULTIMATELY...ULTIMATELY...God's will for us will never be defeated because God always has the last word. The cross is the reminder to us that it was God's intention for Jesus to come to us and show us the way to eternal living. The circumstances of his time showed that there were those who were threatened by him and his radical message of God's love...and they had him killed. But death did not have the last word. Evil does not have the last word. Cancer does not have the last word... God does. The last word is Easter. Resurrection. New life. Eternal life. God can work with us to transform suffering, pain and death into means of grace and salvation.

Pope Francis said "I say to you, carry this certainty ahead: The Lord is alive and walks beside you through this life. This is your mission! Carry this hope onward. May you be anchored to this hope: this anchor that is in heaven; hold the rope firmly, be anchored and carry hope forward.[182]

I have always loved the beautiful words from the lips of the Apostle Paul recorded in 2 Timothy 4:1-8: He knows his death is near and he chooses his words carefully:

> *As for me, I am already being poured out as a libation, and **the time of my departure has come. I have fought the good fight, I have finished the race, I have kept the faith.** From now on there is reserved for me the crown of righteousness, which the Lord, the righteous judge, will give me on that day, and not only to me but also to all who have longed for his appearing.*

Paul prepares for his death with the use of nautical language. "the time of my departure has come." That word *departure* is equivalent to a boat being untied from its harbor and set free to travel the unknown and boundless seas.

Paul sees death as a moment for new adventure, not a time for defeat or sadness...it is a ship which has cast off the ropes which bind us to this world to sail into the unknown waters where God becomes present in immortal ways. Only on the seas can the ship fulfill the possibility of its own being and fulfill the purpose for which it was made.

One of the things I have learned over the years is that it is not the DURATION of life that counts as much as the DONATION that matters. Many people can live into their nineties and beyond and not ever truly live. On the flip side of that, I have known those who have packed a huge amount of life into only a few years of existence. They have truly *"fought the good fight, finished the race and kept the faith."*

This is not to say that we have no fears along the way. I have grown to learn that faith and hope are not the absence of fear and sadness, rather they help us to keep going when we are afraid and when we are grieving, indeed, when life seems so full of despair. Faith and hope together allows us to into the uncomfortable and complex questions about life. If this was easy, there would be no need for the multitudes of writers over the centuries seeking to understand it, and hymn writers who try to convey it:

> *When the storms of life are raging stand by me*
> *When the storms of life are raging stand by me*
> *When the world is tossing me, like a ship upon the sea,*
> *Thou who rulest winds and waters stand by me.*[183]

Another:

> *O Sometimes the shadows are deep, and rough seems the path to the goal.*
> *And sorrows, sometimes how they sweep, like tempests down over the soul!*
> *O then to the Rock let me fly, to the Rock that is higher than I;*
> *O then to the Rock let me fly, to the Rock that is higher than I.* [184]

One more of the "older" hymns:

> *Have faith in God my heart, trust and be unafraid.*
> *God will fulfill in every part; each promise he has made.*
>
> *Have faith in God my mind, tho' oft the light burns low.*
> *God's mercy holds a wiser plan, that we can fully know.*
>
> *Have faith in God my soul, his cross forever stands.*
> *And neither life nor death can pluck his children from his hands.*
>
> *Lord Jesus make me whole, grant me no resting place.*
> *Until I rest heart, mind and soul the captive of thy grace.* [185]

A more contemporary one:

> *Jesus is the Rock and He rolls my blues away*
> *(bop shoe bop, shoe bop, whoo!)*
>
> *When you're out on the street and you really feel down an low*
> *(bop shoe bop, shoe bop, whoo!)*
>
> *When you're out on the street 'cause there's nowhere else to go*
> *(bop shoe bop, shoe bop, whoo!)*
>
> *When you're out on the street, well, Jesus gonna save your soul,*
> *Cause... (refrain)* [186]

Heratio Spafford lived in the 1800's. He and his wife and four daughters were going on a vacation to England. He was called back to New York and sent them on ahead. While at sea, their ship collided with another one and all of his daughters drowned. His wife was the only one that survived.

He immediately got on a ship to England to see her in the hospital. He had asked the captain of the ship to tell him when they got to the place where the ship went down and where his daughters lost their lives. After a couple of days, the captain brought Mr. Spafford on deck and pointed out in the ocean.

Spafford sat down and looked for a while and then got out a paper and pen and began to write these words that have become one of the great hymns of Christendom.

> *When peace like a river attendeth my way*
> *When sorrows like sea billows flow*
> *Whatever my lot, Thou hast taught me to say*
> *It is well, it is well, with my soul.*[187]

How could he write such a phenomenal hymn in the midst of deepest grief? As people of Easter, we believe that death is not the end. We know that nothing is ever wasted that is important to God. Grief and hope can coexist.

I have given instructions to my family that when I die, I wish the marker that will bear my name will look something like this:

My name
Birth date – death date,

Did you notice the "comma" after my date of death? It is there intentionally. Why? Because God is never finished with what God loves. God is never finished with WHO God loves, and God loves us all! I trust the scripture to be true where Jesus said, *"I am the resurrection and the life,* *he who believes in me, though he is dead, **yet shall he live**. And whoever lives and believes in me **will never die**.[188]*

Perhaps one of the most comforting scriptures of all and especially in a time of death is found in John 14. Look closely at these words:

> *14'Let not let your hearts be troubled. Believe* in God, believe also in me. ²In my Father's house there are many dwelling-places. If it were not so, would I have told you that I go to prepare a place for you?* ³And if I go and prepare a place for you, I will come again and will take you to myself, so that where I am, there you may be also. ⁴18 ²⁷Peace I leave with you; my peace I give to you. I do not give to you as the world gives. Do not let your hearts be troubled, and do not let them be afraid. [18928]*

I want to share an excerpt from a eulogy I gave for a person who exemplified a future with hope. She was just 68 when she died of metastatic cancer. She was married and the mother of two grown sons and one grandson. Throughout her entire time of great suffering she never lost the joy of life nor the joy of having Christ at the center of her life. Here is what I said to a sanctuary packed to capacity with people who loved her dearly:

"Calvin Coolidge once said, "No one was ever honored by what they received, but by what they gave." We are here to honor one who gave generously her whole life.

She was an encourager to the clergy of the church. I could count on her to smile while I preached. Do you know how wonderful that is? Some people sit there like stones, but she listened to every word and always encouraged me. I am confident that many times she was praying "Help him Lord, help him now!!!"

Friday, January 12, the doctors at Emory Johns Creek Hospital told her that there was nothing else they could do. They were stopping all treatments and the time had come for hospice to do their part. Her husband texted me, and my wife and I immediately jumped in the car and drove to the hospital.

When we walked in, she smiled and held out her arms to hug and kiss us. An aura of Christ was shining around her. I asked her how she was handling this news. She said, "I am at peace."

My friends, that doesn't just happen. Could we say that? Having a faith like that doesn't just happen. She spent her life studying God's Holy Word, walking daily with Christ, living without regrets, and preparing for the day she would go home into God's eternal kingdom.

I thought when she said those words to us of Jesus' parable of the wise and foolish builders found in Matthew 7:24-27.

Listen to them:

> *Everyone therefore who hears these words of mine, and does them, I will liken him to a wise man who built his house on a rock. The rain came down, the floods came, the winds blew and beat on that house; and it did not fall...for it was founded on the rock.*

> *Everyone who hears these words of mine and does not do them will be like a foolish man, who built his house on the sand. The rain came down, the floods came, and the winds blew and beat on that house; and it fell and GREAT WAS ITS FALL.*

I have known too many people who built their lives on the sand and when crisis came: the loss of job or health, or a marriage, or a loved one who died, they were blown away. They had no anchor to steady them. Certainly, we all can be shocked and saddened, but those who build their lives on the rock of Christ, grieve but not as people with no hope. She knew that. She built her life on solid rock. Nothing, nothing could shake her faith. Her husband said to me over and over in this journey with her, her faith is amazing.

"I am at peace." Even dying, she was a tremendous witness to us and all who took care of her. She said, "I don't' want to leave my family, but I am ready. I do not fear. I trust the future.

She had the peace Jesus talked about in his last will and testament. The only thing Jesus left us in his last will and testament was *his peace*.

Remember: *"My peace I leave unto you...not as the world gives do I give unto you, let not your hearts be troubled, neither let them be afraid."* She had that peace. She wanted every person to have that peace and assurance.

I believe the words of St. Paul are apropos for us today: "I have fought the good fight, I have finished the race, I have kept the faith." She fought the good fight by living life to the best of her abilities; she was a giver, a helper, and one who loved deeply.

As people of Easter...it is our belief that death is not the end at all... rather the beginning of life with God in God's eternal kingdom.

On January 28, 2018, a light in our lives went out, but for her; it was because the dawn of eternity had come. Since love never dies, let us find peace that one day the dawn will come for us all and we shall feast together at the banquet of heaven. Until then, let us continue to fight the good fight, let us finish the race, let us keep the faith. Amen."

How refreshing to be able to have a true service of "celebration" for one who lived life to the fullest. Even as I write these words, her life continues to teach and inspire others and me. The "seeds" of love that she planted along her life, continue to grow and to bear fruit.

My father died fifteen years ago. He was a United Methodist minister for over fifty years. *Though he is dead, yet shall he live!* Over these many years, I continue to learn new things about him and from him. Numerous people have told me things he did for them that I never knew. He began several ministries that are still presently offering strong programs to help those in need that I never knew he began! I have even had people quote from his sermons that he gave over fifty years ago! I've had people say, "he helped me get into college, or seminary or spent time with me during my wrestling with a call to ministry.

And it hit me. Though dad is dead, yet he lives...in the lives of the many people he has touched throughout his life. His life is ingrained in mine and the lives of many and will be for generations to come. Because of him, I have a new understanding of "life beyond death."

Every Easter, when I was a pastor, I invited the best singer I knew to sing "The Holy City." Its words are stirring, and the music forever puts

chills on my skin and in my heart. Notice the power of hope within this
glorious resurrection hymn:

Last night, I lay a-sleeping, there came a dream so fair
I stood in old Jerusalem, beside the temple there
I heard the children singing and ever as they sang
Me thought the voice of angels from heaven, in answer rang
Me thought the voice of angels from heaven, in answer rang

Jerusalem, Jerusalem, lift up your gates and sing
Hosanna, in the highest, Hosanna to the king
And then me thought my dream was changed
The streets no longer rang
Hushed were the glad hosannas, the little children sang
The sun grew dark with mystery, the morn was cold and chill
As the shadow of a cross arose upon a lonely hill
As the shadow of a cross arose upon a lonely hill

Jerusalem, Jerusalem, lift up your gates and sing
Hosanna, in the highest, Hosanna to the king

And once again the scene was changed
New earth, there seemed to be
I saw the Holy City beside the tideless sea

The light of God was on its streets
The gates were opened wide
And all who would might enter and <u>no one</u> was denied

No need of moon or stars by night, nor sun to shine by day
It was a new Jerusalem that would not pass away
It was a new Jerusalem that would not pass away

Jerusalem, Jerusalem, <u>**sing for the night is over**</u>
Hosanna, in the highest, Hosanna to the king.[190]

One day we shall gather at the river, the banquet of heaven, in the holy city, the new Jerusalem and there will be no more crying, no more grief, no more suffering and no more death.

When John Todd, a nineteenth-century clergyman, was six years old, both his parents died. A kind-hearted aunt raised him until he left home to study for the ministry. Later, this aunt became seriously ill, and in distress she wrote Todd a letter. Would death mean the end of everything, or could she hope for something beyond? Here, condensed from *The Autobiography of John Todd*, is the letter he sent in reply:

"It is now thirty-five years since I, as a boy of six, was left quite alone in the world. You sent me word you would give me a home and be a kind mother to me. I have never forgotten the day I made the long journey to your house. I can still recall my disappointment when, instead of coming for me yourself, you sent your servant, Caesar, to fetch me.

"I remember my tears and anxiety as, perched high on your horse and clinging tight to Caesar, I rode off to my new home. Night fell before we finished the journey, and I became lonely and afraid. 'Do you think she'll go to bed before we get there?' I asked Caesar.

'Oh no!' he said reassuringly, 'She'll stay up for you. When we get out o' these here woods, you'll see her candle shinin' in the window.'

"Presently we did ride out into the clearing, and there, sure enough, was your candle. I remember you were waiting at the door, that you put your arms close about me—a tired and bewildered little boy. You had a fire burning on the hearth, a hot supper waiting on the stove. After supper you took me to my new room, heard me say my prayers, and then sat beside me till I fell asleep.

"Someday soon God will send for you, to take you to a new home. Don't fear the summons, the strange journey, or the messenger of death. God can be trusted to do as much for you as you were kind enough to do for me so many years ago. At the end of the road, you will find love and a welcome awaiting, and you will be safe in God's care."

Father Richard Rohr puts it this way:

"Yes, we are going to die, but we have already been given a kind of inner guarantee and promise even now that death is not final—and it takes the form of love. Deep in the heart and psyche, love, both human and divine, connotes something eternal and gratuitous, and it does so in a deeply mysterious and compelling way. We are seeing this now in simple acts of love in this time of crisis (Covid-19), such as people volunteering to make masks and deliver food, or people cheering hospital workers arriving for their shift. Isn't it amazing how a small act of love or gratitude can imprint a deeper knowing on our soul?" [191]

Christian hope is not just wishful thinking. It is surrender. It is getting rid of the "stuff" that deprives us from living so that we can have the best life possible.

In his book, *Christ in Crisis*, Jim Wallis says:

"Hope is not a feeling, but a decision; not a mood, but a choice; and one based on faith. It is a choice, a decision, an action based on faith. Hope is the very dynamic of history. Hope is the engine of change. Hope is the energy of transformation. Hope is the door from one reality to another."[192]

For Wallis, and millions like him, the greatest hope the world has ever known is summed up in one word: resurrection. Resurrection is the door of hope! Wallis points out "That the early disciples first called this reaction to the women at the tomb as "nonsense." Hope unbelieved is always considered nonsense. Yet, this nonsense of the Resurrection became the hope that shook the Roman Empire and established the Jesus Movement. The nonsense of slave songs in Egypt and Mississippi became the hope that let the oppressed go free. The nonsense of a confessing church stood up the state religion of the Nazi regime. The nonsense of prayer in East Germany helped bring down the Berlin Wall. The nonsense of another confessing church in South Africa helped end apartheid. The nonsense of a bus boycott in Montgomery, Alabama, became the hope that transformed a nation, and the nonsense of saying, *Black Lives Matter* defends and continues that transformation today.

Suffering and hope are always joined in human history. The cost of moving from one reality to another, in our personal lives and in history, is always great. But it is the only way to walk through the door of hope.

The resurrection of Jesus Christ teaches us that there always is and always will be hope, we do not carry that hope in vain. And that resurrection hope is one we can see mirrored in our lives and current events, if we know where to look."[193]

Hope is having the mindset that our lives are being shaped by God's love and not our fears.

Jamie Prickett

Paul, in the book of Romans, says it like this:

> **Now hope that sees for itself is not hope.**
> **For who hopes for what one sees?**
> **But if we hope for what we do not see,**
> **we wait with endurance.**
> Romans 8:24-25

One of my favorite Christian writers was the late Brian Doyle. He was a marvelous writer and recipient of many awards including the American Academy of Arts and Letters Award in Literature. He won the Oregon Book Award-winning novel *Martin Marten.* Perhaps Mink River is the one he is most loved for writing. He was editor of Portland Magazine, the University of Portland publication that he helped to put on the map by inviting famous authors to write in it. The University awarded him and honorary doctorate for his accomplishments.

I have followed his writings not only in his books but his devotions in Guideposts Magazines. His articles are scholarly written, yet with a touch that gives the feeling of being at home with him.

He was diagnosed with a brain tumor and died at the age of 60. On his deathbed he wrote "Last prayer."

"I would complain a little here about the long years of back pain and the occasional awful heartbreak, but Lord, those things were infinitesimal against the slather of gifts You gave me, a muddle of a man, so often selfish and small. But no man was ever more grateful for Your profligate generosity, and here at the very end, here in my last lines, I close my eyes and weep with joy that I was alive, and blessed beyond measure, and might well be headed back home to the incomprehensible Love from which I came, mewling, many years ago."[194]

Hope is a decision we make, a choice to believe that God can take the adversity, the disappointment, the heartache, and the pain of our journeys and use these to accomplish his purposes.

Once again let me turn to Jim Wallis who said,

"When we are both preserving what is good and shining a light on what is bad, we offer hope for both nurture and change. We are not limited by what is, nor do we need to destroy all of what is to change what needs to be changed; rather, we can have the 'prophetic imagination,' as Walter Brueggemann has taught us, to see how things could and should be different and better. Like salt preserving the food we need to eat, and light ending the darkness and showing us the way forward, we are called to be in the presence of Jesus Christ and his kingdom in the world. When we demonstrate both perseverance and courage in these roles of salt and light we can help both sustain and transform people's lives, root our communities in the most important values, and keep moving our world toward the kingdom of

God, which both here and yet to come, and which was always intended to change the world that God so loves.

To preserve, to shine a light, and to make the decision to hope; these are the substances of our vocation as Jesus followers."[195]

The brilliant Roman Catholic scholar Hans Kung point out that:

"Our joy derives from a threefold perspective that should characterize the People of God: the past—recollection and thanksgiving for how God has acted, especially in the life and death of Jesus. The present—is the celebration of the community, and the One who draws it together and unites the separate individuals into one church. The future—brings the joy of anticipation, the anticipation of the future consummation of history and the eternal reign of the Messiah. As a link to the future this Eucharistic (joy filled) meal already anticipates in the present that which is not yet fully known. This meal is tha "fellowship, koinonia, communio" with the risen Christ and his present community.[196]

One day, we shall as Walter Brueggemann says:

"have the laugh of Sarah, the Easter laugh of Jesus, the cosmic laugh of God whose kingdom will have no end. We shall, along with our tired world, be remade for singing and praising and yielding, and communing and obeying. We shall be remade along with our world which is now too prudent, too cunning, too coercive. We shall be remade according to God's powerful hope. We can in our fear and complacency resist the cry to so preclude the laugh, and hope for business as usual, world without end. But in that way lies only killing and dying. It is "this other way': that leads us to say with our community: "Beloved, we are God's children now; it does not yet appear what we shall be, but we know that when he appears we shall be like him with fear finished, like him with bread abounding, like him learning war no more...like him, but it begins in the way of the loss we cry for the whole failed creation. It begins there. It ends in utter joy. It ends in a laugh that echoes the gracious majestic laugh of God.[197]

Therefore, we can proclaim with Habakkuk (3:17)

> *though the fig tree does not blossom,*
> *and no fruit is on the vines;*
> *though the produce of the olive fails,*
> *and the fields yield no food;*
> *though the flock is cut off from the fold,*
> *and there is no herd in the stalls,*
> *yet I will rejoice in the LORD;*
> *I will exult in the God of my salvation.*
> *GOD, the Lord, is my strength;*
> *he makes my feet like the feet of a deer,*
> *and makes me tread upon the heights.*

It is hope that gives us a song to sing in the midst of great disaster.

It is hope that moves us to rebuild from ruins.

It is hope that enables us to move forward even in despair.

It is hope that renews us, restores us, re-creates us, and redeems us.

It is hope that lets us see, taste, smell and feel the presence of God. surrounding us.

It is hope that invites us to the banquet of life, on earth as it is in heaven.

Morning has broken

Morning has broken like the first morning
Blackbird has spoken like the first bird
Praise for the singing
Praise for the morning
Praise for them springing fresh from the Word
Sweet the rain's new fall, sunlit from heaven
Like the first dew fall on the first grass
Praise for the sweetness of the wet garden
Sprung in completeness where His feet pass

Mine is the sunlight
Mine is the morning

Born of the One Light Eden saw play
Praise with elation, praise every morning
God's recreation of the new day

Morning has broken like the first morning
Blackbird has spoken like the first bird
Praise for the singing
Praise for the morning
Praise for them springing fresh from the Word

Chapter 18

My prayer for Hope

———◇———

Prayer is hope.
It is the dawn of life. It sows the
seeds of happiness. Those who challenge
the future with prayer are sure to see
continual improvement in their lives.

Daisaku Ikeda

Joyce Rupp says, 'Hope resides at the core of who we are. We are meant to be hope-filled people. Yet the question looms large before us; is it possible to have persistent hope when we live in a society where divisiveness and hostility doggedly work against the likelihood?"[198]

That is the final question in the quest for hope. How can "persistent hope" continue to exist in a society filled with hate and fear? How do we help those who prefer to live in their bitterness instead of trying to seek help and reconciliation? Do we simply "wipe the dust off of our feet" and move on with our lives or do we continue to offer hope without being a pest or violating the boundaries of another's space?

We must never take hope for granted, lest we lose her and not only our world, but our place in the world will be lessened and destructive. J.

307

Alfred Smith, Sr., once said, "When hope dies, the pregnant mother of time dies with the unborn child of a redeemed future."[199]

The artist, George Frederic Watts entitled one of his paintings "Hope."

At a glance, it seems that the painting is a study in contradictions because "what is designated as the title of the painting and what is depicted on the canvas seem to be in direct opposition to each other. It shows a woman who is playing a harp and sitting on top of the world. She is powerful and in control. But when you look at the painting more closely, 'when the illusion of power starts giving way to the reality of pain,' the world she is sitting on –our world—is one 'torn by war, destroyed by hate, decimated by despair and devasted by distrust.' The world is, in fact, on the brink of destruction, and Watts, the artist, has contradicted the tile, "Hope" by depicting that despair on the canvas. Then one sees that the harpist is sitting in rags: her clothes are tattered as though she herself has been a victim of Hiroshima or the Sharpeville massacre.' When one examines her closely, one sees a bandage on her head, with blood beginning to seep through. Scars and cuts are visible on her face, arms and legs, and the harp she is playing has all but one of it strings ripped out and dangling down. Even her instrument has been damaged by what she has been through, and she is more the classic example of quiet despair than anything else. Yet the artist dared to entitle this painting "Hope." A seemingly hopeless contradiction."[200]

Pastor Jeremiah Wright in using this painting as an illustration in one of his sermons says,

"See, in spite of being on a world torn by war; in spite of being on a world destroyed by hate; in spite of being on a world devasted by mistrust and decimated by disease; in spite of being on a world where famine and greed were uneasy bed partners; in spite of being on a world where apartheid and apathy fed the fires of racism; in spite of being on a world where nuclear nightmare draws closer with every second; in spite of being on a ticking time bomb with her clothes in rags, her body scarred, bruised, and bleeding, and her harp all but destroyed except for that one string that was left – in spite of all of these things, the woman had the audacity to hope. She had the audacity to hope and to make music and praise God on the one string she had."[201]

That image speaks to the truth about the world in which we live. Yet in spite of all the wrong that flows continuously down the streets of life, it is hope that gives way to possibilities of re-creation, renewal, restoration, and repurposing.

It is my belief that prayer sustains those who wish to be agents of hope even with only "one string on our harps!" For decades, many of the people of Germany prayed for the destruction of the Berlin wall. In

1989, the wall began coming down. Finally, East and West Germany were united!

The civil rights movement began in a church in Birmingham, Alabama, from the prayers of Black people seeking equality in every aspect of life. Their leader, Martin Luther King, Jr., was a man of prayer and action. He could never undertake such a magnanimous project alone but called for all church people of every race and culture and denomination to join him in prayer for the healing and elimination of injustice of all.

We must never take prayer lightly. The only thing Jesus' disciples asked him to teach them was how to pray.[202] His most famous prayer, the "Lord's Prayer" is prayed throughout the world in churches, homes, and in the hearts of many. The old adage is true: "prayer changes things." It can change the life of the one who prays it, it can change the churches who pray it sincerely, and it can change the world by those who stive to live out this prayer in daily living with intentional acts of kind and actions of love.

I keep a sign in my office that says, "God, who would you have me love for you today?" That is my prayer. It is said that Martin Luther read the paper in one hand and the Bible in the other. Each day as I read the paper, I jot down situations and people for whom I need to pray, and for whom I need to reach out and touch. Prayer calls us to action. How can we read in the paper about a family burned out of their home without finding ways to help them, or homeless freezing on the streets without seeking them a place to stay or going through our closets and giving coats, hats, gloves, and other clothing items, or see that a child has died in the community without reaching out with a card, flowers, or other expressions of sympathy?

When Alex Trebek revealed that he had stage-4 pancreatic cancer, he often thanked all for their prayers. He knew the power of prayer and he credited them for his strength and fortitude to fight the disease.

Since my relative's words to me, I have not assumed that I have brought hope to anyone. I try, like the Apostle Paul says, "to be constantly in prayer." (I Thessalonians 5:17) To do that, life itself must become a prayer. Thus, I pray daily that my life will become hope for those in need. I cannot read people's minds, nor can I always stop and ask someone what their hope is, so I must strive to simply live as hope.

The apostle Paul summarized the "love chapter" of the Bible with the words "faith, hope and love remain forever, but the greatest is love." (I Corinthians 13) I would argue that love seeks to offer hope. Hope enables love. When we love another, it is our hope to surround them with all that is good and healthy in a relationship. We want to share what we have to offer to the highest benefit of the other.

Hope is the work of Jesus

In several places in the gospels, we read of Jesus doing the "work of God." What is that "work"?

1) Pointing to the kingdom of God
2) Living the way of God's kingdom: Matthew 25
3) Pointing to the cross (deny self, take up a cross, follow me)
4) Offering hope through his very life: preaching, teaching, serving) and the messianic hope.
5) Suffering, dying, Easter and Pentecost... we can't achieve a better world by ourselves, we need the community of faith.

Faith also is a steppingstone to hope. Let me illustrate this:

When I was in seminary, my mother was diagnosed with breast cancer. She found the lump one evening, went to the cancer specialist the next day and nine days later my siblings, father and I took her to Emory University Hospital for her to have a biopsy. She knew that if the biopsy was positive for cancer, the physician would immediately perform a radical mastectomy.

In the car on the way to the hospital, my mother turned to us, her children, and said, "I don't know what is going to happen to me today. I may be home this afternoon free from any worries, I may lose a part of my body, or I may be told I have a short time to live. What I want you to know is that I have lived a great life. I have few regrets. I am okay with whatever happens. I don't want you to worry. I know God is with me."

In the midst of the great unknown, her faith shined brightly for us. She offered us hope from her strong faith.

Interestingly, she had cancer and surgery was performed. She was fine for fifteen years until the cancer reappeared and she had another biopsy. This time, the news was not good. Her cancer specialist told her that the cancer had metastasized and that she was "at the end of the road." He challenged her to get things in order for most people in this stage of the disease, did not live more than six months to a year. Interestingly, she outlived him! She lived fifteen more years terminally ill!!! Her doctors called her the "miracle woman" and she lived life to the fullest. Her faith in God during those thirty years inspired many who were diagnosed with cancer to have hope of living much longer than expected. Today, numerous women wear her name on their shirts as they walk in the "Breast Cancer Walk" each year. Truly faith is a steppingstone, indeed a springboard, to hope.

Throughout the years of my mother's illness, I carried hope with me that she would not just survive, but that she would live, really live. To merely exist, is not to live. And live she did! She danced at my daughter's wedding just six months before her death. She kept her little garden at the nursing home until just a few weeks before she was moved to hospice care.

When I have had people betray me, walk away from the church because of minor things, or believe false things, I still carry within me a ray of hope that one day the light will come and reconciliation will be made. It is never easy to see those who have hurt others... thrive. It is difficult to be in the room with one who has stolen from you, abused you and discounted you in front of others. But I believe deep within all of us, there is a place under all the hurt and sadness that is reserved for hope.

"Hope is the hardest love we carry."

Jane Hirshfield

Friends of silence newsletter, March 2020

During my years of theological training, I was a chaplain at Children's Hospital of Atlanta at Egleston, the "terminal cancer" floor of Emory University Hospital (and the hospital in general), Wesley Woods geriatric facility, Georgia Mental Health, Henry Grady Hospital Emergency room and Atlanta Medical Center. I cannot remember ever telling a patient or the family that "everything would be just fine." I visited as one human to another. I visited as a clergy to a patient. I visited with the "hope" that all would improve and if not, that their suffering and pain would be transformative for good in some way, similar to the suffering of Jesus on the cross. Unfortunately, there are few instruments to measure if any chaplain, pastor, priest, rabbi, or imam, successfully brings hope to anyone.

Jesus himself, hanging from a cross in deepest pain and agony, prayed. He knew that though his work was "finished," there was still much to do for the world to prepare for God's kingdom to come on earth as it is in heaven. He prayed: "Father forgive them, they know not what they do."[203] He prayed the psalms[204] and in short, he prayed with his whole being for the salvation of the world.

We must take up His prayers even when we feel a failure or that God is all too silent and distant. Prayer does more for the cause of healing, hope, peace and love than we can ever know.

Let me call all of us to put our prayers into action and to work for a world where "the lion and the lamb" can live in peace with one another.

Vision peace. Vision hope. I believe such can happen and that such is the kingdom of God.

I see hope in the ministry of presence. Just showing up is vital. Words are secondary.

I believe that listening is one of the greatest ministries available in this age of noise upon noise.

I believe a picture (image) is better than a thousand words.

I believe music is the language of the soul.

I believe bread and wine are agents of transformation

I believe the smells that remind us of home can lighten our load.

I believe that hope is the "glue" between faith and love.

I believe that love covers all wrong and that hope is packaged in love.

I believe the mystery of the ocean, shells, a bird in the air, and the laughter of children can heal better than prescriptions from a pharmacy.

I believe in God, even when God is all too silent.

I believe, like Anne Frank, that deep down, humans are basically good.[205]

I believe that all of us can offer hope to others.

I believe in second chances to do just that!

I believe hope is all around us!

It is my heartfelt prayer that all of humanity will open our eyes, our ears, our hearts, indeed, our whole being and receive hope. Bathe in it, envelop it, feast on it, breathe it in, cast your eyes upon it, feel it and trust it. In doing so, you will find the true meaning of life and you will not be able to keep from sharing it with others. Always offer hope in all the ways you can even if there are those who do not recognize it or reject it. It will change the world! In the name of God: Faith, Hope and Love! Amen.

***So, in the end I am left only
with hope.***
I hope the nights are transformative.
I hope every dawn brings deeper love,
for each of us individually and for
the world as a whole. I hope that
John of the Cross was right when
he said the intellect is transformed
into faith, and the will into love
and the memory into - hope.

*~ by Gerald May in **The Dark Night of the Soul***

Suggested Reading

———————◇———————

Billings, J. Todd. The End of the Christian Life: How Embracing our Mortality Frees us to Truly Live. Brazos Press, 2020.

Boesak, Allan Aubrey. Dare We Speak of Hope: Searching for a language of Lie in Faith and Politics. William B. Eerdemans Publishing Company, 2014.

Boisen, Anton. Out of the Depths an Autobiographical Study of Mental Disorder and Religious Experience. Harper, 1960.

Bourgeault, Cynthia. Mystical Hope, trusting in the Mercy of God. Cowley Publications, 2001.

Bourgeault, Cynthia. The Holy Trinity and the Law of Three, Discovering the Radical Truth at the Heart of Christianity. Shambala Publication, 2013.

Brueggemann, Walter. A Gospel of Hope. Westminister John Knox Press, 2018.

Brueggemann, Walter. From Judgment to Hope: A Study on the prophets. Westminster, John Knox Press, 2019.

Buechner, Frederick. Wishful Thinking. Harper Collins, 1973.

Chittister, Joan D. Scarred by Struggle, Transformed by Hope. Wm. B Eerdmans Publishing Company, 2003.

Cuncic, Arlin. The Anxiety Workbook: A 7-Week Plan to Overcome Anxiety, Stop Worrying, and End Panic. Althea Press, 2017.

De Beauvoir, Simone. All Said and Done: The Autobiography of Simone De Beauvoir. deCapo Press, 1994.

Francis, Pope. New Beginning, New Hope. Our Sunday Visitor, 2014.

Gaines, Joanna. Homebody: A Guide to Creating Spaces You Never Want to Leave. HarperCollins Publishers, 2018.

Gaines, JoAnna and Marah Stets. Magnolia Table: A Collection of Recipes for Gathering. HarperCollins, 2018.

Gaines, Joanna. <u>Magnolia Table, Volume 2: A Collection of Recipes for Gathering</u>

Grinnan, Edward. <u>The Promise of Hope. How true stories of Hope and inspiration saved my life and how they can transform yours.</u> Guideposts, 2011.

Hamilton, J. Wallace. <u>Still the Trumpet Sounds.</u> Fleming H. Revell Company, 1970.

Hong, Howard v. and Edna H. Hong, editors. <u>The Essential Kierkegaard.</u> Princeton University Press, 1979.

Jenson, Robert W. <u>The Knowledge of Things Hoped For: The Sense of Theological Discourse.</u> Wipf and Stock Publishers, 1969.

King, Jr., Martin Luther. <u>A Testament of Hope, the Essential Writings and Speeches of Martin Luther King, Jr.</u> Harper Collins, 1990.

King, Jr. Martin Luther. <u>Letter from a Birmingham Jail</u>. ????? 1963.

Laine, Sam B. <u>Hope Realized</u>. Lighthouse Leadership Series, 2012.

Mayfield. D. L. <u>The Myth of the American Dream: Reflections on Affluence, Autonomy, Safety and Power</u>. Intervarsity Press, 2020.

Moltmann, Jurgen. <u>Ethics of Hope</u>. SCM Press, 2010.

Moltmann, Jurgen. <u>Hope for the Church.</u> Abingdon, 1979.

Moltmann, Jurgen: <u>The Spirit of Hope: Theology for a World in Peril</u>. Westminster Johns Knox Press, 2019.

Moltmann, Jurgen. <u>The Theology of Hope: On the Grounds and Implicaton of Christian Eschatology</u>. Fortress Press, Minneapolis, 1964.

Murphy, Timothy Charles. <u>Sustaining Hope in an Unjust World.</u> Chalice Press, 2019.

<u>One Hundred Meditations on Hope.</u> The Upper Room, 1995.

Owensby, Jake. <u>Looking for God in Messy Places: A book about Hope, how to find it. Practice it and grow it.</u> Abingdon Press, 2021.

Rawle, Matt, Juan Huertas, Katie McKay Simpson. <u>The Marks of Hope.</u> Abingdon Press, 2018

Nouwen, Henri J. M. <u>The Road to Daybreak, A Spiritual Journey</u>. Image Books, 1990.

Rohr, Richard. The Universal Christ: How a forgotten reality can change everything we see, hope for and believe. Convergent, 2019.

Rupp, Joyce. Constant Hope: Reflections and Meditations to strengthen the Spirit. Twenty-third Publications, 2019.

Sanchen Joni S. Words that Heal: preaching Hope to Wounded Souls. Abingdon Press, 2019. Nations Books, 2004.

Solnit, Rebecca. Hope in the Dark: Untold Histories, Wild Possibilities.

Spoelstra Melissa. Dare to Hope, Living Intentionally in an Unstable World. Abingdon Press, 2019.

The United Methodist Book of Hymns. The United Methodist Publishing House, 1989.

Wallis, Jim. Christ in Crisis, Why We Need to Reclaim Jesus. HarperOne, 2019.

Weatherhead, Leslie D. The Will of God. Abingdon, 1944 and 2011.

Winner, Lauren. Wearing God; clothing, Laughter, Fire and Other Overlooked Ways of Meeting God. HarperOne, 2015.

Wright, N. T. Surprised by Hope. Rethinking Heaven, the Resurrection, and the Mission of the Church, Harper Collins, 2010.

Zimmerman, Bill. Lifelines: A Book of Hope. Bantam Books, 19

Endnotes

———————⋈———————

1 Dickenson, Emily. The Complete Poems of Emily Dickinson. "Hope is the Thing with Feathers". Belknap Press, Harvard University Press, 1951, 1955, 1979, 1983.

2 God the good parent: see Matthew 18 and 19

3 Ibid

4 Galatians 5:22-23

5 Price, Robert Preston. "Abnormal Psychology" LaGrange College, 1974.

6 Ibid

7 Merriam-Webster Dictionary. —Merriam-Webster Publisher, Springfield, Massachusetts, 1964.

8 Laine, Sam. Hope Realized. Lighthouse Leadership Series, 2012.

9 Interpreter's Dictionary of the Bible, Volume 2, page 885

10 Rohr, Richard. The Universal Christ: How a Forgotten Reality can Change Everything We see, Hope for and Believe. Convergent, New York, 2019.

11 Bourgeault, Cynthia. Mystical Hope: Trusting in the Mercy of God. Cowley Publications, 2001. P 3, 4, 9-10, 17, 20, 41.

12 I John 4:7-8

13 I Corinthians 13

14 Kierkegaard, Soren. Fear and Trembling. 1843.

15 Keller, Helen. "Optimism" The Story of My Life. C. P. Crowell and Company, 1903.

16 Macy, JoAnna, and Chris Johnstone. Active Hope, How to face the Mess We are in Without Going Crazy. New World Lib. 2005

17 Havel Vaclar. "Summer Meditations." Share International #3, Volume 25

18 Chittister, Joan. Scarred by Trouble, Transformed by Hope. William B. Eerdmans Publishing Company, 2005.

19 Solnit, Rebecca. Hope in the Dark: Untold Histories Wild Possibilities. Haymarket Books, 2019.

20 I Corinthians 13

21 Attributed to St. Francis of Assisi 1181-1226.

22 Merriam- Webster Dictionary. Merriam Webster Publisher, Springfield, Massachusetts, 1964.

23 Moltmann, Jurgen. The Theology of Hope: on the Ground and the Implications of A Christian Theology. Fortress Press, 1964.

24 Bowsher, Karla. "Highest Suicide Rates: Some of the Nation's most dangerous jobs are also those with the highest suicide rates." July 5, 2016.

25 Anderson, Pauline. "Doctors' Suicide Rate Highest of Any Profession". WEBMD Archives, May 8, 2018.

26 Shiparo, Mark. Dome Magazine, May/June 2019.

27 Ibid.

28 Brown, Elizabeth. Share. TweetSnap. March 28, 2017.

29 The United Methodist Book of Worship. "The sacrament of Christian Baptism" The United Methodist Publishing House, 1992, p.95

30 Mark 2:17 "When Jesus heard this, he said to them, "Those who are well have no need of a physician, but those who are sick; I have come to call not the righteous but sinners."

31 Matthew 18:22 " Jesus said to him, "Not seven times, but, I tell you, seventy-seven[a] times"

32 Kierkegaard, Soren. The Essential Kierkegaard. Princeton University Press, 1997. p 357.

33 Ibid. "Call it Grace " by Serene Jones p 76-77

34 Moltmann, Jurgen. The Theology of Hope: on the Ground and the Implications of A Christian Theology. Publishers. 1964. Pages 77-78.

35 Ibid. P 31

36 Ibid

37 Ibid p 29

38 Kierkegaard, Soren. The Essential Kierkegaard. Princeton University Press, 1997. p 361

39 Losch, Andreas. (Baeck, Leo. Institute Year Book Vol. 60,) "What Is behind God's Name? Martin Buber's and Franz Rosenzweig's Reflections on the Name of God University of Bern, 2015.

The Martin Buber Archive in Jerusalem holds a draft of Buber's translation of Exod. III:3 which shows the later corrections Buber made. In another extant manuscript there, these corrections are already worked into the original writing. According to these manuscripts, Buber proposed Luther's "I will be the one that I will be" for hyha r?a hyha in Exod. III:14a, and "I-will-be" for hyha in Exod. III:14b. This was then corrected to"I will be-there, as the one being there",33 and "I-am-there", or in the clean copy, "I AM THERE" He also comments on Exod. III:12: "In order to grasp this in the sense of 'being there, present', [one should translate]: 'Certainly, I shall be there at your side.'"

Behind God's name is the assurance of God's always being there, especially in times of need. To express this, Buber and Rosenzweig chose personal pronouns for its translation. This choice probably lay with Rosenzweig, who was also in charge of word choice in the translation project, but was also prepared by Buber's enduring struggle with the term ani va-ho in the Mishnah, which he interpreted as a primitive form of naming God. As Buber phrases it: "The insight into the pronominal character or content of the original name form paved the way. That is why in our translation it is written I and MY, where God speaks, THOU and YOUR, where he is spoken to, and HE and HIS where he is spoken of." Another important aspect is the oft-neglected relevance of (Rosenzweig's and) Buber's dialogical philosophy as background to these decisions, as shown by the ties between the ¢rst unpublished typescript and I and Thou. The translation of Exod: III:13f (I will be there howsoever I will be-there) in the joint project therefore demonstrates Buber's core ideas as well. The God that is omnipresent.

40 Lucado, Max. Dad Time. Thomas Nelson, 2014.

41 Rupp, Joyce. Constant Hope: Reflections and Meditations to Strengthen the Spirit. Twenty-Third Publishers. 2018 , p.1

42 Ibid. p 20

43 Wesley, Charles. "And Are We Yet Alive." The United Methodist Hymnal. P 552

44 Bourgeault, Cynthia. Mystical Hope: Trusting in the Mercy of God. Cowley Publications, 2001.

45 Nouwen, Henri. Daybreak: A Spiritual Journey. Image Books, 1988. P204-205.

46 Brown, Robert McAfee. Spirituality and Liberation: Overcoming the great fallacy. Westminster, 1988. Page 136.

47 Boesak, Allan Aubrey. Dare We Speak of Hope: Searching for a language of Life in Faith and Politics. William B. Eerdmans Publishing Company. 2014.

48 Sacky, Jonathan. The Dignity of Difference: How to Avoid the Clash of Civilization. Continnum, 2006. page 29.

49 Boesak, Allan Aubrey. Dare We Speak of Hope: Searching for a language of Life in Faith and Politics. William B. Eerdmans Publishing Company. 2014. Page 65.

50 Ibid. page 70

51 Ibid. page 73

52 Follis, Don. "10 Great Ways to Give People Hope". Cutting Edge Magazine, July, 2016.

53 Cunic, Arlin. "Ten Great Ways to Give People Hope." Lifestyle

54 Buechner, Frederic. Wishful Thinking. Harper and Row Publishers, 1973.

55 "Susan G. Komen for the Cure: New name, renewed mission to fight breast cancer". Brainerd Dispatch. January 27, 2007. Archived from the original on July 8, 2011.

56 Ruth :1-12

57 Mattthew 27:46

58 Weatherhead, Leslie D. The Christian Agnostic. Abingdon Press, 1965.

59 Buber, Martin. I and Thou. Martino Publishers, 1923.

60 Areas, Keith Urban. "Over 100 Names for God." Christian Study Topics. 2016.

61 Dylan, Bob. "Blowing in the Wind." Columbia Records, 1962.

62 Bourgeault, Cynthia. The Holy Trinity and The Law of Three: Discovering the Radical Truth a the Heart of Christianity. Shambhala, 2013. P 20

63 Ibid. p. 38

64 Ibid p. 16

65 John 2:13-16 "The Passover of the Jews was near, and Jesus went up to Jerusalem. In the temple he found people selling cattle, sheep, and doves, and the money changers seated at their tables. Making a whip of cords, he drove all of them out of the temple, both the sheep and the cattle. He also poured out the coins of the money changers and overturned their tables. He told those who were selling the doves, "Take these things out of here! Stop making my Father's house a marketplace!"

66 O God the movie (based on the novel by Avery Corman, 1971).

67 Bruggemann, Walter. A Gospel of Hope. Westminster John Knox Press, 2018. p 96

68 1 John 4:7-21

69 I Corinthians 13

70 Song of Solomon 8:6

71 John 4:4-26

72 Luke 19:1-10

73 Mark 5:1-20 (The Gerasene Demoniac)

74 John 13: 1-17

75 Luke 15:11-32

76 Luke 10:25-37

77 Luke 15:8-10

78 Luke 15:3-7

79 Matthew 13:1-23

80 Matthew 20:1-16

81 Rohr, Richard. The Divine Dance: The Trinity and Your Transformation. Whitaker House, 2016

82 Genesis 4:1-16

83 "First Day of Rosh Hashanah" September 25, 2014

84 CNN broadcast, Eric Leverson November 17, 2018

85 Dylan, Bob. "Blowing in the Wind." Columbia Records, 1962.

86 "A Message of Healing and Reconciliation" December 2000. (see also, A Long Walk to Freedom.)

87 Service of ordination, Glenn Memorial United Methodist Church, Bishop William Ragsdale Cannon, presiding. June, 1977.

88 Mandela, Nelson. "The Healing of our Land." A service of healing and reconciliation dedicated to sufferers of HIV/AIDS, Johannesburg, December 6, 2000.

89 Harline, Leigh and Ned Washington. "When You Wish Upon A Star" (Disney Studios.)

90 Ancient Greek Mythology

91 Jamestown: the life and Death of People's Temple. "James Warren Jones: Leader of the People's Temple Cult". 2007.

92 Noa, Madeline. "The Branch Davidian Cult". 2010

93 "Assemblies of God Defrok Bakker." United Press International. 2018

94 Encyclopedia Britannica. "Jimmy Swaggart: Biography, Ministries, and Scandals," 2020.

95 Colorado Springs Gazette, 2006.

96 Bruni, Frank. "A Gospel of shame: children, Sex abuse, and the Catholic Church", 2020.

97 John 4:24

98 I John 4:7-21

99 I John 4:19

100 Nova, Annie. Personal Finance. August 13, 2018.

101 McHale, Tom. International Law, American University. Gun Training: the Dangers of a false Sense of Security, May 30, 2017.

**The most expensive wars in U.S. history – in order of spending/lives lost

John Harrington and Grant Suneson Wall Street: June 13, 2019.

War of 1812

- U.S. war spending (2019 dollars): $1.78 billion
- Duration: 2 years, 8 months
- U.S. military deaths: 15,000

Mexican-American War

- U.S. war spending (2019 dollars): $2.72 billion
- Duration: 1 year, 9 months
- U.S. military deaths: 13,283

American Revolution

- U.S. war spending (2019 dollars): $2.75 billion
- Duration: 8 years, 5 months
- U.S. military deaths: 4,435

Spanish-American War

- U.S. war spending (2019 dollars): $10.33 billion
- Duration: 4 months
- U.S. military deaths: 2,446

American Civil War (Confederacy)

- U.S. war spending (2019 dollars): $22.99 billion
- Duration: 4 years
- U.S. military deaths: 750,000 (North and South)

American Civil War (Union)

- U.S. war spending (2019 dollars): $68.17 billion
- Duration: 4 years
- U.S. military deaths: 750,000 (North and South)

Persian Gulf War

- U.S. war spending (2019 dollars): $116.6 billion
- Duration: 7 months
- U.S. military deaths: 383

World War I

- U.S. war spending (2019 dollars): $381.8 billion
- Duration: 1 year, 7 months
- U.S. military deaths: 116,516

Korean War

- U.S. war spending (2019 dollars): $389.81 billion

- Duration: 3 years, 1 month
- U.S. military deaths: 36,574

Vietnam War

- U.S. war spending (2019 dollars): $843.63 billion
- Duration: 17 years, 9 months
- U.S. military deaths: 58,220

War in Afghanistan

- U.S. war spending (2019 dollars): $910.47 billion
- Duration: Since 2001
- U.S. military deaths: 2,285

Iraq War

- U.S. war spending (2019 dollars): $1.01 trillion
- Duration: 7 years, 5 months
- U.S. military deaths: 4,410

World War II

- U.S. war spending (2019 dollars): $4.69 trillion
- Duration: 3 years, 9 months
- U.S. military deaths: 405,399

102 Hess, Abigail. "Here's Why Lottery Winners go broke." August 25, 2017.

103 Martin, Jomell. The Washington Post

104 Zagorsky, Jay. US World and News Report

105 McNay, Don. Life Lessons from the Lottery. Time Magazine.

106 Ibid.

107 Conrad, Charles. Sazrks Financial.

108 Hayes, Sandra. Associated Press

109 Ibid.

110 Frost, Robert. Mending Wall. "Fences" 2014.

111 Markum, Edward. The Man with the Hoe. Poem: He drew a circle. 1859.

112 Benedict. The Rule of St. Benedict. 546 ce.

113 John 19:30

114 John 5:17

115 From a sermon by Davis Chappell, pastor Brentwood United Methodist Church, Brentwood, Tennessee. November, 2020.

116 Fraga, Juli. "False Hope Syndrome: Why We'll quit our New Year's Resolutions This Weekend." The Guardian, 2016.

117 De Beauvoir, Simone. All Said and Done: the Autobiography of Simone De Beauvoir. Putnam Press, 1974.

118 Wikipedia

119 The United Methodist Book of Hymns. The United Methodist Publishing House, 1989. Page 881

120 Ibid, page 885

121 The Hour of Power

122 Stephen Ministers are lay congregation members trained to provide one-to-one care to those experiencing a difficult time in life, such as grief, divorce, job loss, chronic or terminal illness, or relocation.

Stephen Ministers come from all walks of life, but they all share a passion for bringing Christ's love and care to people during a time of need.

Since 1975, more than 600,000 people from more than 13,000 congregations and other organizations have been trained as Stephen Ministers.

123 The United Methodist Book of Discipline. Abingdon Press, 2016.

124 Mark 16:17-18

125 Luke 12:10

126 Matthew 5:30

127 2 Corinthians 11:24-32

128 Wesley, John. The Journal of John Wesley. "I look upon all the world as my parish; thus far I mean, that in whatever part of it I am, I judge it meet, right, and my bounden duty to declare unto all that are willing to hear, the glad tidings of salvation." –Journal, June 11, 1739.

129 Demotrescu, Camilion. "Symbols in sacred Architecture and Iconography," The Institute for Sacred Architecture, The Sacred Art Journal.

130 The Jubilate Group. Hope Publishing, 1982, 1987.

131 Romans 10:17

132 Wallis, Jim. Christ in Crisis, Why We Need to Reclaim Jesus. HarperOne, 2019. Pages 284-285.

133 Ibid. page 284

134 Lagace, Maxime. Quotes via the world-wide-web.

135 Kniestede, Karen. Aired May 26, 2018

136 CBS NEWS. "Patients with Cognitive Impairment Benefit from Singing." December 28, 2012.

137 Coss, Brandon. "Cindi Lauper and Hope for the Holidays" December 7, 2019.

138 Winner, Septimus. "Whispering Hope" 1868.

139 Tindley, Charles Albert. "We Shall Overcome", 1900.

140 Dylan Bob and Tom Petty. "Blowing in the wind", Columbia Records, 1962.

141 Newton, John. "Amazing Grace." Olney Hymns, 1779

142 Imber, Naftali,. "Hope" Hetz, 1878.

143 Winner, Lauren. Wearing God: Clothing Laughter, Fire and Other Overlooked Ways of Meeting God. Harper Collins, 2015. P92

144 Exodus 16

145 Psalm 23

146 Isaiah 25:6-8

147 Revelation 19:6-9

148 Ibid 21:4

149 John 6:31

150 Matthew 26:29 and Mark 14:25

151 Luke 22:16-18

152 Luke 14:15

153 Luke 22:29-30

154 Luke 13:29-30

155 Luke 12:37

156 Matthew 25:10

157 John 6:55

158 John 21:1-12

159 Luke 24:13ff

160 John 6:25-59

161 The United Methodist Hymnal. The United Methodist Publishing House, Nashville, Tennessee, 1989. The Order for the Sacrament of Holy Communion. Page 11

162 I Corinthians 11:26

163 Revelation 2:7

164 Revelation 19:6-9

165 Winner, Lauren. Wearing God: Clothing, Laughter, Fire and Other Overlooked Ways of Meeting God. Harper Collins, 2015.

166 Acts 2

167 here are over 100 Biblical passages about not being drunk. Here is a sample:

Proverbs 20:1 – Wine a mocker, strong drink a brawler, and whoever is led astray is not wise.

Galatians 5:21- Envy, drunkenness, orgies and thing like these, I warn you, as I warned you before, that those who do such things will not inherit the kingdom of God.

I Peter 5:8 – Be sober-minded.

I Corinthians 6:10 – Nor thieves, nor the greedy, nor drunkards, nor revilers, not swindlers will inherit the kingdom of God.

168 Payne, Jacqueline. "Child attachment disorder" The Information Standard. January, 2019.

169 The United Methodist Book of Worship. Abingdon Press. 1992.

170 John 13:1-17

171 Field, Tiffany. "touch is the first and most profound language" Touch Research, The Institute at Miller School of Medicine. 2017.

172 Ibid. (with Jay Skidmore) December 2017

173 Linden, David. The Touch: Science of Hand, Heart and Mind.

174 Ibid.

175 John 20:24-27

176 300 Quotes to Make you Laugh. June 2019

177 Rosen, David. 'Humor Can Increase Hope, Research Shows" Texas A & M University, February 2005.

178 Rosen, David, Alexander P. Vilaythong, Randolph C. Arnau and Nathan Mascaro, studied nearly 200 subjects ranging in age from 18-42. Texas A & M University. April 13, 2005.

179 Marano, Hara Estroff. Psychology Today. published April 5, 2005 -

180 One Hundred Meditations on Hope. The Upper Room, 1995.

181 Kerslake, Camilla, Michael Damien Hedge, Robert Lowry, Sally Herbert. "How can I keep from Singing." BMG Management.

182 Francis, Pope. New Beginning, New Hope. Our Sunday Visitor, 2014.

183 The United Methodist Hymnal. "When the Storms of Life are Raging." The United Methodist Publishing House, 1989.

184 Ibid, 1939. Erastus Johnson "O Sometimes the Shadows how deep," 1909.

185 The United Methodist Hymnal. "Have Faith in God my Heart: The United Methodist Publishing House, 1968.

186 Noman, Larry. "Jesus is the Rock and He Rolls My Blues Away."

187 The United Methodist Hymnal. "It is Well with My Soul" The United Methodist Publishing House, 1989.

188 Scripture: I am the resurrection and the life

189 John 14

190 – Revelation 21: The Holy City

191 Rohr, Richard. "Reality Initiating Us" Part II, "Nothing Can Come Between Us. April 10, 2020.

192 Wallis, Jim. Christ in Crisis. Page 248

193 Ibid. pages 264-265

194 Fate, Tom Montgomery. The Christian Century. "Brian Doyle's Rivers of Words." Page 37.

195 Wallis, Jim. Christ in Crisis. Pages 248-249

196 Kung, Hans. 222

197 Bruggeman, Walter. The Gospel of Hope. Page 104.

198 Rupp, Joyce. Constant Hope: Reflections and Meditations to strengthen the Spirit. Twenty-third Publications, 2019, page 1

199 Boesak, Allan Aubrey. Dare We Speak of Hope: Searching for a language of Lie in Faith and Politics. William B. Eerdemans Publishing Company, 2014.

200 Ibid

201 Jeremiah Wright sermon "The Audacity to Hope. March, 2008.

202 Matthew 6:9-13

203 Luke 23:34

204 Psalm 22

205 Frank, Ann. The Diary of A Young Girl. Contact Publishing, Amsterdam, 1947.